# INDUSTRIAL EVOLUTION

# STUDIES IN INDUSTRY AND SOCIETY

GLENN PORTER, *General Editor*

Published with the assistance of
THE ELEUTHERIAN MILLS-HAGLEY FOUNDATION

1. Burton W. Folsom, Jr.
*Urban Capitalists: Entrepreneurs and City Growth
in Pennsylvania's Lackawanna and Lehigh Regions, 1800–1920*

2. John Bodnar
*Workers' World: Kinship, Community, and Protest in an Industrial
Society, 1900–1940*

3. Paul F. Paskoff
*Industrial Evolution: Organization, Structure, and Growth of the
Pennsylvania Iron Industry, 1750–1860*

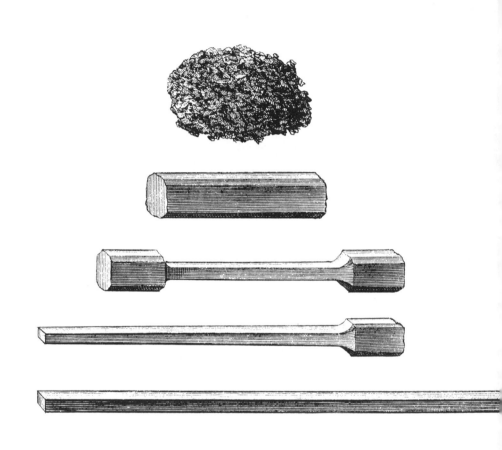

# INDUSTRIAL EVOLUTION

Organization, Structure, and
Growth of the Pennsylvania
Iron Industry, 1750–1860

## PAUL F. PASKOFF

THE JOHNS HOPKINS UNIVERSITY PRESS

Baltimore and London

© 1983 by The Johns Hopkins University Press
All rights reserved
Printed in the United States of America

The Johns Hopkins University Press, Baltimore, Maryland 21218
The Johns Hopkins Press Ltd, London

**Library of Congress Cataloging in Publication Data**
Paskoff, Paul F.
   Industrial evolution.
   (Studies in industry and society; 3)
   Bibliography: p. 163
   Includes index.
   1. Iron industry and trade — Pennsylvania — History.   I. Title.   II. Series.
HD9517.P4P37   1983        338.4'7669141'09748   83-48058
ISBN 0-8018-2904-6

Illustrations on pp. iv and v are details from Denis Diderot's *Encyclopédie,*
vol. 4, *Forges,* sec. 4, p. 4.

*To my mother
and to the memory
of my father*

# Contents

# List of Illustrations

# List of Tables

# Foreword

Paul Paskoff was a fellow at the Regional Economic History Research Center during the period when our research was concentrated on the 1750–1850 era in the Mid-Atlantic states. Through the generosity of the National Endowment for the Humanities and the Andrew W. Mellon Foundation we were able to offer fellowships to many scholars interested in the early beginnings of industrialization in our area. Professor Paskoff was among the first of the center's fellows, and it is most appropriate that our association with him has continued to the point where his work on the early iron industry of Pennsylvania is being published as part of this series undertaken jointly by the center and The Johns Hopkins University Press.

Paskoff's study provides a detailed look at a number of firms that were active in that important regional industry during its formative years. This work attempts to blend economic history with business history, to examine the minute in the context of the whole. By investigating the experience of individual firms in detail, Paskoff is able to document the phenomenon of early industrial managers learning by doing, improving productivity by careful attention to the rhythm of production. The businesses described here existed in an extremely uncertain economic world, in which they were constrained by the highly imperfect systems of communication and transportation that prevailed until the very end of the era considered in this book. In that uncertain world the managers of early iron enterprises, like most businessmen at most times, did everything they could to reduce the risks they faced. Despite a largely static production technology, many succeeded in that effort, albeit modestly by later standards. Many of the foundations of what would for a time be the world's most productive iron and steel industry were laid in Pennsylvania in the period Paskoff analyzes.

It is now almost half a century since the publication of Arthur C. Bining's *Pennsylvania Iron Manufacture in the Eighteenth Century.* Paskoff's study updates and extends that classic work, adding carefully compiled new data and carrying the story forward to the era of the Civil War. Given the importance of the Pennsylvania iron industry to the economic history of the Mid-Atlantic states, it is fitting that the Regional

Economic History Research Center should assist in making Paul Paskoff's work available to a wide audience.

GLENN PORTER
Director, Regional Economic History Research Center
Eleutherian Mills-Hagley Foundation

# Preface

In writing this history of the early Pennsylvania iron industry, I have derived considerable comfort from the fact that the subject is an important one. Although iron-making in America first began on a signifi- cant scale elsewhere, notably in Massachusetts, the iron industry of eighteenth- and early nineteenth-century Pennsylvania laid the technolog- ical, organizational, and structural foundation upon which the post–Civil War American iron and steel industry rested. Moreover, this industry played a substantial role in the national economy long before the transpor- tation revolution, rapid industrialization, and urbanization altered so decisively the economic setting in nineteenth-century America. One of my main purposes is, indeed, to study very closely the development of firms in this industry prior to the events generally associated with the beginnings of the industrial revolution or "take-off." Of particular interest to me is the role of technology in that setting.

Economic and business historians have customarily agreed that firms of that early vintage did not achieve significant advances in technology and, hence, in productivity, but the reasons for this have not been at all clear. By examining in detail the iron industry before, during, and after the great transition of the nineteenth century, I hope to throw some light on this important question. I try also to show how forms of business organization and technological innovation are related, if at all.

It is generally accepted that in any industry the firms with the most advanced form of organization — joint-stock companies or chartered cor- porations — were the first to adopt and successfully exploit new tech- nologies and that therefore the technical progress of an industry depended in great part on the appearance of these corporate entities. I have not found this to be a very reliable assumption as regards the development of the Pennsylvania iron industry. Of related interest is the way in which iron firms in the eighteenth and early nineteenth centuries managed their opera- tions and coped with an external economic environment that was often hostile to their interests and always mercurial. Again, the conventional wisdom is that early industrial firms could do little if anything to increase productivity in the face of rising costs or falling prices. Although there is more validity to this notion than to the idea that technical progress is associated mainly with complex organizational forms, considerable evidence exists to suggest that while early iron producers were largely passive in their response to the market, they were not entirely helpless.

The period 1750–1860 was an almost natural choice for the study's temporal bounds. In 1750 England's Parliament, bowing to pressure from that country's iron producers, passed the Iron Act in an attempt to inhibit the further development of iron-making in the North American colonies, thereby formally acknowledging that colonial iron production had come of age. The selection of 1860 as a terminus was dictated by the significant changes that took place in the industry during the 1850s. During that decade the modern industry began to take shape very quickly, marking a significant departure from the path along which iron-making had developed since 1750.

I fully expected to find, in keeping with what we know of the general course of nineteenth-century American economic growth, that the transit of the iron industry from its modest eighteenth-century beginnings to its more robust state of 1860 had occurred in a burst of activity after 1830. Although the growth in output between 1830 and 1850 was rapid, the evidence argues more persuasively for gradual change than for some sort of Rostovian "take-off" or an industrial revolution. Continuity, then, and not discontinuity, is the book's theme. The changes that took place between 1830 and 1850 were closely linked to previous developments in the industry. To a lesser extent, the same can be said for the more dramatic transitions of the 1850s.

In charting the changes of the fifties, I have drawn heavily upon Peter Temin's masterful study, *Iron and Steel in Nineteenth-Century America: An Economic Inquiry* (1964). Also, I have not thought it necessary to present my own computations of profits or aggregate output of the iron industry after 1830, because these quantities have already been computed by Peter Temin and Robert Fogel, respectively. I am convinced by their results and am grateful for them. I have made less use of Arthur C. Bining's classic work, *Pennsylvania Iron Manufacture in the Eighteenth Century* (1938), largely because of that account's descriptive nature. Instead, I have tried wherever possible to supplement Bining's study with quantitative data on production and marketing drawn from the records of eighteenth-century firms.

As a study of the operations and organizational structure of individual firms, this book is a form of business history, leavened by a concern for the broader technological and organizational development of the industry as a whole and for the interplay of iron producers, markets, and the larger economy in which they functioned. In this sense, then, it is also an economic history. The blending of these two approaches has permitted the probing of some important but neglected aspects of the iron industry's development and has largely determined the content and format of the book. I wished to focus on what I consider to have been the critical aspects of the industry's development, that is, its organizational development, its technological progress, and the interplay of these two. Such concerns of course cover a good deal of ground and cannot be considered apart from the larger world of the market that was their context. Accordingly, this study examines the relationship between the industry's supply side and its demand side throughout the period 1750–1860.

Beginning with the formation of the first substantial iron firms in Pennsylvania and adjacent Maryland and Virginia, chapters 1 and 2 examine their form of organization, the role of the men — in the main, merchants — who invested in them, and their initial attempts to come to terms with the regimen and technology of iron production and with the iron markets abroad, particularly in England. The development of a vigorous, sometimes treacherous domestic market system before the American Revolution and the significance to that system of geography and transportation technology are traced in chapter 3.

In their efforts to cater to the market, the iron producers frequently found themselves hostage to political events that they could not foresee and to conditions of aggregate supply and demand over which they could exert little if any control. However, while the ability to influence market conditions was generally absent, the desire to do so was almost always evident. The search by the producers for a means to that end between 1750 and 1850 is the subject of chapter 4. For much of this period their attempts to achieve some degree of mastery over the market were hampered by the essentially static technology of iron production.

The rapid growth of the market during the first half of the nineteenth century stimulated the adoption of new technology by many firms, while it left many others unmoved. During these decades of technological change the industry's organizational structure also underwent a transformation. But, as chapter 5 suggests, technological change and organizational change were not necessarily related; nor did their conjunction necessarily yield results better than those achieved by firms that had adopted the new production techniques but were still organized along traditional lines. This mixture of the old and the new, of continuity and change, within the Pennsylvania iron industry persisted until at least the Civil War, but as is shown in chapter 6, the last ante-bellum decade was the crucial period in the industry's development. Chapter 7 summarizes the evidence and arguments of the preceding chapters and provides me with the opportunity to say what I think their significance is.

Although this study relies on a variety of manuscript sources, including letters, personal journals, and the business records of individual iron firms, the reader will note the extensive use made of several compilations of statistical and other quantitative data. Although the desirability, as well as the necessity, of using these data is clear enough to me, it may not be so to the reader who is unfamiliar with these quantitative records and who therefore may be curious as to why these particular sources, and not others, are used.

The statistical record of eighteenth- and early nineteenth-century American economic history leaves much to be desired, and more than one student of the period before 1840 has referred to it as a "statistical dark age." The statistical data on manufacturing for the first four decades of the nineteenth century are indeed fragmentary, but for the eighteenth century they are nonexistent. Their absence makes certain comparisons between the Pennsylvania iron industry of 1750–1800 and that of 1800–1850 difficult if not hazardous. The chief problem is essentially one of generalization: that is, can one assume that calculations of the output rates and employment levels of the few eighteenth-century firms for which the necessary manuscript evidence exists are representative of the entire industry's performance? The answer is hardly cut and dried and necessarily depends upon a careful evaluation of the evidence for the eighteenth century and the more extensive data for the first decades of the nineteenth century.

The earliest statistical compilation of nineteenth-century industrial activity, including iron production, is Tench Coxe's *A Statement of the Arts and Manufactures of the United States of America for the Year 1810*, published in 1814. Coxe's report, an addition to the census of 1810, is of only limited value to studies of the structure of the early Pennsylvania iron industry. The data are aggregated according to the type of production or manufacturing process and are by no means complete. Although these considerations preclude any attempt to analyze the performance of individual firms or to estimate the output of the entire industry, the data in Coxe's report are nevertheless valuable. Using them, it is possible to arrive at a reasonably accurate determination of the output of bar iron per forge (as in chapter 2) and of the output of pig iron and castings per furnace (see table 20) in 1810. Moreover, these estimates of output in early nineteenth-century Pennsylvania shed light on the performance of the iron industry in the latter half of the eighteenth century.

Apart from the Coxe report, the statistical record of industrial activity over the next several decades is at best spotty. The census of 1820 included a report of manufactures as an afterthought. Probably for this reason, and also because many citizens refused to cooperate with the census enumerators, the 1820 census report is woefully incomplete and unreliable. The same may be said of the report on manufactures in the 1840 census (the census of 1830 did not include any tabulation of industry); consequently, neither the 1820 nor the 1840 census report is the basis in this study for calculations and conclusions concerning the Pennsylvania iron industry between 1810 and 1840. Instead, more extensive data on the industry's performance, organization, and structure are available in the report on manufactures for 1830, compiled by Secretary of the Treasury Louis McLane in 1832, and in the published compilations by the ironmasters themselves for 1840–47.

Although neither McLane's report nor the various reports by iron producers are comprehensive in covering the industry, the data contained in them permit the calculation of mean output per facility by type and form of business organization for a large number of individual firms. Moreover, the data from the industry reports can be used to compute rates of output per worker for facilities of all types. (These computations and detailed comments concerning the sources on which they are based may be found in the text and notes of chapters 4 and 5.)

The data base for 1849 and 1850 is far more extensive than that for any earlier year. The sixth census of the United States (1850) was the second census to include an enumeration of industry as an integral part of the census schedules (the first was the 1840 census). However, as was true of many earlier censuses and virtually all subsequent ones, it was plagued by the problems of noncooperation; suspicion that the federal government would use the census as the basis for direct federal taxation; and a lack of completeness. In this regard, the caveats of William D. Walsh (*The Diffusion of Technological Change in the Pennsylvania Pig Iron Industry, 1850–1870* [1975]) concerning the use of the census enumerators' reports for the schedule of manufactures merit serious consideration. Walsh notes that illegibility, a lack of completeness, and "definitional ambiguities" are among the major deficiencies in the enumerators' reports (pp. 16–18). Even the superintendent of the sixth census, J.D.B. De Bow, found the report to be seriously flawed, for many of the same reasons cited by Walsh. These defects make the 1850 census, for my purposes, a less than attractive source of data on the Pennsylvania iron industry. This study relies on an alternative source, the 1849 report of a committee of the state's ironmasters.

The 1849 ironmasters' report is superior to the 1850 census enumerators' records in a number of important respects. First, the ironmasters' report is far more complete in terms of the number of firms covered — 350 firms operating 495 facilities of all types. For example, the ironmasters' report included data on furnaces "out of blast" as well as those "in blast"; the census enumerators' records covered only those furnaces "in blast." The greater number of furnaces included in the ironmasters' report proves to be of considerable consequence in the characterization of the engineering technology of blast furnaces presented in chapters 5 and 6. Considerations similar to these argued against the use of data from the seventh census (1860) and in favor of an alternative source, the exhaustive compilation by J. P. Lesley, *The Iron Manufacturer's Guide to the Furnaces, Forges and Rolling Mills of the United States* (1859).

My use of these sources and a large body of manuscript collections was made the more profitable through the assistance of many hands. My debts to others are therefore legion, but I owe the most to Louis Galambos. He and Jack P. Greene started this hare. Daniel J. Wilson and Robert A. Becker read most of the manuscript and offered valuable criticism, as did David Dauer, Paul Hoffman, and André-Philippe Katz. Wayne Austerman, who provided needed sources on the manufacture of firearms during the Revolution, has my thanks, as do Carolyn Becker, Lawrence Falkowski, Douglas Harrison, and Sam B. Hilliard. Wardell Jones performed yeoman service as a keypuncher. The Regional Economic History Research Center, its director, Glenn Porter, and its assistant to the director, William Mulligan, provided essential support while I was a fellow at the center during the summer of 1977. Glenn Porter has my appreciation also for his incisive criticism and sensitive editorial eye. Alfred D. Chandler, Jr., Stanley Engerman, Robert Gallman, Albro Martin, and Henry Tom, social sciences editor for The Johns Hopkins University Press, have my thanks for their respective critical readings of the manuscript. I also thank Joanne Allen, copy-editor for the Press, who cleared a path for me and others through sometimes obtuse text and tables. The assistance of archivists and librarians in many local and state depositories is deeply appreciated, but I owe a special debt to Peter Parker and Lucy Hrivnak, of the Historical Society of Pennsylvania. Both were indefatigable in introducing me to many of the manuscript sources used in this study. To my children, Catherine and Martha, go my thanks and admiration for their tolerance. To my wife, Beth, goes my deepest gratitude. No one has lived longer or more bravely with the Pennsylvania iron industry.

# INDUSTRIAL EVOLUTION

# Acts of Faith: The Early Industrial Enterprise

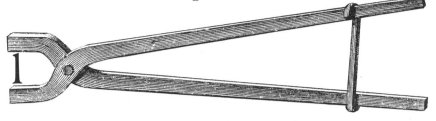

*I resolved to try a method for securing
a reputable Income by means that might
at ye same time be advantageous to ye
Public [which] was by carrying on one
fourth part of a large Iron works.*

James Logan, merchant

Iron-making in America began as a supplement to commerce. Merchants in England and in the North American colonies, particularly in Massachusetts Bay, quickly saw it as an opportunity to cater to increasingly hungry English markets. In 1724 English investors raised substantial amounts of capital for an iron venture in Maryland and Virginia — the Principio Company — destined to be one of the largest eighteenth-century industrial enterprises in the New World. From the outset the efforts of this company were bent in the direction of meeting the mother country's demand for iron; the possibility of serving a local American market never played any part in the thinking of the company's owners.

Much the same attitude characterized the approach of the slightly younger Baltimore Company, founded in 1731 by five wealthy and influential Maryland men. The absence of any conveniently located home market for the Baltimore Company's pig iron dictated that this company follow the lead of the Principio Company in search of a market overseas.[1] Maryland, along with much of the South, lacked the population centers and the smaller but nonetheless vibrant hinterland settlements which could have absorbed the iron produced in the colony. To the north, however, in Pennsylvania, the iron that poured from that colony's furnaces was consumed in the form of cast ironware by thousands of households and as pig iron by forges, where it was refined into bar iron for a variety of uses. By

1

mid-century these facilities were landmarks for travelers in Pennsylvania's interior.

In the early autumn of 1748 Peter Kalm, a young Swedish naturalist, made his way west out of Philadelphia to begin what would be a two-year journey through the cities, countryside, and wilderness of British North America. On October 6, just outside the "little market town" of Chester, he came upon "an iron forge, which was on the right by the roadside. It belonged to two brothers, as I was told. The ore however is not dug here but thirty or forty miles away, where it is first melted in a furnace and then carried to this place. The bellows were made of leather, and both they and the hammers, and even the hearth, were but small in proportion to ours. All the machines were worked by water. The iron was wrought into bars." [2] The forge might have impressed Kalm more had he known that it was only one of some thirty-four furnaces, forges, and ironworks which had been erected in the thirty years before his arrival. [3]

These facilities, punctuating the landscape of rural southeastern Pennsylvania, were usually built along the region's many streams. The streams provided the necessary waterpower, while the rural setting assured a readily available and inexpensive supply of the essential raw materials for iron production: iron ore and wood. At the time when Kalm saw his forge Pennsylvania iron-making was under way in six counties; within a few years it would spread further west across the Susquehanna River to two more (see map 1). [4] By 1775 iron-making had become an industry that was intimately bound up with the larger economy of the colony, employing well over two thousand workers — about 1 percent of Pennsylvania's population, the overwhelming majority of which were farmers. [5]

Iron-making in Pennsylvania began along much the same lines as in Virginia and Maryland, and from an identical motive. In 1716, when the colony's first forge is thought to have been erected, and in the years immediately thereafter Pennsylvania ironmasters sought many of the same markets as did ironmasters in the South. [6] These years of initial development could, then, be cited as evidence supporting the staples thesis — the theory of economic development that stresses the crucial role of commodities produced for export. [7]

By the middle of the eighteenth century, however, the Pennsylvania iron industry was charting a new course, one that could no longer be explained by the staples thesis. The settlement of Pennsylvania had progressed to a point where the colony's population constituted a significant home market for the iron producers' products. Consequently, although English markets represented a potentially larger aggregate demand, they had relatively little allure for Pennsylvania's ironmasters, who in the first instance could have no assurance of success in competing there with Southern producers. More to the point, however, were the greater convenience and lower costs associated with the growing local markets. This is not to say that Pennsylvanians ignored the overseas trade in iron, but most of the ventures at this time were not geared to the production of iron for sale in England. Although a number of these firms were partly financed by merchants who acted as passive partners and who might have been able to arrange shipment of iron to England, most of the furnaces and forges — twenty-six of thirty-four by 1750 — were owned by individuals or two-member partnerships.[8] These firms usually had no contractual connections with merchants engaged in the export trade and relied instead upon local markets of small-scale buyers. They arranged their production and other aspects of their business to suit that particular market.

From the point of view of the individual firm, the choice of better-known and perhaps more predictable local markets over distant markets was a means of reducing risk — an understandable decision in this economic setting. Profits would probably be smaller, but the demand would be relatively steady when one supplied a local market. Debts might be hard to collect, but at least the producer would have firsthand knowledge of those to whom he extended credit. The English market held out the lure of greater profits, along with the threat of much greater losses. It took more faith, as well as more capital and better commercial contacts, to venture into that distant market. Given the poor communications and slow transportation of that era, the producer could never make the rational calculations about his market that seem so essential from our modern perspective. Every aspect of the eighteenth-century businessman's activities was shaped by the high degree of uncertainty he faced every day.

Despite the risks, a few works, such as those of the Durham Iron Company, on the northern reaches of the Delaware River, were organized specifically to supply iron to overseas markets. These firms were almost always owned by multi-member partnerships of the colony's merchants. For these men, an ironworks offered what few other investments could: direct control over the supply of a commodity much in demand. They in turn could supply credit and contacts overseas — crucial factors in dealing with a distant market.

Even the substantial merchants of this ilk sought of course to reduce their risks, and one way was by diversifying their capital investments. For James Logan of Philadelphia, later an owner of Durham Company, this meant acquiring a brief (and unsatisfactory) interest in tobacco to supplement his longstanding activities in the fur trade. Similarly, Dr. Charles Carroll, an Annapolis surgeon and later a partner in the Baltimore Company, who described himself to a London merchant in 1729 as being "conveniently seated for Business [with] a desire to fall into a little trade," thought it wise to consider exporting tobacco and furs, particularly the latter, because "I can purchase of them considerably."[9] Carroll also tried his hand at shipbuilding, an interest that he maintained sporadically after becoming a partner in the Baltimore Company. Carroll, like Logan and so many other merchants who sought alternative investment areas to commerce, became especially active in land speculation.[10] Land, even unimproved land, offered a generally secure outlet for capital, appreciating modestly in value under normal conditions and sharply under speculative pressure. So long as he did not tie too much of his capital up in land, the colonial businessman was able to protect his capital in this way. Merchants large and small thus normally dealt in land as well as commodities.

Accustomed as they were to these kinds of investments, merchants were receptive to the idea of ventures in iron production. Because the largest single initial expense involved in erecting an ironworks was usually the purchase of land for timber and ore supplies, a merchant's experience in assessing and acquiring vast tracts prepared him for this facet of an otherwise novel enterprise. For the more substantial merchants, iron was a particularly attractive commodity for export because, like furs, it was often accepted by English merchants in lieu of specie for settling outstanding accounts. Moreover, during the first half of the eighteenth century in both the English and American iron markets there were relatively few competitors, and entry costs were low.[11] Thus, numbers of colonial merchants, particularly those in Maryland and Pennsylvania, began to look upon iron as a viable means of securing "a reputable Income."[12] The interested merchants frequently pooled their resources with others of a similar mind, which was another means of spreading the risks of doing business. Generally, the members of these partnerships were well acquainted with one another through prior commercial arrangements, friendship, or family ties. Such familiarity notwithstanding, business was seldom consumated merely by a handshake or a verbal agreement. Instead, the concerned parties entered into formal, written contracts by which they legally formed themselves into companies for, as one contract put it, "the Melting, Casting and making of iron."[13]

The contracts were shaped by the problems of doing business in the face of a high degree of uncertainty and risk. With varying degrees of specificity, these contractual agreements described the obligations and rights of a company's membership, as well as the regulations under which the affairs of the firm and its operation were to be governed.[14] For the most part, the agreements dealt with only two major aims: iron was to be produced at a profit, and the financial and personal integrity of each partner was to be maintained. Little, if anything, could be written down about the company's anticipated but highly changeable markets. The existence of a market was taken for granted, and responsibility for charting changes in market conditions was left by implication in the hands of the several members. Almost all of the members of the Durham and Baltimore companies were men of considerable mercantile experience who were accustomed to dealing with these sorts of markets. Decision making was left decentralized, in the hands of the members, and the articles of agreement merely safeguarded their rights. The organization was thus very flexible. It sacrificed the efficiency of a centralized, high-volume operation in order to stay in touch with its varied, far-flung, ever-changing markets.

Even this degree of decentralization proved to be insufficient in some cases. The companies made decisions by reference to majorities of the shareholders, whose votes were weighted proportionately according to the number of shares owned.[15] In this way all members could know the affairs of the company and have a say in its operation, especially in the sale of its iron and the distribution of the profits. But this was a cumbersome form of organization, and its practical weakness quickly became apparent. In 1742, within a decade of the Baltimore Company's establishment, the partners voted to abandon the policy of selling iron as a company and embarked on a "policy of apportionment and separate sales."[16] This enabled each of the merchants to deal on his own account. While the total sales might not be greater, each had the assurance that he could make his own decisions on the spot, without reference to his fellow investors.

This centrifugal tendency made any attempt to coordinate market information with the operating schedule of a firm's production facilities extremely difficult. The amorphous nature of the formal organizational structure of the large colonial iron firm was perhaps a constraint upon improvements in productivity. Clearly, the system was oriented to the marketing functions of the firm, which was where the company's greatest losses and gains were to be realized. It would be several decades before this changed. A new organizational arrangement would then grow out of the practical experience of owners and manager as they came to grips with the regimen of iron production and the pressing demands of their iron markets. Initially, however, the problems of coping with these markets dominated every facet of the industry in Pennsylvania.

Understandably, many of these ventures in iron were unsuccessful, and the roster of losers and the magnitude of their losses must have been sobering for potential investors. One such failure, that of Peter Hasenclever in New York and New Jersey, amounted to approximately fifty thousand pounds. A similar end befell Charles Read, who, like Hasenclever, had invested heavily in New Jersey ironworks.[17] Aside from the extent of their respective losses, the two men seem to have had little else in common. When all competitors were coping each day with such high degrees of uncertainty, disaster appears to have been almost blind in its choice of victims.

Although the losses suffered by Read and Hasenclever were exceptional by virtue of the amounts involved, they were far from unique. Failure in ironworks was not uncommon, and the danger was sufficiently great for Benjamin Franklin to warn his friends against investing in such enterprises.[18] Some men acquired this wisdom the hard way. In the summer of 1728 James Logan, buoyed by having at last sent Durham Company iron to England, suggested that his company and others might soon be able "to supply England with a great part of what they occasion for."[19] It was not to be, and little more than a year later Logan cataloged his woes in a letter to a friend. Despite a personal investment of eighteen hundred pounds (Pennsylvania currency), a shallow Delaware River and unsatisfactory freight rates had combined to frustrate his hopes. He now predicted, "I am likely to be intirely [sic] disappointed."[20] He survived, but with considerably less enthusiasm for the iron business than he had had when he first became involved in it.

Given these experiences, it was little wonder that many of the businesses that survived in the 1750s were those that looked to local, less risky markets. As new firms came into the industry, they too tried to reduce their risks. They did not hesitate to solicit advice from more experienced iron producers, and the responses they received were more often than not words of caution concerning what not to do.[21] Given the complexities of the trade and the difficulties of production for the first time, we can only marvel that any of these early firms survived. Robert Erskine, the manager of the British-owned American Company in New York, summarized the complexities of an ironworks operation in a letter to his employers:

> I design to follow the natural order of things as they arise. Wood, Charcoal and Ore are the First in Course the furnace its Construction & appurtenances the Roasting mixting smelting of ore into pig metal come next, together with a variety of other articles which may occur during are in [sic] Blast, then come the Forge with all their Connections, which will include the processes of the Manufactory of Bar Iron faults improvements &c. &c. Provisions and necessaries, Farms, Horses, Cattle, Carriages, Roads, Mills, Dams, Houses &c &c must follow, and no doubt several miscellanious observations what cannot be ranged under particular heads, must necessarily be interspersed. The Workmen in the various Branches must be included in the Articles to which they belong.[22]

If Erskine's description seems lacking in the specificity we might have hoped for, it accurately reflects conditions in a risky industry in which most of the crucial decisions had to be left in the hands of the man on the ground. Centralized control was too cumbersome. Distant markets were too changeable. All one could do was join hands with men of good judgment, work hard, and hope for the best. This brand of early capitalism was characterized more by faith and intuition than by calculation.

Even the most talented group of well-connected and well-heeled merchants who organized an ironworks encountered challenges that were foreign to mercantile affairs. Management of a new sort was required. Organization loomed larger; personality became a less certain key to profits. In this sense, industrialization, even before the industrial revolution, had revolutionary implications for the mercantile brand of capitalism that had held sway in Europe and its colonies for several centuries. Frequently, solving the problems of management had as much to do with the success of the enterprise as did the firm's encounters with the market at home or abroad.

Iron-making was a continuous process in which the flow of inputs had to be closely regulated to ensure their adequate supply and timely arrival at the furnace or forge. In great part, the profitable operation of an ironworks depended upon the degree of coordination of the various materials, routines, and labor at the two production sites within the works, the furnace and forge. Often, both units were contained within a single ironworks, although it was not uncommon for an ironworks to consist of one or two furnaces or forges alone.

The furnace was the facility at which iron ore was smelted to make pig iron by mixing specific amounts of ore with measured amounts of charcoal fuel and a flux of lime or limestone. The furnace itself was a brick structure, usually about thirty to thirty-two feet in height, which was loaded from the top with ore, fuel, and flux and then fired at the base.

Once the furnace was lit, a semicontinuous blast of cold air from a pair of water-powered bellows entered it through the tuyère, a nozzlelike air pipe near the base, and raised the furnace's internal temperature to the point necessary for smelting. The flux coagulated the waste material and impurities in the ore and formed a surface of slag on the now-molten iron. The iron itself was tapped from the crucible at the bottom of the furnace, where it collected, and the molten iron was allowed to run into channels made in the sand floor around the hearth. The pattern of these channels and the appearance of the cooled iron in them were evidently evocative of suckling pigs around their mother, and the furnace product was therefore called pig iron. Some of the furnace iron generally was run into sand molds for cast-iron articles such as stove plates, which were then sold in local or other colonial markets. For the most part, however, the output of a furnace consisted of pigs.

Once pig iron was produced at an ironworks, the ironmaster shipped it to colonial forges or to English markets, principally London. Frequently the pigs were refined into bar iron at the ironworks's forges. There were generally two hearths at a forge: a refinery, or finery, and a chafery. At the finery the pig iron was heated to a semimolten state, pounded by a massive water-powered hammer, reheated, and then hammered again into anconies, thick bars with bulbous ends. The ancony was one form of bar iron, and its fabrication often marked the final step of production at a forge. Frequently, however, the anconies comprised semifinished input material for the chafery, where they were heated and hammered again and then cut into various-sized bars for sale.

An extremely important decision that an entrepreneur establishing such an ironworks had to make was exactly where to locate it. An iron producer wanted his products to leave the works with minimal expense and risk of loss or damage. Access to inexpensive water transportation was particularly desirable, since iron was a relatively high-bulk, low-value product. Of course the location of an ironworks was determined by more than the presence of navigable waterways or terrain conducive to road construction. Although the lay of the land, like the weather, was something about which little could be done, ironmasters were sometimes able to alter inhospitable natural features for roads, provided they had enough money and manpower and could exert influence in the right places. Even so, this was not always enough. In 1745 the owners of the Durham Iron Works, near the Delaware River in Bucks County, Pennsylvania, petitioned and contracted for the construction of a road from the works to a point eight miles below it on the Delaware. Local townspeople protested, however, and the project was abandoned.[23]

Of fundamental importance in determining the location of an ironworks was the proximity of sufficient suitable ore, wood for making charcoal, and waterpower. The question of which of these physical endowments was the single most significant locational criterion has been a source of disagreement among students of the charcoal iron industry, although the argument has centered on the relative importance of the supply of wood as compared to that of ore.[24] Admittedly, the selection of any one geophysical factor is difficult and always susceptible to counterargument. Nevertheless, it is a question worth pursuing because an ironworks's success, whatever measure of it was due to skilled labor and acute management, rested in the first instance on a foundation of geographical and physical advantages. There is much evidence to suggest that Arthur C. Bining's argument for the primacy of iron ore as a locational determinant is valid. Both timber and swiftly moving streams were common enough in eastern North America; their proximity to an ore deposit was to be expected. It was only after an ironworks had been in operation for a number of years that the supply of timber became a cause for real concern.[25] Thus, for the most part, furnaces were located on or near land that was known for its iron ore content and offered an outlet to a market.

Once the site for a furnace or forge had been selected and the initial surveying and acquisition of the land had been accomplished, the actual construction of the facility and its ancillary structures was begun. The expenses incurred in erecting an ironworks varied somewhat with location and, of course, with time. This last point is significant for what it implies about the scale and level of competition within the iron industry during the last twenty-five years of British rule. Questions of scale of operation and competition will be considered at length in chapter 4; for now, it is useful to note that although the Baltimore Company was initially capitalized at thirty-five hundred pounds sterling in 1731, it represented about thirty-five thousand pounds sterling in capital by 1764.[26] This capital appreciation was due not only to the company's expansion of its physical plant but also to its aggressive program of land acquisition: between 1734 and 1751 it gathered in about fifty-five hundred acres beyond its initial holdings.[27] Growth such as the Baltimore Company experienced (a 900 percent increase in capitalization) was evidence of an unusually well-run, profitable enterprise. However, the scale of the Baltimore Company's operations in the 1760s also suggests that by that time the initial capital requirements that confronted a new competitor for the London market — in which the Baltimore Company occupied a fairly strong position — were very high.

The initial expense involved in the erection of a furnace or forge was probably greater in the years after 1750 than during the preceding quarter-century, and the relatively high cost of entry on a truly competitive basis in any of the major English markets no doubt encouraged many firms to stress production for local buyers. At home they would face limited competition. Abroad they had to compete with well-capitalized businesses like the Baltimore Company. To match the latter firm, the newcomer would have to make large quantities of high-quality iron. The degree of coordination and control, as well as the number of skilled and unskilled workers, required to conduct an enterprise the size of the Baltimore Company or the Cornwall works of Pennsylvania taxed even these established firms. A partial explanation for Peter Hasenclever's failure in New York and New Jersey may well lie in his attempts to begin iron production on a scale comparable to that of the larger established American works without providing for a commensurate level of operational control.[28] The safer course was to be satisfied with the more modest profits provided by the growing market at home.

The perils of opting for the larger but riskier markets abroad were illustrated by the misfortunes of the Durham Iron Company. After a seemingly well-planned expenditure of four thousand pounds in 1727 and 1728, the company soon encountered serious problems, to the profound frustration of James Logan, one of the company's major shareholders. The Durham Company's problems were due in part to the fact that the Delaware River, on which the works were located, was too shallow downstream from the works to take ships heavily laden with iron.[29] A more important problem, however, seems to have been the company's inability to find shipping to England at acceptable freight rates. This unwillingness to pay what must have been the standard freight charges is curious, since in 1735 the Baltimore Company was prepared to pay at a rate of ten shillings per ton — about 10 percent of the selling price — of pig iron from their works on the Patapsco River to England.[30] The Durham Company's owners decided not to pay this much, however, and gave up the idea of extensive sales to English buyers. The company seems to have done well enough selling in the Philadelphia market, but by the early 1770s it was out of business.[31]

As the experience of the Durham Iron Company illustrates, it was essential to have efficient operations under the control of a capable resident manager. In this business, administration was of far greater importance than was normally the case with mercantile investments. The manager's concerns included the flow of materials, the scheduling of each routine and subroutine of the production process, and the assignment and discipline of the labor force. Only rarely was an ironworks manager who was not also an owner of the works given any extensive responsibility for marketing the iron produced at the forge or furnace.[32] This was just as well, since the other demands upon a manager's time and energy were considerable, and none of these was more complex and important than the management of labor.

Iron-making at the larger colonial ironworks was a self-contained activity in that most if not all of the raw materials and the intermediate and final products were usually produced within the confines of the ironworks themselves. This was true even at the smaller ironworks. Because of the variety of functions involved in iron production, ironworks employed labor forces composed of skilled, semiskilled, and unskilled workers.[33]

With the exception of the very skilled workers, the labor forces of furnaces and forges were quite similar. Both facilities employed relatively unskilled workers such as woodcutters, carters, or haulers, and laborers. The semiskilled work force consisted of stockers, who fed charcoal to the furnace or forge, and the assistants to the founders and forgemen as well as fairly skilled workers, such as colliers, who made charcoal, and assorted craftsmen, including carpenters, wheelwrights, masons, and blacksmiths.

Of course, there were some workers — skilled, unskilled, and semiskilled — who were peculiar to a furnace alone, including miners, ore breakers and cleaners, and furnace fillers.[34] The most important distinction, however, between the labor forces of a furnace and those of a forge lay in the types of highly skilled work that each facility's operation required. A founder's job required considerable experience in running iron into pigs or castings. No less demanding of experience but quite different in terms of the type of skill required was the work of finers, chafers, and hammermen at a forge: they transformed pig iron into anconies and from them made bar iron.

TABLE 1

Wages and Prices in Pennsylvania, 1730–74, Selected Years (in £ Pa.)

| Year | Wholesale Price Index[a] | Bar-Iron Price per Ton | Woodcutter's Wage per Cord | Collier's Wage per Cbu. | Finer's Wage per Ton |
|------|------|------|------|------|------|
| 1730 | 100[b] | – | 0.111[c] (2) | 0.572 (1) | 1.000 (1) |
| 1746 | 95 | 19.50 | [d] | 0.583 (1) | – |
| 1748 | 117 | 27.32 | [e] | [f] | 1.500 (1) |
| 1760 | 125 | 32.50 | [g] | 0.494[h] (1) | 1.250 (1) |
| 1768 | 121 | 23.71 | 0.110 (8) | – | 1.250 (1) |
| 1769 | 117 | 23.35 | 0.111 (4) | 0.435 (1) | 1.635 (1) |
| 1770 | 122 | 23.17 | 0.101 (1) | – | – |
| 1772 | 138 | 27.07 | 0.100 (2) | – | 1.349 (1) |
| 1773 | 134 | 26.43 | 0.100 (2) | 0.401 (9) | 1.999 (1) |
| 1774 | 131 | 26.12 | – | 0.440 (3) | – |

Sources: Wage data are from Hopewell Forge Coal, Iron & Time Book, Etc., 1768–75, and Hopewell Forge Ledgers, A–F, 1765–74, in Grubb Furnace and Forge Account Books, Grubb Collection, Historical Society of Pennsylvania; New Pine Forge Cole Book, 1744–60, New Pine Forge Time Book, 1760–63, and New Pine Forge Ledger A, 1760–62, in Forges and Furnaces Account Books, ibid.; Arthur Cecil Bining, *Pennsylvania Iron Manufacture in the Eighteenth Century,* Publications of the Pennsylvania Historical Commission, vol. 4 (1938; reprint, Harrisburg: Pennsylvania Historical and Museum Commission, 1973), pp. 105–13; and Keach Johnson, "The Genesis of the Baltimore Ironworks," *Journal of Southern History* 19 (1953): 167. The data on iron prices and the wholesale price index are from Anne Bezanson, Robert D. Gray, and Miriam Hussey, *Prices in Colonial Pennsylvania* (Philadelphia: University of Pennsylvania Press, 1935).

*Note:* Cbu. = 100 bushels. Figures in parentheses indicate the number of observations for each class of worker in a given year.

[a] To closest integer.

[b] Extrapolated value.

[c] Bining, in his *Pennsylvania Iron Manufacture* (p. 110), cites several instances of woodcutters' wages of 2s.6d., or £0.125. The Durham Company, ca. 1730, paid £0.083 (see Johnson, "The Genesis of the Baltimore Ironworks," p. 167).

[d] Two observations – one of 28 August 1740 and the other of 6 January 1743 – show a wage rate of £0.100 per cord (see Colebrookdale Furnace Ledger, 1750–52, Forges and Furnaces Account Books, p. 51).

[e] Two observations – of 24 and 29 April 1751 – show a wage rate of £0.100 (ibid., pp. 14 and 2, respectively).

[f] One observation – of 25 November 1751 – shows a wage rate of £0.500 per load (ibid., p. 11). Colebrookdale Furnace was in eastern Bucks County.

[g] Seventeen observations – in March–May 1762 – show a wage rate of £0.104 per cord (see Potts Grove Ledger B, XVII, 1762, Potts Manuscripts, Historical Society of Pennsylvania).

[h] Six observations show a wage rate of £0.55 per load (ibid.), Pottsgrove was in Berks County.

As the above suggests, the colonial ironworks had a well-defined division of tasks and, at the higher levels of skill, of labor. This division was reflected in the different wage rates for the various jobs, which in many instances did not vary significantly from one facility to another.[35] Unfortunately, specific wage data for the colonial iron industry are rare, and some of the surviving data are ambiguous. Workers were often paid in kind rather than in cash, wages having been credited to their accounts with the ironmaster. For example, one such account in 1773 showed: "126 Loads [of charcoal], the Yield of 362 Cords of Wood, coal'd by Craft Achenback @ 2/p [2 shillings per] Cord & ent [entered] to his C[r] 28th Oct[r] 1773."[36] On other occasions a worker might receive half of his payment in cash and half in goods. There were, however, a fair number of cases in which the worker was paid in cash and had to furnish himself with provisions.[37]

Because of the admixture of arrangements for wages, it is extremely difficult to determine average wages and wage differentials with precision.

TABLE 2

Percentage Changes in Wages and Prices in Pennsylvania, 1730–74 (in £ Pa.)

| Period | Wholesale Price Index | Bar-Iron Price per Ton | Woodcutter's Wage per Cord | Collier's Wage per Cbu. | Finer's Wage per Ton |
|---|---|---|---|---|---|
| 1730–46 | − 5.0 | − | − | + 1.9 | − |
| 1730–48 | + 17.0 | − | − | − | + 50.0 |
| 1730–60 | + 25.0 | − | − | − 13.6 | − |
| 1730–68 | + 21.0 | − | − 0.9 | − | + 25.0 |
| 1730–69 | + 17.0 | − | 0 | − 24.0 | − 0.6 |
| 1730–73 | + 34.0 | − | − 9.9 | − 29.9 | + 99.9 |
| 1730–74 | + 31.0 | − | − | − 23.1 | − |
| 1746–60 | + 31.6 | + 66.7 | − | − 15.3 | − |
| 1746–74 | + 37.9 | + 33.9 | − | − 24.5 | − |
| 1748–68 | + 3.4 | − 13.2 | − | − | − 16.7 |
| 1748–73 | + 14.5 | − 3.3 | − | − | + 33.3 |
| 1768–69 | − 3.3 | − 1.5 | + 0.9 | − | + 30.8 |
| 1768–72 | + 14.0 | + 14.2 | − 9.1 | − | + 7.9 |
| 1768–73 | + 8.3 | + 11.5 | − 9.1 | − | + 59.9 |
| 1769–70 | + 4.3 | − 0.8 | − 9.0 | − | − |
| 1769–72 | + 17.9 | + 15.9 | − 9.9 | − | − 17.5 |
| 1769–73 | + 14.5 | + 13.2 | − 9.9 | − 7.8 | + 23.3 |
| 1769–74 | + 12.0 | + 11.9 | − | + 1.1 | − |
| 1770–72 | + 13.1 | + 16.8 | − 1.0 | − | − |
| 1772–73 | − 2.9 | − 2.4 | 0 | − | + 48.2 |
| 1773–74 | − 2.2 | − 1.2 | − | + 9.7 | − |

Sources: See table 1.
Note: Cbu. = 100 bushels.

Moreover, wages at colonial ironworks behaved erratically over time; the wage rates for some jobs remained fairly stable, while those for others changed markedly. Unless we compare the movement of wages with that of prices, trends in wage rates by themselves do not reveal very much about the relative positions of unskilled, semiskilled, and skilled workers.[38] This comparison is presented in tables 1, 2, and 3. In each table the wage rates for unskilled, semiskilled, and skilled workers are represented by those for woodcutters, colliers, and finers, respectively. As table 2 reveals, wages, with the exception of those for finers, declined even as the wholesale price index and the wholesale price per ton of bar iron increased substantially. In view of this, the 23 percent rise in the wage for finers appears anomalous. The increase was probably due, at least in part, to the fact that finers were highly skilled workers and not particularly numerous in Pennsylvania or any other colony during the eighteenth century. Thus a premium would have been paid for their labor, particularly during the 1760s, when Pennsylvania "became the leading colony in the export of bar iron to England."[39] During this period of expansion, production could not be increased without employing more of these scarce workers, and

TABLE 3

Daily Wages of an Unskilled, a Semiskilled, and a Skilled Worker in Pennsylvania, 1730–73, Selected Years

| | Daily Wage of Worker (£ Pa.) | | | | | |
| | Unskilled | Semiskilled | Skilled | Ratio of | | |
| Year | Woodcutter (3 cords per day) | Collier (210 bushels per day) | Finer (1.0 tons per day) | Collier to Woodcutter | Finer to Woodcutter | Finer to Collier |
|---|---|---|---|---|---|---|
| 1730 | 0.333 | 1.201 | 1.000 | 3.61 | 3.00 | 0.83 |
| 1768 | 0.330 | – | 1.250 | – | 3.79 | – |
| 1769 | 0.333 | 0.914 | 1.635 | 2.75 | 4.91 | 1.79 |
| 1772 | 0.300 | – | 1.349 | – | 4.50 | – |
| 1773 | 0.300 | 0.842 | 1.99 | 2.81 | 6.63 | 2.36 |

*Sources:* The daily-output figure for a woodcutter is from Bining, *Pennsylvania Iron Manufacture,* p. 110; he also notes a 2-ton-per-week figure for finers (p. 109). The figure of 1.0 tons/day used here is an estimate derived from the variable weekly output of a finery hearth at Hopewell Forge – from 1.0 to 16.5 tons in 1774 – divided by the 6 work days in the week. Although Bining's figure of 2 tons per week is a good approximation, it does not reflect the actual number of days worked in the week (see Hopewell Forge Coal, Iron & Time Book, Etc., 1768–1775, pp. 59–75). The output figure for a collier is derived from Hopewell Forge Coal, Iron & Time Book, Etc., 1768–75.

manufacturers were doubtless bidding for their services. Less-skilled workers such as woodcutters and colliers were far easier to find, and the general decline in their wage rates probably reflects population growth in Pennsylvania throughout the period 1725–75.

Despite the higher wages paid to their finers, ironworks such as Cornwall Furnace, Hopewell Forge, New Pine Forge, the Baltimore Company, and others continued to be profitable enterprises; the wage increases for their very skilled workers did not eliminate profits for the owners.[40] Nor were the increases possible because of proportional increases in the price per ton of bar iron. In fact, the wage increase for finers from 1768 to 1773 was five times as great as the increase in the price of bar iron for the same period. It seems very likely that the manufacturers were able to increase wages in this way because of savings on the labor costs of less-skilled workers, a conclusion confirmed by the data in tables 3, 4, and 5.

From 1730 to 1773 the wage bill for woodcutters and colliers necessary to produce one ton of bar iron fell by £0.86 (Pennsylvania currency). The concomitant increase in the combined wage bill for finers and chafers was almost £2.00 (Pennsylvania), a difference of about £1.14. It is reasonable to assume that much if not most of this difference consisted of savings on the wage bill of unskilled and semiskilled workers (similar to those realized on the wage bill of woodcutters and colliers). A part of these savings may also have been due to increased efficiency in one or more of the several operations of iron production. In general, however, the higher wages of the skilled forge workers were possible largely because of the savings realized in the wages of the less-skilled workers.

TABLE 4

Labor Time Necessary to Produce One Ton of Bar Iron, 1730–73

| Worker | Number of Days' Labor | Percentage of Total Days |
|---|---|---|
| Woodcutter | 3.75 | 48% |
| Collier | 2.06 | 26% |
| Finer | 1.00 | 13% |
| Chafer | 1.00 | 13% |
| Total | 7.81 | 100% |

Sources: See table 1.

TABLE 5

Wages Necessary to Produce One Ton of Bar Iron, 1730–73,
Selected Years (in £ Pa.)

| Year | Bar Iron Price (Pounds per Ton) | Wage of | | | |
|---|---|---|---|---|---|
| | | Woodcutter | Collier | Finer | Chafer |
| 1730 | — | 1.249 | 2.471 | 1.000 | 1.000 |
| 1768 | 23.71 | 1.238 | — | 1.250 | 1.250 |
| 1769 | 23.25 | 1.249 | 1.879 | 1.635 | 1.635 |
| 1772 | 27.07 | 1.125 | — | 1.349 | 1.349 |
| 1773 | 26.43 | 1.125 | 1.732 | 1.999 | 1.999 |

Sources: See table 1.

The desire to achieve such economies was undoubtedly one reason for the use of indentured servants and slaves in many colonial ironworks. Thus on 8 December 1773 Charles Carroll, of Carrollton, in a letter to his partners in the Baltimore Company, strongly recommended the purchase of forty slaves to save the company the annual expense of employing "hirelings," that is, free laborers.[41] Although slaves worked for the most part at the unskilled and semiskilled jobs, such as mining, cutting wood, and making charcoal, many were employed as highly skilled finers and chafers at forges such as Hopewell and New Pine.[42] At the latter forge, as at others, slaves learned their skills by working as assistants to free, skilled forgemen. At New Pine the June 1760 labor agreement of Samuel Barford stipulated that he was to be given £1.25 (Pennsylvania) per ton of bar iron, as well as a house and the "usual customs of other forgemen," provided that he assumed "charge of a Negro man called Tom and promises to use his utmost Endeavors to Learn him the Said Negro."[43] To the ironmaster a skilled slave doubtless represented a profitable investment, especially in light of the increase taking place in the wages of his skilled craftsmen.[44]

There was of course a major disadvantage to the use of slaves and indentured servants: many of them ran away from what could not always have been pleasant conditions.[45] In July 1745 Richard Croxall, manager of the

Baltimore Company's Patapsco works, placed an advertisement in the *Maryland Gazette* offering a reward for the return of "Three *Irish* Servant-Men belonging to *Benjamin Tasker,* Esq., and Company," who had run away on June 25. Croxall noted that one was "a butcher by trade" and another "wears a truss for Rupture."[46]

Ultimately, running away was the only course of action available to slaves and indentured servants confronted with what they considered to be intolerable conditions; flight was their protest. A free ironworker of course enjoyed considerably more latitude in expressing dissatisfaction with his situation. At the very least he could approach his employer about a wage increase, as the carters at the American Company's works did in the early 1770s.[47] Failing in that, the worker could deliberately do inferior work, refuse to work, or simply leave. Peter Hasenclever, then the resident manager of the American Company, described his trouble with the German workers he had imported on a contract basis, complaining that "they pretended to have their wages raised, which I refused. They made bad work; I complained, and reprimanded them; they told me they could not make better work at such low wages; and, if they did not please me, I might dismiss them. I was, therefore, obliged to submit, for it had cost me a prodigious expense to transport them from Germany; and, had I dismissed them, I must have lost these disbursements, and could get no good workmen in their stead."[48]

Although such instances of friction between labor and management are arresting, they were probably not very numerous or, generally, very severe, because apart from cases where workers — free or chattel — ran away, the records of the ironworks contain little or no mention of serious disputes. For the most part, work at a furnace or forge was a physically taxing and monotonous affair relieved only by various diversions, including frequent bouts of drunkenness. Curttis Grubb, owner and manager of Cornwall Furnace, complained one day that his clerk "is such a drunken Fellow . . . he Gits Whiskey Amongst the People & [is] hardley Ever Sober . . . ."[49] Severely tried and also disgusted, Grubb summed up his feelings in a letter to his brother Peter, saying simply, "I have the worst luck with drunken clerks of anybody."[50] Drunkenness may have fueled the passions of the workers of "Ringwood Iron-Works, in New Jersey," at which "a fray happened among some of the workmen . . . which continued some time by which one man lost his life, and several were badly wounded."[51] Alcohol, then, provided a release from the drudgery and monotony of work at a furnace or forge. Whereas the arduousness of the jobs was a function of their almost completely manual character, their monotony was a reflection of the industrial discipline intrinsic to the work schedule of iron-making: continuity of process and regularity of step — in short, reliability — were demanded by the rhythm of successful iron production.

This type of discipline, relatively new in the eighteenth century, was alien to mercantile or agrarian endeavors. For the entrepreneur first engaging in iron-making it must always have been a confusing problem to operate such a business. If he and his partners put the wrong man in charge of their operations, they could anticipate problems that would soon undermine their marketing efforts, however successful they were. Only through efficient management of production could they provide iron of the quality and quantity demanded by their customers. A firm could fail even if its production were well-managed; it could never succeed if this were not the case. This was a new set of relationships for the merchant to master. Given these new relationships, what is most surprising about colonial iron-making is not that so many enterprises failed but that as many succeeded as did.

# Innovation and the Rhythm of Production

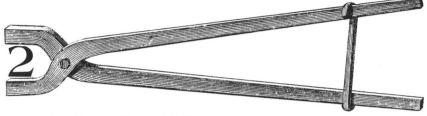

*. . . the forge Stood Idle*
*7½ days for want of Coal*

Peter Grubb, ironmaster

As we have seen, the merchants who ventured into iron-making encountered in the productive process a situation that was for the most part alien to their commercial experience. In commerce they had to make a series of discrete decisions any one of which might well mean their downfall but few of which were interrelated as part of a continuous social process. They might need to buy pork wisely one day and sell one of their ships the following week. If they made a good decision about accepting the bills of exchange they were offered in payment, they would make a good profit. But tomorrow they would have another such decision, and the two would be in large part autonomous. This was not so in manufacturing, where the opportunities for a quick profit did not exist and the major decisions about industrial operations could have a cumulative, long-term effect. Even small improvements in technique or organization might mean substantial savings over time. It is critical to understand the manner in which the colonial businessmen made these improvements as they sought to increase their profits in iron-making.

Innovators in the iron industry had to take account of the fact that the fundamental schedule that governed pig- and bar-iron production was controlled to a great extent by nature. Many of the major operations at an ironworks could be performed only during particular months. This seasonal dependence was a direct outgrowth of the nature of iron production technology, which rested on a base of charcoal fuel and waterpower.

The production of charcoal entailed the controlled firing of wood in domelike mounds for three to ten days. Because of the nature of the operation and the time involved in its execution, charcoal-making required dry

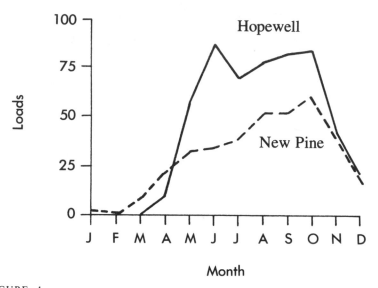

FIGURE 1
MEAN MONTHLY LOADS OF CHARCOAL ARRIVING AT HOPEWELL FORGE, 1768–74, AND NEW PINE FORGE, 1751–59
Data from New Pine Forge Cole Book, 1744–60; and Hopewell Forge Coal, Iron & Time Book, Etc., 1768–75.

weather with a minimum of wind. Consequently, most charcoal was made during the late spring, summer, and early fall (see fig. 1, for Hopewell and New Pine forges). The colliers could not begin their work, however, until the woodcutters had cut timber into cordwood size. Once in this form — called "ranks" — the wood was inspected for flaws by a foreman. Those ranks that were accepted, or "taken up," were then termed "cords." Usually, woodcutters were about 96 percent efficient; that is, only 4 percent of all ranks were rejected.[1]

The peak period of activity for woodcutters preceded that for colliers by about a month and, as figure 2 makes clear, the jobs of woodcutting and charcoal-making required the largest number of an ironworks's laborers.[2] Because charcoal was of central importance to iron-making, its production schedule largely determined the rhythm of production of pig iron and therefore of anconies and bar iron as well. The nature of these interrelationships can be demonstrated by using the records of Cornwall Furnace and Hopewell Forge, in Lebanon County, Pennsylvania, for the period 1768–75.[3]

As figure 3 indicates, pig iron arrived at Hopewell Forge from Cornwall Furnace with a significant degree of seasonal regularity. The peak tonnage was consistently received during the winter months of December, January, and February (March 1775 is the single exception). This pattern had its

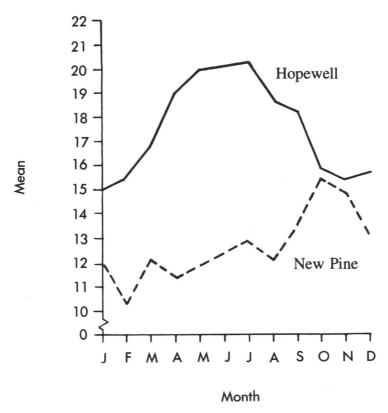

FIGURE 2
MEAN MONTHLY NUMBER OF WORKERS AT HOPEWELL FORGE, 1768–75, AND NEW PINE FORGE, 1760–62
Data from Hopewell Forge Coal, Iron & Time Book, Etc., 1768–75, passim; and New Pine Forge Time Book, 1760–63, passim.

origin in the blast schedule of Cornwall Furnace; one of the two major blast periods, during which the furnace produced iron, began in October and ended in December (the other blast period probably began in April and lasted until late July or early August).

A similar pattern is evident in the monthly record of ancony production at Hopewell Forge. With only a few exceptions, the level of output of anconies (see fig. 4) coincides with or lags behind by one month the peak months of pig-iron deliveries to the forge from Cornwall. This coordination between the two facilities made for an efficient operation at both forge and furnace, but it demanded a high degree of integration among the several component routines of each.

The extent to which the various activities at Hopewell Forge were integrated is apparent from the ancony-production figures presented in table

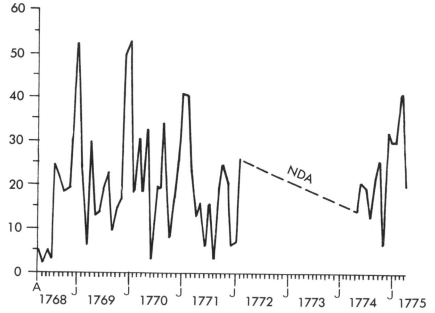

FIGURE 3

MONTHLY TONS OF PIG IRON RECEIVED AT HOPEWELL FORGE FROM CORNWALL FURNACE, 1768–75

Data from Hopewell Forge Coal, Iron & Time Book, Etc., 1768–75.

6.[4] The predicted values and the actual number of tons produced for each year are in fairly close agreement, suggesting that Hasenclever's estimates of required quantities of inputs were reasonably accurate. The significance of table 6 lies in what the figures given there reveal about the production process for bar iron.

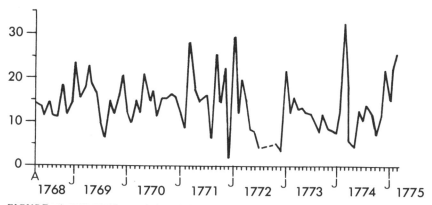

FIGURE 4

MONTHLY ANCONY OUTPUT AT HOPEWELL FORGE, 1768–75, IN TONS
Data from Hopewell Forge Coal, Iron & Time Book, Etc., 1768–75.

TABLE 6

Actual and Predicted Ancony Output at Hopewell Forge, 1768–74

| | | | | Predicted Values | |
|---|---|---|---|---|---|
| Year | Cbu. of Charcoal[a] | Tons of Pig Iron Received | Tons of Anconies Produced | Based on 4.32 Cbu. per Ancony Ton | Based on 1.5 Tons Pig Iron per Ancony Ton |
| 1768 | 811.11 | 130.75[b] | 119.85[c] | 187.76 | 87.17[b] |
| 1769 | 726.44 | 271.25 | 193.18 | 168.16 | 180.83 |
| 1770 | 762.00 | 277.75 | 175.73 | 176.39 | 185.17 |
| 1771 | 713.74 | 227.75 | 169.71 | 165.22 | 151.83 |
| 1772 | 476.25 | 33.00[d] | 106.22[e] | 110.24 | —[f] |
| 1773 | 606.75 | 0.00[g] | 148.88 | 154.34 | — |
| 1774 | 571.50 | 154.75[h] | 157.36[i] | 132.29 | 103.17 |
| Total | 4,727.79 | 1,095.25 | 1,070.93 | 1,094.40 | — |

*Sources:* Hopewell Forge Ledgers A–F, 1765–74; Hopewell Forge Coal, Iron & Time Book, Etc., 1768–75.
*Note:* Cbu. = 100 bushels.
[a] Bushels have been calculated from the number of "loads" of charcoal carted to the forge. One load usually equaled 127 bushels, or 1.27 Cbu.
[b] March–December only; January and February were two of the months in which the largest number of pig-iron tons generally arrived at Hopewell Forge. Consequently, the pig-iron tons listed are probably not the year's total.
[c] Data available for April–December.
[d] January and February only.
[e] No output listed for August–October.
[f] Insufficient data for calculations.
[g] No data listed.
[h] Data available for May–December only.
[i] Actual tons for May–December amounted to 97.11.

For three of the five years the predicted values are similar, but in two years they diverge to a substantial degree. This disparity arises partly from the fact that they are estimates derived by using two constants — 432 bushels of charcoal and 1.5 tons of pig iron — to predict the tons of anconies produced each year. This method rests on the assumption that Hopewell Forge used the same amount of each of these input materials every year to produce one ton of anconies. This was obviously not the case. The number of bushels of charcoal consumed in the production of one ton of anconies was a function of the quality of the wood from which it was made, as well as of the skill of the collier.[5] Even if we assume a uniformly high level of skill among the colliers, no such uniformity characterized the various types of wood. Thus, the number of bushels of charcoal required to make one ton of anconies would probably have been less than 432 bushels in one year and more in another.

The predicted values calculated on the basis of pig-iron tons received present a more difficult problem and one of another kind. Unlike charcoal, pig iron did not have to be used soon after its arrival at the finery or chafery. Consequently, a calculation of predicted ancony production on the basis of the number of pig-iron tons received at the forge would probably be inaccurate for some years because pig iron already at the forge has been excluded from consideration.[6] Moreover, we can have no assurance that the production of a ton of anconies at Hopewell Forge required exactly 1.5 tons of pig iron each year (or month). At most furnaces the quality of the product was variable, albeit within a certain general set of standards, a fact of which ironmasters were very much aware. For example, the owners of the Carlisle Iron Works instructed their manager to run tests on the pig iron from their furnace by making bar iron from the pigs. Further, they advised him that "if the quality should not prove good in such Tryal for Bar Iron, then to make as many castings & as few Piggs as possible — ." [7]

Nevertheless, the predicted values are useful because when compared with the actual production, they suggest that the entire operation of Hopewell was conducted with a degree of control not usually associated with enterprises of a preindustrial economy. The amount of coordination achieved in a variety of separate operations is surprising. This precision suggests that Curttis and Peter Grubb were doing an excellent job of short-term planning as managers of Cornwall Furnace and Hopewell Forge, respectively. Their accomplishment is all the more impressive in view of the complexity of their task.

The production of anconies was a continuous process requiring that the inputs — pig iron and charcoal — be on hand in the appropriate amounts when needed. Because an existing supply of charcoal could spoil if stored in the coal house for too long or if exposed to the elements, ironmasters desired that the production of fresh quantities of charcoal proceed at a rate not much faster than that of consumption. Thus knowledge of how much pig iron could be obtained and when it would arrive was important to the manager of a forge. Even more important, however, was the availability of a sufficient supply of charcoal, since pig iron stored at a forge represented unproductive capital and, often, an outstanding debt. The same considerations applied to a furnace; unused ore and lime meant an outstanding wage bill undiminished by earnings through pig-iron sales, and unconsumed charcoal was a similar liability.

The arrival of the various inputs at a furnace or forge in the necessary amounts and at the correct time required the careful scheduling of the labor force. Reliability meant more than the mere presence of the seasonally appropriate number of workers; it also meant the efficient employment of these workers over the course of each month. Most months comprised twenty-six twelve-hour work days. [8] Consequently, the true measure of the monthly employment level of the labor force at an ironworks was not the number of workers employed during any one month but the number of man-days worked. The two need not have been proportional; and often, as figure 5 indicates, an increase or decrease from one month to the next in the number of workers was accompanied by the opposite movement in the number of man-days worked. [9]

Moreover, although both variables reflect the seasonality of employ-

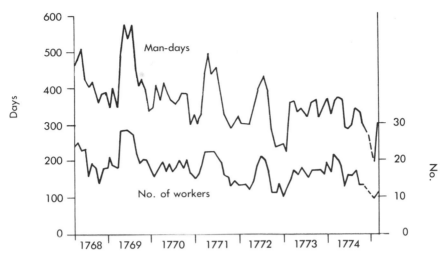

FIGURE 5
MONTHLY MAN-DAYS WORKED AND NUMBER OF WORKERS AT HOPEWELL FORGE, 1768–75
Data from Hopewell Forge Coal, Iron & Time Book, Etc., 1768–75.

ment with about equal fidelity, the number of man-days worked is the
more finely resolved of the two, especially because it is the measure of
actual labor time consumed in production. The careful use of this time was
one of the most demanding tasks confronting producers in an industry
characterized by increasing competition, falling prices, and a static technology.

The absence of significant technological change effectively deprived iron
producers of what was potentially the most fruitful avenue to increased
productivity. That the attainment of productivity increases was a matter of
no little moment to them is evident from their letters and memoranda.[10]
If, as some economic historians have contended, necessity is the mother of
invention, then the colonial iron industry should have been a scene of
rapid technological change.[11] But this was not the case.

There was apparently little change in the material technology of production. Manuscript sources for four eighteenth-century iron production
facilities in southeastern Pennsylvania — Cornwall Furnace; its allied facility, Hopewell Forge; New Pine Forge; and Mary Ann Furnace — reveal
that except for routine maintenance at the forges and furnaces and the
rebuilding of the furnace stacks after each blast period, the owners made
no modifications of or additions to their physical plants.[12] Moreover, the
performance of these facilities was not surpassed until well into the 1830s.
For example, during the period 1768–74 Hopewell Forge produced about
8.5 long tons of bar iron per worker — a mean annual product of 153 tons;
in 1810, more than thirty years later, the mean output per forge for sixty-

six charcoal forges in southeastern Pennsylvania was almost precisely the same — about 152 tons.[13] As late as the early 1830s published data on Pennsylvania's charcoal forges revealed that little if anything had changed in the technical relationships involved in the production of bar iron. The mean annual output of bar iron at twenty-one charcoal forges in Berks County — the center of this sector of the charcoal iron industry in Pennsylvania — during the three-year period 1828–30 was about 8.8 tons per worker and 180 tons per forge.[14]

Much the same situation probably prevailed in the pig-iron sector of the industry, although the data for the eighteenth-century furnaces leave a good deal to be desired. Because of their uneven and fragmentary nature, only rough comparisons between eighteenth- and nineteenth-century performance levels are possible. Still, the data suggest that the rate of output per furnace during the late eighteenth century at Cornwall Furnace and at neighboring Elizabeth Furnace was typical of those rates reached in the first decade of the nineteenth century.

During the thirty-one years of production when Cornwall was in operation, between 1766 and 1800, its mean annual output of pig iron and castings was about 650 long tons; that of Elizabeth Furnace was slightly more than 530 tons for the period 1780–90.[15] The disparity between the two sets of figures, however, can be misleading. In some years prior to the Revolution Cornwall produced more than 900 tons, and in the best year within the 1780–90 period Elizabeth ran in excess of 750 tons of pig iron and castings.[16] Also, a comparison of annual output levels per furnace yields reliable results only when the values of two variable quantities are known: (1) the proportion of a furnace's output in the form of castings, the production of which was more time-consuming than the running of pig iron, and (2) the furnace's output per day in blast. The two are obviously related. Unfortunately, no data concerning product mix are available for Cornwall, Elizabeth, or any of the twenty-six furnaces covered in the 1810 report. Moreover, the data necessary for the calculation of tons of output per day in blast only cover operations at Cornwall and Elizabeth, and they present anything but a clear picture. Only Elizabeth Furnace achieved a prolonged increase in output per day in blast, almost doubling daily production from about 1.9 tons in 1780 to almost 3.6 tons in 1790.[17] This may very well have been a result not only of increasing efficiency but also of an altered product mix. At best, the spotty corresponding data for Cornwall Furnace reveal little change in that facility's performance.

A firmer basis for assessing the degree, if any, of change in furnace technology is provided by data on the size of eighteenth- and nineteenth-century furnaces. The two critical dimensions of a charcoal furnace were the height of its stack and the diameter of its bosh, or the widest part of its interior. A rough but logical rule of thumb is that, other things being

TABLE 7

Cold-Blast Charcoal Furnaces in Eastern Pennsylvania, 1737–1849

| Period Constructed | Number | Mean Bosh (ft.) | Mean Stack (ft.) | Mean (Bosh/Stack) |
|---|---|---|---|---|
| 1737–70 | 7 | 8.3 | 30.4 | 0.28 |
| 1785–97 | 10 | 8.0 | 30.2 | 0.27 |
| pre-1800[a] | 9 | 7.6 | 30.1 | 0.25 |
| 1800–1819[a] | 9 | 8.2 | 30.8 | 0.27 |
| 1820–29[a] | 9 | 7.9 | 31.4 | 0.25 |
| 1830–39[a] | 18 | 7.8 | 29.8 | 0.26 |
| 1840–49[a] | 9 | 7.4 | 29.8 | 0.24 |

Sources: Data for furnaces constructed between 1737–70 and 1785–97 and not in use in 1850 are from Bining, *Pennsylvania Iron Manufacture,* p. 177; and Jeffrey Francis Zabler, "A Microeconomic Study of Iron Manufacture, 1800–1830" (Ph.D. diss., University of Pennsylvania, 1970), p. 39. Data for all other furnaces are from "Documents Relating to the Manufacture of Iron in Pennsylvania," *Journal of the Franklin Institute,* 3d ser., 21 (January 1851), tables following p. 72.
[a] In use in 1850.

equal, the output capacity of a furnace was in large measure a function of its size. The question then arises as to why charcoal-furnace dimensions remained virtually unchanged throughout the eighteenth century and well into the nineteenth. In his study of the iron industry during the period 1800–1830 Jeffrey Zabler answered simply that the iron industry's continuing reliance on charcoal fuel effectively limited the size of furnaces.[18] The consistency of charcoal was such that a full load in a blast furnace of much more than thirty-two feet in height almost certainly would have pulverized the chunks of charcoal, thereby preventing the weak blast from being effective. It is not surprising, then, that the common dimensions of charcoal furnaces during the early eighteenth century persisted throughout that century and well into the next (see table 7). For example, while the average height and diameter of seven furnaces erected between 1737 and 1770 were 30.4 and 8.3 feet, respectively, the corresponding values for ten post-Revolution eighteenth-century furnaces were 30.2 and 8.0 feet.

The persistence of these values well into the nineteenth century is clear from the data available for fifty-four charcoal furnaces operating in eastern Pennsylvania in 1850. Although height and bosh diameter decreased slightly over the first half of the century, they remained remarkably stable through about 1820, with approximate mean values of 7.9 feet for the bosh and 30.4 feet for the height, thereby providing still more evidence of technological stasis within the charcoal iron industry.[19]

Because little, if anything, could be done to improve the performance of the physical plant at an ironworks, the ironmaster sought productivity increases in those aspects of his operation over which he had some control: the size and cost of his labor force. There is, in fact, considerable evidence indicating that the iron producers of this time sought to impose tighter control over the process of production — increasing managerial efficiency — through learning by doing. To understand fully the preoccupation of ironworks owners with labor costs, we must first realize that despite the high initial capital requirements and the continuing need for new investment, iron-making was a labor-intensive activity. Wages comprised a substantial part of the unit production costs of pig and bar iron, about 70 percent and 40 percent, respectively, of the total expenses.[20] Consequently, as wholesale prices for pig and bar iron fluctuated along a generally declining path after 1760, ironworks owners found themselves in a frustrating position. Aggregate demand for their products was probably higher than ever before, yet prices continued to drop. The reason, of course, was that iron-making had become a very attractive investment for a growing number of individual entrepreneurs, partnerships, and companies, with the result that more iron firms were organized in Pennsylvania during the last twenty-five years before the Revolution than during the preceding thirty-five.[21] Falling prices forced the owners to seek means of lowering their costs.

Most of the ironworks owners were well aware that attempts to produce more iron simply by consuming more inputs ran up against an unyielding wall of obstacles associated with the technological structure of the industry, especially its reliance on charcoal fuel. These were the considerations under which the owners of Hopewell Forge operated during the period 1768–75. As the records of the forge make clear, the owners were preoccupied with the cost and management of the facility's work force.

Constrained by a static technology and confronted by the rising cost of skilled labor and by depressed prices, Hopewell's owners fixed on the sole means available to them of surmounting their difficulties: they attempted to minimize their use of labor, particularly unskilled and semiskilled labor. Labor costs were the only component of the overall cost of bar-iron production susceptible to their manipulation; wherever and whenever possible, as the forge's production data suggest, the owners examined their use of labor and whittled away at the excess.

Because of limitations on hearth size occasioned by the use of charcoal fuel at forges, and the consequent restriction on the rate of output to about two tons of anconies per week, a finery forge — a forge at which anconies, or semirefined bar iron, were made from pig iron — had a limited requirement for charcoal, which in turn meant a limited demand for cordwood.[22] And because woodcutting and charcoal-making employed the largest number of workers at an ironworks, the continuous employment of these workers over the course of several months contributed nothing to increasing the output of anconies and meant an operating loss as well.

For this reason, the maximization of the number of man-days worked each month by each worker was simply not in the interest of a forge

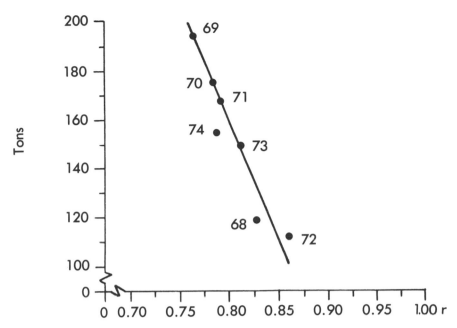

FIGURE 6
ANNUAL ANCONY OUTPUT BY *r* AT HOPEWELL FORGE, 1768–75, IN TONS
$r$ = total man-days worked/maximum possible man-days.
Data for $r$ were derived from the actual figures contained in Hopewell Forge Coal, Iron
& Time Book, Etc., 1768–75.

owner. In fact, as figure 6 illustrates, Hopewell Forge's best years in this period were those in which the total number of man-days worked in a year was between 75 percent and 80 percent of the maximum possible number (equal to the number of workers employed during each month multiplied by the twenty-six working days in each month and summed over the twelve months). Moreover, from 1768 through 1774 Hopewell Forge achieved a substantial decrease in the number of man-days worked per ton of anconies produced, the required labor time having been reduced from more than twenty-eight days to fewer than twenty-five days (table 8). In the absence of any alteration of the forge's physical plant, this increase in labor productivity could have come about only through an increase in organizational efficiency on the part of Hopewell's resident owner-manager. Unlike in nineteenth-century instances of increased labor productivity accomplished through a combination of increasing managerial efficiency and a learning curve for workers, workers at Hopewell had little if any responsibility for the increase in their productivity. Like their counterparts at other ironworks, unskilled and semiskilled workers at

TABLE 8

Labor Productivity and Fuel Consumption at Hopewell Forge, 1768–74

| Year | $r^a$ | Tons of Anconies | Tons per Man | Man-days per Ton | Number of Months | Cbu. of Charcoal | Cbu. of Charcoal per Ton |
|------|------|------|------|------|------|------|------|
| 1768[b] | 0.81 | 119.85 | 5.99 | 31.67 | 9 | 811.11 | 6.77 |
| 1769 | 0.76 | 193.18 | 8.65 | 27.55 | 12 | 726.44 | 3.67 |
| 1770 | 0.78 | 175.73 | 9.72 | 25.12 | 12 | 762.00 | 4.34 |
| 1771[c] | 0.79 | 169.71 | 11.77 | 25.84 | 11 | 713.74 | 4.21 |
| 1772[d] | 0.85 | 106.22 | 7.24 | 36.74 | 9 | 476.25 | 4.48 |
| 1773 | 0.81 | 148.88 | 9.65 | 26.05 | 12 | 606.75 | 4.08 |
| 1774 | 0.77 | 157.36 | 9.68 | 24.90 | 12 | 571.50 | 3.63 |

Source: Hopewell Forge Coal, Iron & Time Book, Etc., 1768–75, pp. 59–75.
[a] Ratio of man-days worked to maximum possible man-days.
[b] April–December.
[c] June not included.
[d] August–October not included.

Hopewell Forge seldom stayed long enough to even partly effect the significant changes under way at the forge before the Revolution.[23]

We might suspect that a firm able to achieve economies in its use of labor would also be able to economize in its consumption of raw materials, especially charcoal, in the production of iron. Although the records for Hopewell Forge bearing on the relationship between iron output and fuel consumption are limited to the seven years from 1768 through 1774, they nevertheless yield a result that is statistically significant and consistent with both the above hypothesis and the performance records of twenty-one forges and eleven furnaces in Berks County during the years 1828–1830 and those of twenty-three rolling mills in western Pennsylvania in 1850.[24]

For each set of facilities, as well as for Hopewell Forge, output measured in tons per worker is inversely related to the quantity of fuel consumed per ton of output by an asymptotic exponential function.[25] The asymptotic character of the regression line arises from the physical, or engineering, limitations of the production process: a minimum level of fuel consumption had to be achieved before any iron could be produced in a furnace or forge. Similarly, there was a minimum production rate of iron per worker below which no production and fuel consumption would occur. Thus, when Hopewell Forge operated most efficiently, a minimum quantity of charcoal — between 350 and 420 bushels — was consumed in the production of a ton of anconies. At such times the forge attained its highest rate of output, 9.6 to 11.7 tons of anconies per worker.

Furnace and forge owners who had achieved economies in one aspect of their operations had the greatest likelihood of realizing higher levels of efficiency in other aspects. This probably explains in part the observed connection between levels of output per worker and fuel-consumption rates. Still, the complete explanation is not so straightforward, and like so much else about the charcoal iron industry, it has much to do with the use of charcoal as a fuel.

The sequence of operations involved in the making of charcoal at a furnace or forge was always the most time-consuming and, after the purchase of pig iron by a forge, the single most expensive aspect of iron-making. More than half of the work force at a furnace or forge was directly or indirectly concerned with the production of charcoal.[26] At Hopewell Forge in 1768 and 1769 expenses incurred in the making of the necessary charcoal to produce a ton of bar iron represented about 22 percent of the total per-ton cost of production (see table 9). Obviously, the achievement of any economies in this facet of iron-making was bound to have a profound and salutary effect upon a firm's operations. Even a modest reduction in the wage bill for wood and charcoal haulers could result in significant savings and increased profits. Although haulers' wages accounted for only 5.65 percent of the per-ton production cost of bar iron at Hopewell in 1768, they totaled £188 for an annual output of 173.6 tons of bar iron and a production cost of £3300. More impressive is the fact that the wage bill for hauling in 1768 represented 30 percent of that year's net profit of £569.5.[27] Even a 25 percent reduction in hauling wages would have saved about £47, which would have increased net profits by 8.25 percent.

A more efficient use of charcoal, brought about in part by reducing waste, not only reduced a forge's or furnace's charcoal consumption per ton of iron produced but also enabled the owner to reduce the size of his work force without reducing the quantity of iron produced. The result, therefore, was that those facilities that operated at the higher rates of output per worker necessarily enjoyed the lowest rates of fuel consumption per unit of output. When we consider this result in conjunction with the evidence presented above concerning the attainment of productivity increases at Hopewell Forge, measured in man-days worked per ton of output, we should not be surprised to learn that Hopewell's owners realized still another increase in factor productivity during this same period. Nor should it surprise us that in this instance the means to this very desirable end was not augmentation or modification of the physical plant but rather the prosaic yet very effective process of learning by doing.

As the evidence presented here suggests, the entrepreneurs in this industry were improving productivity in spite of a largely static technology. Compared with the productivity increases of the nineteenth century, these efficiencies were not very impressive. In a tight market, however, they could mean the difference between business success and failure. In the eighteenth-century industry, savings of this sort were important, and they indicate just how successful the commercial capitalists of that time were in making their transition from a mercantile to an industrial brand of capitalism. This is not the sort of development we usually associate with the colonial economy. Insofar as this important industry is concerned, we

TABLE 9

Decomposition of Per-Ton Production Costs of Bar Iron at Hopewell Forge, 1768 and 1769 (in £ Pa.)

| Item (Wages/Cost) | 1768 | | | | 1769 | | | |
|---|---|---|---|---|---|---|---|---|
| | Unit Cost | Total Cost | Material Cost | Labor Cost | Unit Cost | Total Cost | Material Cost | Labor Cost |
| 1.5 tons pig iron | 6.800/ton | 10.20 | 10.200 | – | 6.500/ton | 9.75[a] | 9.750 | – |
| 4.32 Cbu. charcoal | 1.020/Cbu. | 4.41 | 0.078 | – | 0.998/Cbu. | 4.31 | 0.078 | – |
| 11.25 cd. cutting wood | 0.110/cd. | – | – | 1.238 | 0.111/cd. | – | – | 1.249 |
| 11.25 cd. hauling wood | 0.029/cd. | – | – | 0.326 | 0.033/cd. | – | – | 0.371 |
| Coaling | 0.465/Cbu. | – | – | 2.009 | 0.435/Cbu. | – | – | 1.879 |
| Haul charcoal | 0.175/Cbu. | – | – | 0.756 | 0.170/Cbu. | – | – | 0.734 |
| Forgemen's wages | 1.250/ton | 2.50 | – | 2.500 | 1.635/ton | 3.27 | – | 3.270 |
| Salaries and repairs[b] | 1.390/ton | 2.08 | – | – | 1.390/ton | 2.08 | – | – |
| Subtotal | | 19.19 | 10.278 | 6.829 | | 19.41 | 9.828 | 7.503 |
| Total | | 19.19 | | | | 19.41 | | |
| Wages/total cost | | 35.60% | | | | 38.60% | | |
| Hauling wages/charcoal cost | | 24.60 | | | | 26.00 | | |
| Hauling wages/charcoal wages | | 25.00 | | | | 25.50 | | |
| Hauling wages/total wages | | 15.90 | | | | 14.70 | | |
| Hauling wages/total cost | | 5.65 | | | | 5.67 | | |

Sources: Hopewell Forge Coal, Iron & Time Book, Etc., 1768–75; Hopewell Forge Ledgers A–G, 1765–75; and Peter Hasenclever, The Remarkable Case of Peter Hasenclever, Merchant (London, 1773), Special Collections, New York Public Library, p. 82.

Note: Here Hopewell Forge is regarded as a separately owned facility having no connection with Cornwall Furnace. The lack of specific production data for Cornwall Furnace makes this approach necessary.

[a] Unfortunately, the records of Hopewell Forge provided the cost per ton of pig iron from Cornwall Furnace for 1768 only. Thus, the 1769 cost per ton of pigs, listed as £9.75, represents an estimate. This estimate has been arrived at by subtracting the Cornwall price for pigs in 1768 from the annual average wholesale price in Philadelphia and then subtracting this £1.7 difference from the 1769 Philadelphia price.

[b] These figures are of doubtful accuracy and are probably too high. They represent the cost per ton of the pig-iron input charged to salaries and repairs of buildings and roads for making bar iron and are derived from Hasenclever's figure for this operation. More specifically, the £1.39 (Pa.) is a mean value per ton of Hasenclever's £3.0 (N.Y. currency, ca. 1765) and no overhead charges at all. Clearly, there were always overhead charges of some sort. However, the upper bound estimate of £3.0 (N.Y.), when converted somewhat arbitrarily into £1.39 (Pa. currency, 1768), is itself improbably high because (1) it would have included the salary of the forge's clerk, paid on an annual basis, which would have come to £0.30 (Pa.) per ton at most; and (2) Hopewell Forge had a far less extensive road network and considerably fewer buildings than Hasenclever's works. Thus, maintenance charges at Hopewell would have been lower than this figure.

should revise this part of our general view of the pre–industrial revolution economy in America.[28]

Notwithstanding the substantial benefits derived from improving productivity, the most widespread and probably the most effective method of reducing costs in iron production was through quality control of inputs and outputs. Although its results — largely in the form of savings on labor costs — might be less dramatic than those achieved at Hopewell Forge, they could nevertheless be significant to the profit margin of a firm. Quality control also took some of the risk out of marketing iron. An established reputation for high-quality products eased sales in the domestic as well as in the English market. In the hinterland market in particular — and this, as the years passed, was an increasingly important part of the trade — a reputation for good iron and iron products helped to shield the producer from competition.

The implementation of quality control through careful inspection at various steps in the production process ensured that wages would be paid only for work that met established standards. This condition was usually incorporated in the contracts of skilled and unskilled workers, irrespective of whether a worker was paid by the unit of output or by the day, the month, or the year. For example, an agreement in 1773 with a collier at Hopewell Forge stipulated that he was to be paid "for every Hundred Bushels of good Coals." [29] A similar condition was included in an agreement between the manager of New Pine Forge and a young wagon driver, William Williams, who was to be paid twenty-four pounds for one year and forty shillings "if the Said Williams is faithful in the Business reposed in him." [30] Thus, woodcutters were paid not by the number of ranks cut but by the number of cords accepted. Similarly, colliers were paid only for the number of bushels of good charcoal that they produced and were docked either because of dirt mixed in with the charcoal or because of short loads, that is, containing too few bushels.[31]

Quite clearly, the application of quality control to an operation such as woodcutting resulted in economies, but even greater savings could be realized in its application to making charcoal, running pig iron, and drawing bar iron. By the time a cord of wood reached the coaling pit considerable labor costs had already accumulated in the form of wages for cutters and haulers. If this same cord were then made into bad coal, and this bad coal rejected, the wage bill for that cord quite literally went up in smoke, and operations at the primary production site of a furnace or forge might well be delayed. As the owners of the Principio Company recognized, such delays entailed losses:

> The profits of such works are found in its continuance at work and the
> short time that intervenes between y^e time of Blowing out [the furnace]

and getting into Blast again and this depends on proper influence over all about the works concerned but especially yᵉ wood cutters Colliers & miners if there cou'd be a certain dependence had on yᵉ Assiduity of these, sure there might be some certainty of the works going on to proffit.[32]

More important, bad coal that somehow escaped detection before being used made bad iron or, at best, greatly increased the difficulty of making good iron. This problem was encountered at Hopewell Forge in May 1769 and was recorded in a memorandum in the forge's coal book regarding the charcoal of one collier, Edward McFarland. He had forwarded to the forgeman thirty loads — approximately thirty-eight hundred bushels — that were "Esteemed by the finers to be the worst Coals ever they wrought." [33] Although learning at such a late date that a particular collier's coals were of inferior quality was better than not knowing until the firm's iron had been spurned in the market, such knowledge was purchased dearly.

The problems of quality control in the actual production of pig and bar iron were similar to those encountered in the making of charcoal, but they were even more acute. Recalling table 9, we see that in the drawing of one ton of bar iron more than 75 percent of the production cost was accumulated before the forgemen began their work. Consequently, improperly drawn bar iron represented an enormous waste of capital and labor. Fortunately, although the entire antecedent cost was not recoverable, a substantial part of it — probably between 40 percent and 50 percent — could be salvaged by reworking the metal.[34] This technique was standard operating procedure at the Carlisle Iron Works in Cumberland County, Pennsylvania, and the owners' instructions to the manager specified that "the Broken and brittle Bar Iron shall be wrought over again." [35]

Quality control over the pig- and bar-iron output resulted in direct and indirect savings. Managers achieved direct savings by paying wages to founders and forgemen only for each acceptable ton of iron, an arrangement that was stipulated in the articles of agreement between forge owners and forgemen.[36] Thus, the production cost of a ton of substandard bar iron did not include the wages of finers and chafers. Moreover, labor contracts between forgemen and the owners or managers of a forge frequently included a clause requiring that the worker pay a penalty for waste.[37]

The indirect savings stemmed from the ease with which efficient ironworks managers could market their product after establishing a reputation for its quality. They accomplished this through experimentation to find the best iron-making techniques and by a crude form of product testing to ascertain the iron's strength. To this end, the owners of the Carlisle works instructed the manager "that no Bar Iron shall be sent to Town [probably York, Pennsylvania] till after reasonable Tryal made of its toughness to bear Carriage & throwing out of the wagons —." The manager, Robert

Thornburg, was also instructed as to the kinds of experiments to perform on the company's pig iron, and he was further directed "to pursue that matter by every manner of working that his Ingenuity & Art may suggest, to make the Iron tough Bar Iron, & if his Tryals succeed that he shall oblige the Forgemen to pursue the same method." [38] Experiments had also been conducted by the newly formed Baltimore Company in the 1730s to determine how its pig and bar iron compared with that of the Principio Company and Swedish firms. [39]

All such efforts at research and testing were attuned to conditions in the major colonial iron markets, as well as to those in the English market, centered in London. With the formation of more and more firms in the Colonies, particularly after 1750, competition for the lucrative London market became severe. The colonial domestic market for bar iron and iron manufactures burgeoned after 1750, and colonial iron firms found themselves in sharp competition not only with one another but with English firms as well. In the Philadelphia market the reputation of an ironworks's product was everything, and it was jealously guarded. Thus, on December 16, 1767, Curttis and Peter Grubb, of Cornwall Furnace and Hopewell Forge, respectively, bought space in the *Pennsylvania Chronicle* to inform "the Public, especially those who deal in BAR IRON, that the Public, as well as the Subscribers have been grossly imposed upon by persons who have sold Bar Iron as and for the Subscribers Iron which was neither of so good a Quality, nor so well drawn as that which they have heretofore made, and do now make — ." The brothers concluded their notice by assuring one and all that in the future a buyer of Hopewell bar iron would know it by the mark "C.&P.G.," which would be stamped into each piece. This measure, they hoped, would restore "the Character of their Iron . . . to its former Credit." [40]

The contest among many colonial ironworks was aggravated by the availability in American and English markets of Swedish iron, which was competitively priced and highly esteemed for its purity and malleability. [41] Not surprisingly, colonial iron firms regarded Swedish iron as a standard against which to measure the quality of their own iron, and they cherished their valuable reputations in the market for producing pig and bar iron equal to that of Sweden. The good reputation of a colonial ironworks's product was indeed valuable in an age that was devoid of industry journals and annual technical reports and in which a favorable personal recommendation could propel a career or a product. The maintenance of a good reputation was all-important, and in London especially a colonial firm's standing could be easily lost if it allowed the quality of its product to slip. [42]

Soon after the Baltimore Company began production, the owners shipped about forty tons of pig iron to the Bristol, England, merchant firm of Lyde & Cooper. In March 1734 the English firm wrote to Charles Carroll informing him that it intended to have the Baltimore iron tested and evaluated because "its value [was] not to be known by inspection." Lyde & Cooper further advised Carroll that in view of the variable quality of pig iron, "one Furnace cannot be a president [sic] for the value of another, and [we] are fully satisfied of its real worth."[43] Although these formal tests quickly validated the company's claims for the quality of its iron and ensured initial acceptance in the market, the testing process never really ended. Instead, the formality that characterized the first tests was superseded by more informal but nevertheless effective trials by buyers in the market. The verdict was not always to the Baltimore Company's liking. In June 1751 the company received a letter from an unhappy merchant in Liverpool who handled the firm's iron there. He said that he had written only the previous month to say that he had received their shipment of pig iron. But, he said, "I have not Since been able to Sell it none offering me more than £5 [per] Tun for it complaining its but very indifferent. when a Pig is broke theres in the midle a black spot which they say is dross & a fault in the refining."[44]

Whether or not the company knowingly had shipped the defective iron is a moot question. In either case, quality control had not been effective, and the firm had permitted substandard iron to reach the English market, which gave it an unenthusiastic and, for the Baltimore Company, an unprofitable reception. The importance of quality control and its relationship to success in the market were clearly recognized by the owners of the Carlisle Iron Works. They urged their new manager to "be careful that none of the old trash of Scraps and other old pieces of Iron, which were made from the Bad ore are worked up. This would injure the credit of the works, and be a means of hurting us in the price, if we should incline to dispose of them."[45]

Although the findings of individual buyers percolated through the various centers of the English iron market — London, Liverpool, and Bristol — the market per se had no central clearing house for information nor, for that matter, even a uniform set of standards by which to grade iron. The hearings conducted by Parliament in the 1730s, 1740s, and 1750s did in a sense serve as an instrument for gathering and disseminating information about iron. However, for the most part this information was of a general nature, pertaining to the economic advantages and disadvantages of encouraging colonial bar-iron production.[46] In the absence of an official system, the Royal Navy became the most important source of standards. The navy, in order to meet its own needs for iron, "operated an extensive program of testing to ascertain the quality of iron from many different sources."[47] Notwithstanding that the navy's criteria were somewhat different from those of most other buyers, the verdict given by the navy yards on a brand of iron had considerable influence in the market. Very likely, two important reasons for this were the presumed impartiality of the Navy Board and its rigorous standards. The major reason for the navy's influence on the iron market was, however, its active participation as a frequent and lavish buyer.[48]

Because the navy contracted for wrought iron in large quantities and from several firms, its standards necessarily became those of the wrought-iron manufacturers, who through their own purchases of iron in the market determined the quality standards of English ironmasters and iron merchants.[49] These merchants in turn communicated these standards to colonial producers. In this roundabout way a degree of uniformity was imposed upon English and colonial iron. Moreover, news of orders for iron and information concerning the quality of specific brands moved along the same channels that carried the navy's quality standards. For example, in the late 1750s Caleb and Edward Dorsey, owners of the Elk Ridge iron company in Maryland, received a letter from a London correspondent who informed them that "in regard to Bar Iron the Navy Board has lately refused Several parcells. Some on account of [illegible] drawn and [improper?] Sizes."[50]

Nor were all the responses negative; good products elicited a swift reaction. Soon after Peter Hasenclever had informed his partners in England of the development of a process for making bar iron from furnace and forge cinders and had sent them a sample, they were able to respond enthusiastically "that it is universally allowed by the trade to be the best drawn Iron, by far, that ever made its appearance in the London Market from America; it has been tried and found of exceedingly good quality."[51] Evidently news of Hasenclever's discovery soon retraced its route from America to England, for the technique of making "cinder bar-iron" was adopted in the Colonies.[52] At about the same time or a few years later the method was tried in England, after one of Hasenclever's managers "returned . . . and built a stamping-mill, and manufactured this sort of iron in Staffordshire."[53]

Hasenclever's process was important, but it was atypical of an American industry whose basic technology was relatively stable. In England there were more dramatic changes as coal and coke were being substituted for charcoal fuel. But even this important innovation was not adopted by American producers, one of whom — Barrister Carroll — dismissed an English merchant's plan to make pig iron with coal instead of charcoal, asserting that "your project for Running Pigg with Pit Coal will I believe meet with the fate of many of that Fraternity But even should they succeed the Iron they will be able to make as it Can never be fit for any thing but Castings will by no means Lower the Price of Ours which is of the Tough Malleable Kind."[54]

Carroll's opinion of the quality of pigs run with coal was well-founded.[55]

American ironmasters also could have employed a sound economic argument for their unwillingness to substitute coal or coke for charcoal. Unlike their English counterparts, colonial ironworks still enjoyed an abundant supply of timber for charcoal-making and had little reason to shift to a more expensive fuel.[56] Perhaps the only material innovation in furnace design adopted by American producers was the substitution of the English-invented blowing cylinder, or tub, for bellows. The tub was a more efficient means by which to generate a blast of air for a furnace because it provided a more continuous flow of compressed air.

Those few innovations in material technology that were adopted by American ironmasters were much less dramatic than the substitution of coke for charcoal and were probably indigenous to the Colonies. Predictably, these techniques were directed at the problem of cost reduction. Thus, Peter Hasenclever's procedure for making "cinder bar-iron" was valuable because of the fine quality of the output and because it enabled producers to use the waste by-products of furnace and forge operation. The Carlisle Iron Works's conversion of "old Hammers and anvils" into pig iron — that is, the cannibalization of depreciated capital — was similarly important.[57] We can get a rough idea of the savings achieved through such techniques by comparing Hasenclever's figures for the production of pig, bar, and cinder bar iron presented in table 10.[58]

The cost advantage of producing cinder bar iron rather than standard bar iron is evident from the results presented in table 10.[59] In fact, the cost structure of cinder bar iron was more akin to that of pig iron than of bar iron. Although labor costs were 27 percent higher for cinder bar iron than for bar iron, these higher costs were outweighed by the savings on the cost of input materials, which totaled only 37 percent of the cost of those for standard bar iron. The higher labor costs for the production of cinder bar iron had two sources. First, this process required 19 percent more charcoal per ton of output than the production of standard bar iron. Second, as Hasenclever notes, "the working of this Iron being more tedious, the forgemen have more wages one-third per ton than for the common bar-iron."[60] The net result was lower production costs for the new technique. Further, the production of cinder bar iron resulted in still another form of savings because the consumption of waste materials relieved the pressure on convenient ore deposits, thereby increasing their period of profitable exploitation. An ironworks's application of this kind of innovative production method enabled it to cut costs while actually improving the quality of its product and simultaneously enhancing its reputation in markets at home and abroad.

Increasingly, the most important markets for most of the iron producers were in the Colonies themselves. For most of the Pennsylvania producers, that meant the Philadelphia market and the growing markets in the city's

TABLE 10

Decomposition of Per-Ton Production Costs for Pig, Bar, and Cinder Bar Iron
(in Pounds Sterling)

| Input | Input Ratio | Type of Iron | | |
|---|---|---|---|---|
| | | Pig | Bar[a] | Cinder Bar |
| Materials | | 0.64[b] | 4.48 | 1.66 |
| Salaries and repairs[c] | | 0.19 | 2.51 | (0–2.51)[d] |
| Labor | | 2.01 | 4.64[e] | 5.87 |
| Total cost | | 2.84 | 11.63 | (7.53–10.04) |
| | Labor/total | 70.8% | 39.9% | (85.9–58.5%)[f] |
| | Material/total | 22.5% | 38.5% | (22.0–16.5%)[f] |
| | Material/labor | 31.8% | 96.6% | 28.3% |
| Cbu. of charcoal | | 2.88 | 4.32 | 5.12 |

Source: Hasenclever, The Remarkable Case of Peter Hasenclever, Merchant, pp. 79–82.
Note: All figures are derived from those given in the source.
[a] Figures are for bar-iron production at a forge owned independently of a furnace.
[b] Excluding the cost of lime.
[c] Consists of "salaries and reparations of buildings and Roads."
[d] Hasenclever did not list any miscellaneous charges for cinder bar-iron production, but the charges probably fell within the indicated range.
[e] Whether Hasenclever included the wages of pig-iron haulers is unknown.
[f] Because overhead charges must have accrued in the production of cinder bar iron, the lower bound of zero for salaries and repairs can be ignored. However, since about 59 percent (by weight) of the cinder input consisted of forge cinders, the overhead charges on road repairs were almost certainly less than those for making standard bar iron. Therefore, the upper bound of £2.51 is probably unrealistically high. Consequently, the percentages of the total per-ton production cost represented by labor costs and material costs are probably close to, but greater than, their respective lower bounds.

hinterland and, to the south, in Baltimore. Even the largest firms — those that still looked to England in the years after 1750 — were often forced to pay more attention to indigenous demand. This was true even of the Baltimore and Principio companies, which were located in Maryland and Virginia, colonies that (unlike Pennsylvania, New Jersey, New York, and New England) afforded little in the way of a domestic market for iron.[61] As one member of the Baltimore Company observed, writing to his London correspondent in 1762: "the [English] Markets for Pig and Barr are so unpromising that I must sell in the Country to Prepare for next years Remittance."[62] Such reluctance to market iron locally was perhaps typical of the larger Maryland firms, but quite the contrary attitude characterized Pennsylvania's iron firms. By the 1760s the colony's voracious demand for iron offered more than enough encouragement to its iron makers to market locally almost all that they produced.

In catering to local markets, Pennsylvania's iron producers confronted buyers who were as demanding of high-quality products as were those in the larger English markets. In fact, quality control was, if anything, even more important in markets close to the producer than it was in those abroad. In the colony, information traveled more quickly, and levels of supply and demand changed more rapidly. There were fewer buyers and sellers, most of whom were well known to one another. Tied together by an extensive road network, they exchanged both iron and information. Consequently, a load of bad iron could quickly destroy a reputation built up over the years. Conversely, however, a producer could rapidly acquire a reputation for making good iron, a reputation that could ensure sales even in the tensely competitive Pennsylvania markets of the years after 1750.

# The Rise of the Domestic Market

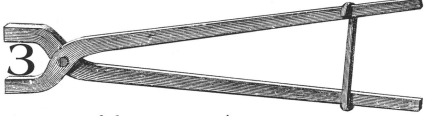

*As a part of the transportation system of the country, the humble rural road has seldom been given its due.*

George Rogers Taylor

Eighteenth-century communications and transportation were slow and erratic, and there was often little or no difference in the means, and consequently the speed, with which messages and commodities moved. Although this was particularly true of transoceanic communications and transportation, a similar situation prevailed in overland movement. To understand the rise of the domestic market for iron in Pennsylvania, one must analyze the geography and technology of distribution in the colonial era.

A significant part of the uncertainty that attended the eighteenth-century relationship between producer and purchaser had its source in the vagaries of winds, weather, and tides. Further, physical geography heavily affected overland movement, determining, as it did, not only the location of routes but also times of travel. Like the technology of iron production, the communication and transportation technologies were only slightly removed from the direct influence of nature; in each case economic agents, lacking the tools with which to confront the natural environment, could, at most, prevail by circumspection. Thus, roads followed terrain and did not cut into hillsides to level grades; ferries, not bridges, crossed rivers and bays. Construction techniques and materials permitted only slight alterations in topography, thereby further limiting overland rates of movement, as did the reliance on animals and winds as sources of motive power.

The extent to which these factors combined to retard the speed with which private and public information could travel is apparent from the travel times between Philadelphia and New York given in table 11.[1] These

39

TABLE 11
Travel Times for the Philadelphia–New York Post

| Year | Number of Days | Frequency of Service | Comment |
|------|----------------|----------------------|---------|
| 1720 | 3.0 | Once a week | Regular mail |
| 1729 | 2.5 | Once a week | Regular mail |
| 1754 | 1.5 | Twice a month<br>Three times a week | In summer and winter<br>— |
| 1764 | 1.0 | Twice a week<br>Every other day | In winter<br>By relay |

*Source:* Adapted from Seymour Dunbar, *A History of Travel in America,* 4 vols. (Indianapolis: Bobbs-Merrill Co., 1915), vol. 1, p. 177, n. 2.

figures must of course be taken with a grain of salt, especially because they represent the *shortest* times achieved and not the mean times.[2] Also, correspondence between the two cities, especially during the first half of the century, did not rely exclusively on the official postal services, as is attested by the numerous instances of letters sent with travelers or commodities.[3] Consequently, the mean number of days required for a letter to travel from New York to Philadelphia would probably have been significantly greater than the times given in table 11.

That this was indeed the case is further suggested by the travel times for passenger service on the New York–Philadelphia stage route. In 1750 the journey from one city to the other by a combination of stage, boat, ferry, and wagon required five days.[4] Six years later this time had been reduced to less than three and a half days, and by 1765 the travel time had been cut to three days.[5] With the introduction in 1767 of the "Flying Machine," an overland stage, the travel time between the cities was further reduced to two days.[6] As its owner proudly advertised, the high speed of "The Flying Machine" was "a Circumstance greatly to the Advantage of the Traveller, as there is no Water Carriage, and consequently nothing to impede the Journey."[7] A regular schedule of departures assured passengers that "they would set off from Philadelphia and New York on Mondays and Thursdays [respectively] punctually at Sun-rise."[8] By 1771 the same trip was advertised as requiring only one and a half days, but "in reality the advertised day and a half was nearly two days."[9]

It took substantially more time to move public information than it did to move private communications (see table 12). An entry listed here represents the mean number of days elapsed, or lag time, between the date of an event at a particular location and the publication of a report of the event in a newspaper in Philadelphia or Annapolis in 1767.[10] The economic significance of these lag times becomes clear when we consider the contents of colonial newspapers. In addition to news concerning political developments in continental Europe, Britain, other colonies, and the local

TABLE 12

Mean Public Information Time Lags at Philadelphia and Annapolis, 1767

| From | To Philadelphia | | To Annapolis | |
|------|-----|-----|-----|-----|
| Annapolis | 14 | ( 5) | — | — |
| Baltimore Town[a] | — | — | 4 | ( 8) |
| Boston | 13 | (15) | 21 | (20) |
| Bucks County[a] | 9 | ( 2) | — | — |
| Charleston, S.C. | 26 | ( 8) | 39 | ( 8) |
| Chester County[a] | 5 | ( 3) | — | — |
| Elkridge Landing[a] | — | — | 2 | ( 4) |
| Hartford, Conn. | 15 | ( 3) | 24 | ( 2) |
| Lancaster County[a] | 10 | ( 2) | — | — |
| Lancaster Town[a] | 8 | ( 2) | — | — |
| London | 69 | (29) | 71 | (39) |
| Newport, R.I. | 16 | ( 7) | 19 | ( 3) |
| New York | 4 | (26) | 11 | (25) |
| Philadelphia | — | — | 10 | (18) |
| Providence, R.I. | 16 | ( 3) | 25 | ( 2) |
| Williamsburg, Va. | 18 | ( 4) | 32 | ( 2) |

Sources: Pennsylvania Chronicle and Universal Advertiser, January–December 1767; Maryland Gazette, January–December 1767.

Note: Time lags are rounded off to the nearest whole day. The figures in parentheses indicate the number of times a dated report or advertisement appeared during the year.

[a] Dated advertisements.

area, papers also carried reports of distant and immediate markets, including information about commodity prices, arrivals and departures of vessels, and mercantile advertisements. If merchants, shippers, and others were to capitalize on an opportunity, obviously they had first to know that it existed. This knowledge was best used while the opportunity was still new, especially in those instances when shipping space was advertised.

The figures in table 12 suggest a high degree of geographic isolation in terms of public information. Of course in one sense the situation was not quite as extreme as the lag times indicate. The newspapers from which table 12 was constructed were weekly publications, and therefore news from New York arrived slightly before its publication in the *Pennsylvania Chronicle* or the *Maryland Gazette*. However, because this news was not sent by one private individual for another's consumption but rather was meant for public consumption, the lag times are probably a valid indicator of the rate at which a significant amount of market information moved.

This was particularly true in transoceanic communications, which were characterized by lengthy delays between the transmission and reception of information. As was pointed out in chapter 1, this could create serious problems for the Atlantic commercial system. Imagine the consternation among Philadelphia's merchants upon reading in a four-day-old dispatch from New York in the May 18, 1767, issue of the *Philadelphia Chronicle* that "both by private letters, and the London prints, we have intimations of the failure in London, of Hagan and Comp. and another great house there, who were the chief contractors for most of the wheat, that have gone lately from Philadelphia, Maryland and this city [New York]; by reason of which we are assured many merchants in these ports will probably be great sufferers, especially if the markets should turn out but low, which by all appearance, will be really the case." Because the information contained in the dispatch arrived in New York by packet from Falmouth, England, after a voyage of nine weeks, at least sixty-seven days had elapsed before Philadelphia's mercantile community received word of the collapse of Hagan and Company. According to the announced sailing schedule of the Falmouth–New York packets, news leaving England for America should have been available four or five weeks later in New York. But it often was not.[11] As table 12 suggests, the packets frequently took much longer to make the crossing, and merchants who put their faith in the announced schedule were either reckless or fools. Yet all the merchants, prudent and imprudent, who shipped to British markets were hampered by the delay intrinsic to transatlantic communications. The transoceanic time-lag figures provide one important reason why doing business in foreign markets was so much riskier for Pennsylvania producers than was selling iron at home.

Even within the Colonies of course communications and transportation fell far short of what the ironworks owners and iron merchants might have desired. Although the nature of their business forced them to give careful attention to the demand for iron in Philadelphia and the other colonies, their efforts to do so were frequently hampered.[12] An examination of the time required for public information to reach Philadelphia and Annapolis from other colonial cities suggests the kinds of difficulties they encountered in obtaining information about the major colonial market centers. The difference between the respective lag times at Philadelphia and Annapolis for news going from one to the other suggests that there was a directional bias in the movement of public information. Moreover, although the physical distances between Philadelphia and New York and Philadelphia and Annapolis were roughly comparable, the lag time at Philadelphia for news from Annapolis was more than three times as long as that for New York news. This disparity was partly economic and demographic in origin. Normally, more postriders and packets emanated with a higher frequency and with a greater specificity of route from the larger commercial and population centers than from the smaller ones.

Even more striking is the time required for information to reach Philadelphia and Annapolis from their respective hinterland regions. Although the figures in table 12 that describe this are derived from dated advertisements and not news items, they are reasonably accurate reflec-

TABLE 13

Geographic Distribution of Southeastern Pennsylvania Iron Production
Facilities, 1720–75

| Miles from Philadelphia | Number of Ironworks | Percentage of Total |
|---|---|---|
| 0–10 | 8 | 12.5% |
| 10–20 | 2 | 3.1 |
| 20–30 | 5 | 7.8 |
| 30–40 | 19 | 29.7 |
| 40–60 | 17 | 26.5 |
| 60–80 | 6 | 9.4 |
| 80–100 | 6 | 9.4 |
| 100–110 | 1 | 1.6 |
| Total | 64 | 100.0% |

Sources: See map 1.

TABLE 14

Distribution of Southeastern Pennsylvania Iron Production Facilities by County,
1720–75

| County[a] | Number of Facilities | Percentage of Total |
|---|---|---|
| Philadelphia | 5 | 7.8% |
| Delaware | 4 | 6.3 |
| Montgomery | 5 | 7.8 |
| Chester | 7 | 10.9 |
| Bucks | 2 | 3.1 |
| Berks | 25 | 39.1 |
| Lancaster[b] | 7 | 10.9 |
| York | 4 | 6.3 |
| Cumberland | 5 | 7.8 |
| Total | 64 | 100.0% |

Sources: See map 1.

[a] With the exception of Bucks County, the counties are arranged in order by their closest distance from the city of Philadelphia. Because of Bucks County's configuration and the fact that its iron production facilities were located along its northeastern side, Bucks has been considered more distant than Chester County.

[b] Lancaster County includes what today are Lebanon and Dauphin counties.

tions of the public-information lag times. As they indicate, the Philadelphia hinterland was disproportionately removed in an informational sense from its metropolitan market.[13] This is particularly significant because Pennsylvania ironworks were located almost exclusively in the colony's hinterland, and therefore the hinterland time-lag values constitute an important measure of the ironworks' access to market information. The physical remoteness of iron production facilities from the main source of market information was especially pronounced in southern Pennsylvania (see map 1 and tables 13 and 14). Of the sixty-four facilities for which a precise or probable location could be determined, over 84 percent were

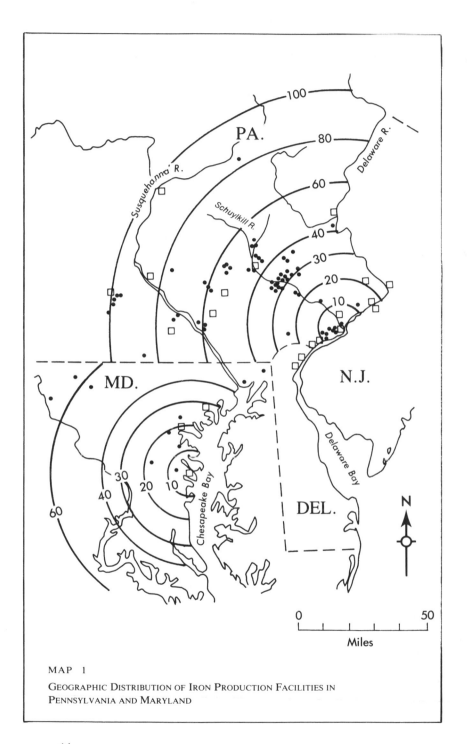

MAP 1

GEOGRAPHIC DISTRIBUTION OF IRON PRODUCTION FACILITIES IN
PENNSYLVANIA AND MARYLAND

more than twenty miles from Philadelphia, and more than half were located between thirty and sixty miles from the city.

Despite a fairly extensive road network in southeastern Pennsylvania (see map 2), the condition of these roads and the vehicles that moved over them still prohibited rapid movement. Under ideal conditions — a good, level road and dry weather — a loaded wagon could travel no more than two and a half miles an hour for twelve hours, or at most thirty miles in a day.[14] Thirty miles per day, however, was an exceptional rate of travel. Twenty miles a day or less probably was a much more common rate of movement, and even that might involve starting at dawn and traveling until after dark.[15] Even this rate of twenty miles per day must be regarded cautiously because of the varying quality of colonial roads, which, particularly in southeastern Pennsylvania and probably also in New Jersey and Maryland, were almost exclusively dirt, clay, or sand and became severely rutted through normal use, and muddy in heavy rains.[16] The maintenance and repair of roads in the Colonies left a good deal to be desired, and the resulting quality of the roads doubtless retarded the rate of movement over them.

Southeastern Pennsylvania was, for the most part, a region that presented itself to its eighteenth-century inhabitants as a fertile and "amply wooded rolling plain" of generally low to moderate slopes.[17] Sixty-five

*(continued from opposite page )*

The term "iron production facility" encompasses furnaces, forges, ironworks, and more specialized facilities such as steel furnaces and plating mills. Each dot represents a facility erected between 1720 and 1775. Data from Robert I. Alotta, *Street Names of Philadelphia* (Philadelphia: Temple University Press, 1975), map following p. 8; Bining, *Pennsylvania Iron Manufacture,* pp. 171–73; Herman P. Miller, *Outline Maps of the Counties of Allegheny, Berks, Bucks, Cambria, Dauphin, Fayette, Lackawanna, Lancaster, Luzerne, Montgomery, Philadelphia, Schuylkill, Westmoreland and York* . . . (Harrisburg: Pennsylvania General Assembly, 1901), pp. 19, 22, 26, 33, 40, 48; Morton L. Montgomery, "Early Furnaces and Forges of Berks County, Pennsylvania," *Pennsylvania Magazine of History and Biography* 8 (1884): 56–81, passim; "A Map of Pennsylvania exhibiting not only the improved parts of that Province, but also its extensive frontiers: Laid down from actual surveys and chiefly from the late map of W. Scull Published in 1770. Published by Robert Sayer & J. Bennett, 10 June 1775," Milton S. Eisenhower Library, The Johns Hopkins University, Baltimore (hereafter cited as "Scull's Map"); U.S. Department of the Interior, Geological Survey, *State of Pennsylvania Base Map with Highways and Contours* (Washington, D.C.: U.S. Department of the Interior, 1955); *The State of Maryland Historical Atlas: A Review of Events and Forces that have Influenced the State* (Washington, D.C.: State of Maryland, Department of Economic and Community Development, Department of State Planning, 1973), pp. 37, 43, 45; and Johnson, "The Genesis of the Baltimore Ironworks," pp. 170–71, passim.

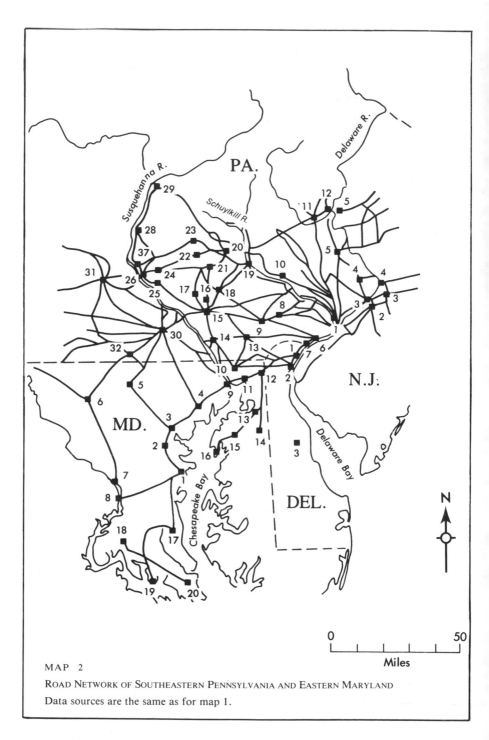

MAP 2

ROAD NETWORK OF SOUTHEASTERN PENNSYLVANIA AND EASTERN MARYLAND

Data sources are the same as for map 1.

46

percent of present-day Chester County and 82 percent of Lancaster County consist of land whose slopes are less than 8 percent and 10 percent, respectively; and such gently sloping land, James Lemon points out, was conducive to intensive agriculture without serious danger of soil erosion.[18]

The same terrain that accommodated agriculture, however, frequently hindered transportation; what was a gentle slope for farming could be a formidable obstacle to wagoners and the iron producers who hired them. This had an important impact on communications and transportation costs, an important factor in shaping access to markets. The courses of roads through level areas were fairly straight, and even over terrain of higher relief routes deviated only slightly and only when absolutely necessary because of land-ownership patterns or extremely obstructive natural features.[19] In the latter case, the road was usually extended to a point where the obstruction gave way. Such situations were not common, however, nor need they have been for the region's topography to have affected transportation to the markets profoundly.

Even minute inclinations of the terrain reduced the speed at which a wagon loaded with iron could travel, and the reduction could be quite pronounced (see table 15). The drawing power listed in table 15 can be prop-

*(continued from opposite page )*

PENNSYLVANIA

| 1 | Philadelphia | 22 | Lebanon (town) | 11 | Charlestown |
|---|---|---|---|---|---|
| 2 | Germantown | 23 | Jones's (Jonestown) | 12 | Elkton |
| 3 | Bristol | 24 | Hummelstown | 13 | Fredericktown |
| 4 | Newton (Bucks County) | 25 | Middletown (near | 14 | Millington |
| 5 | Buckingham | | Harrisburg) | 15 | Chestertown |
| 6 | Chester | 26 | Harris' Ferry | 16 | Rockhall |
| 7 | Marcus Hook | 27 | Fort Hunter–Esther Town | 17 | Prince Frederick |
| 8 | Whiteland Township | 28 | Fort Halifax | 18 | Port Tobacco |
| | (Chester County) | 29 | Fort Augusta | 19 | Cobb Island |
| 9 | Downington | 30 | York | 20 | St. Mary's City |
| 10 | Pottsgrove | 31 | Carlisle | | * *In Virginia* |
| 11 | Bethlehem | 32 | Hanover | | |
| 12 | Easton | | | | NEW JERSEY |
| 13 | New London Crossroads | MARYLAND AND VIRGINIA | | 1 | Glouchester |
| 14 | Drunmore Township | 1 | Annapolis | 2 | Burlington |
| 15 | Lancaster (town) | 2 | Elkridge Landing | 3 | Bordenton |
| 16 | Lititz | 3 | Baltimore (town) | | (Bordentown) |
| 17 | Manheim | 4 | Joppa | 4 | Trenton |
| 18 | Ephrata | 5 | Westminster | | |
| 19 | Reading | 6 | Frederick | | DELAWARE |
| 20 | Middletown | 7 | Georgetown | 1 | Wilmington |
| | (Womelsdorf) | 8 | Alexandria* | 2 | New Castle |
| 21 | Heidelberg | 9 | Havre de Grace | 3 | Dover |
| | (Schaefferstown) | 10 | Nottingham | | |

TABLE 15

Effect of Slope on the Drawing Power of a Horse

| Slope (%) [a] | Drawing Efficiency (%) [b] |
|---|---|
| 0 | 100.0 |
| 1.00 | 90.0 |
| 2.00 | 81.0 |
| 2.22 | 76.0 |
| 2.50 | 72.0 |
| 3.33 | 64.0 |
| 4.00 | 52.0 |
| 5.00 | 40.0 |
| 10.00 | 25.0 |

Source: J. L. Ringwalt, *Development of Transportation Systems in the United States* (Philadelphia: J. L. Ringwalt, 1888), p. 39.

[a] Derived from the gradients used in the source. Thus, a slope of 2.5 percent in this table is equivalent to the gradient of "1 in 40" given by Ringwalt. Slope percentage equals the number of vertical feet divided by the number of horizontal feet and multiplied by 100 percent.

[b] Drawing power is given in the source as a decimal fraction to be used as a multiplicative coefficient with the weight of a load pulled by one horse.

erly regarded as an approximate measure of the transport efficiency of a horse on terrain with various degrees of inclination. For a given distance over ground of constant slope, a loaded wagon moved most efficiently when (1) the load did not exceed the standard pulling capacity of the drawing animals and (2) the speed of travel was not excessive for the load. Clearly, these two conditions were interrelated, but they have been divided here to make an important point more clearly: an increase in speed over any substantial distance required a reduction in load. Similarly, an increase in load resulted in a decrease in speed. The effects of these constraints upon wagon transportation in eighteenth-century Pennsylvania were both direct and considerable. Most wagons hauling iron in the region were drawn by four-horse teams and carried loads of from 1.0 to 1.5 long tons; the usual load was 1.25 tons.[20] This weight limit was not an arbitrary one but, rather, a function of the drawing capacity of the four-horse team and probably of the terrain as well. On a level, sandy road four horses could draw 3,360 pounds, or 1.5 long tons, "at a walk." A four-horse team's capacity was probably somewhat greater on the dirt and clay roads of southeastern Pennsylvania — perhaps as much as 1.7 or 1.9 long tons.[21]

These figures pertain to the movement of a loaded wagon pulled by a team of horses at a walk, or at a rate of about 2.5 miles per hour, over level ground. However, many of the roads in southeastern Pennsylvania followed the contours of the region's rolling hills, and a number of the routes traversed more rugged terrain, which substantially reduced the transport efficiency of a wagon and team. Even a modest slope of 2 percent reduced efficiency by about 20 percent. Although slopes of this magnitude were not uncommon for roads in Lancaster County, they did not typify the terrain of the major iron-producing areas nor of the routes leading from them to the Philadelphia market. About 87 percent of the land area of present-day Chester County had a slope of more than 3 percent; a third of the county had slopes in excess of 8 percent.[22] Both Berks County and the northern part of adjacent Montgomery County were characterized by relatively sharp variations in relief, and although the wagon roads through these areas seem to have been laid out so as to avoid the steeper inclines, a number of the routes necessarily included fairly steep grades that reduced wagon speeds, further increasing the travel time between the ironworks and their markets.[23]

Thus far, everything said about rates of travel has presumed that ideal weather conditions obtained. Naturally, this was not always the case; rain or snow frequently retarded movement and occasionally prohibited any travel whatsoever. For example, on New Year's Day 1761 Charles J. Shippen, of Philadelphia, had to inform his father, in Lancaster, that "the roads have been so bad that no wagons have offered, by which I could send the things I mentioned to you in a former letter."[24] Not quite as dramatic but impressive nevertheless was the four-day journey endured by two Moravians between Bethlehem and Tulpehocken Town (about six miles west of Middletown, now Womelsdorf). The roughly fifty-five-mile wagon trip should have taken less than three full days, but the going was much slower "because it had rained a great deal and the road was very muddy," so muddy that they had to "abandon part of the baggage."[25]

The frequency with which such conditions occurred would naturally have varied somewhat from year to year and markedly from month to month, thereby affecting the movement of iron from southeastern Pennsylvania's production facilities to the region's various markets. Unfortunately, meteorological data for eighteenth-century Pennsylvania are fragmentary, making the construction of a long time series impossible. However, some idea of the incidence of inclement weather can be gained from the available evidence. For example, Peter Kalm maintained a careful daily record of his "meteorological observations" during his investigative journey throughout British North America in 1748 and 1749, and approximately ten of the roughly eighteen months of readings were made in or around Philadelphia.[26] We therefore know from Kalm's journal that of the 315 days of 1749 that he spent in the Philadelphia area, 53, or about 17 percent, were days of severely inclement weather.[27] Roughly the same percentage of days during the first half of 1767 was marred by similar weather conditions.[28]

Because the quantitative meteorological data are so poor for the eighteenth century, cautious improvisation, by way of more recent records, is necessary to shed some light on the possible effects of weather on the iron markets of colonial Pennsylvania.[29] Figure 7 is a plot of the mean monthly

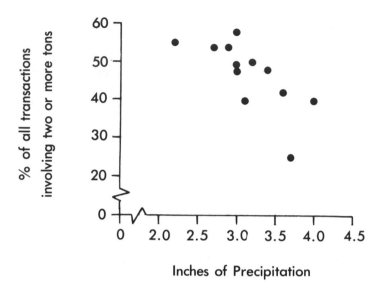

FIGURE 7

LARGE BAR-IRON TRANSACTIONS AND PRECIPITATION IN SOUTHEASTERN PENNSYLVANIA
Precipitation data are from James T. Lemon, *The Best Poor Man's Country: A Geographical Study of Early Southeastern Pennsylvania* (Baltimore: The Johns Hopkins Press, 1972), table 8 (p. 33); bar-iron–transaction data are derived from Hopewell Forge Ledgers B–G, 1767–75.

inches of precipitation at Harrisburg against the monthly mean percentage of all bar-iron transactions involving two or more tons per transaction at Hopewell Forge during the period 1768–75. Although no line of best fit has been drawn through the points, the relationship between the two variables in question is apparent: the number of large bar-iron transactions decreased as the amount of precipitation per month increased. The implications of this observation are significant for two reasons. First, there was no similar relationship between mean monthly precipitation and mean monthly production, nor, for that matter, was there one between bar-iron transactions and ancony production. The absence of such relationships is persuasive evidence for dismissing the possibility of a direct connection between these two sets of variables. Second, and more important, the correlation of precipitation with the ton size of bar-iron transactions strongly suggests that adverse weather conditions reduced the relative number of large bar-iron shipments to the markets.[30] This surmise makes good sense when we consider that the standard heavy load of a wagon carrying bar iron to a market was between 1.25 and 1.5 tons. Transactions involving 2, 3, or more tons necessarily required additional wagons or more than one round trip to the market. Inclement weather may well have discouraged such multiple trips, if only because the teamsters found trips in foul weather grueling and uncomfortable. A more substantial explanation, however, is that muddy or icy roads reduced the traction of a wagon, lengthening travel time but also making reductions in load size imperative.[31]

To some extent, iron manufacturers could turn to the region's rivers and large streams—arteries that also affected information flows, the movement of commodities, and the iron producer's choice of market. We can get a general idea of the waterways' effect on transportation and communication by comparing maps 2 and 3. The dark, wavy lines on the latter are isochrones; that is, they connect points that took an equal number of days' travel by wagon from Philadelphia. The plotting of the isochrones was determined by the road network, physical relief, and the course and location of the major rivers—the Delaware, the Susquehanna, the Schuylkill, and the Lehigh. A comparison of the two maps makes clear that the major waterways did not significantly reduce travel time from Philadelphia. In those areas where the isochrones rise away from the city as they intersect a river—for example, at the Susquehanna near Harrisburg and along the Schuylkill below Reading—the primary cause was usually the presence of a road running parallel to the river. This was the case largely because the flow of these rivers was to the south, making upstream movement, where possible at all, difficult.[32]

Instead of alternative routes, the rivers actually presented additional problems for overland movement, problems that would not have been quite so acute had it not been for the east-west orientation of Pennsylvania's trade.[33] The geographical bias of the colony's internal commerce is evident from the direction of most of the roads shown in map 2 and is further suggested, in map 3, by the far greater extension of the isochrones westward than northward. This was particularly true of the area immediately to the west of the Susquehanna River, which itself represented the largest single obstacle to the movement of commodities within the region. Little freight could be shipped downstream from any point south of Middletown because the river was "unnavigable for fifty miles above its mouth," in the Chesapeake Bay.[34] Similarly, the Schuylkill generally carried freight only after its depth had increased during the spring runoff.[35] Otherwise, the Schuylkill and Susquehanna rivers of southeastern Pennsylvania served, with varying degrees of severity, to divide the region into three parts.

The sharpest division was that made by the larger of the two rivers, the Susquehanna. Its width and rough waters increased travel times between the western and eastern counties of the colony and exacted a stiff tariff from the farmers, iron producers, merchants, and others whose affairs required them to make ferry crossings.[36] The cost of the ferry and the

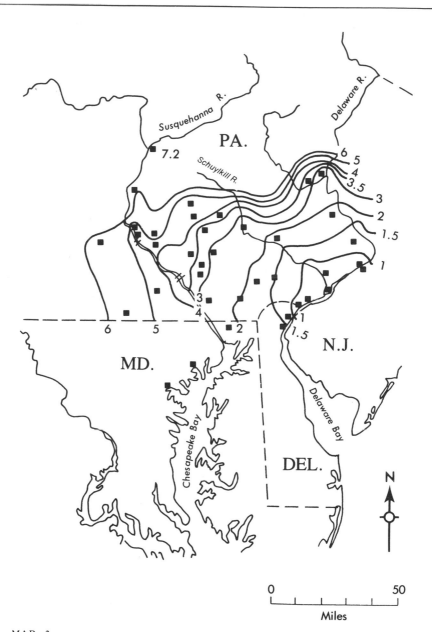

MAP 3

HYPOTHETICAL TRAVEL TIMES BY LOADED WAGON FROM PHILADELPHIA (*in Days*)
Data sources are the same as for map 1.

hazards intrinsic to its operation probably discouraged cross-river traffic so much that Baltimore, which could be reached by road without crossing the river, became an attractive alternative to Philadelphia. Such considerations as these may have been at the bottom of the decision made by the Carlisle Company's owners to ship pig iron to Baltimore in 1765.[37] In any event, the 7.5-shilling-per-ton ferriage charged to cross the Susquehanna was considerable, being equivalent to the cost of transporting iron an additional ten miles overland.[38] The Schuylkill ferry charges of 1.63 shillings per ton added still another 1 percent to the transportation costs from York to Philadelphia.[39] The total ferriage charges from York to Philadelphia therefore raised the transportation cost for bar iron by between 7 percent and 8 percent, or from a base level of approximately £5.8 to about £6.3 per ton.[40]

If these charges are expressed as the costs per ton-mile, a quite different picture results, but the economic impact of the transportation costs remains significant. The £5.8-per-ton base transport cost and the total £6.3-per-ton cost were equivalent to about 1.3 and 1.4 shillings per ton-mile, respectively. Ostensibly, then, ferry charges of about 10 shillings per ton, or 1.2 pence per ton-mile, should not have been a particularly significant consideration to an iron producer near York who wished to sell his iron in Philadelphia. However, more important than the absolute cost of transportation, whether expressed in pounds of currency per ton or per ton-mile, was the effect of this cost on a producer's competitive position in a particular market. Thus, if the production costs in 1768 of a ton of bar iron at a forge near York and at Hopewell Forge near Lancaster were equivalent, that is, at about £19, the decisive factors in determining their relative competitive positions in the Philadelphia market would have been the transportation costs incurred by each facility and the prevailing market price for iron.

For most of 1768 the average wholesale price of bar iron in Philadelphia was about £24 per ton.[41] At this price, Hopewell Forge would have enjoyed a clear advantage over its York County competitor. The base transportation cost for one ton of bar iron from Hopewell Forge to Philadelphia was £3, which with the addition of the 1.63-shilling charge for the Schuylkill ferry was increased by about 2 percent to £3.08.[42] Therefore, the per-ton cost of Hopewell's bar iron — including the cost of production — by the time it reached Philadelphia would have been slightly more than £22, well under the market price. With a production cost of £19 per ton and total per-ton transportation costs of £6.3, the per-ton total cost of the bar iron made by the forge in York County would have exceeded the market price, making it noncompetitive. Of course at a market price of £24 per ton, its bar iron still would not have been able to compete even had there been no ferriage charges. Therefore, a forge in

York and Cumberland counties would have been able to compete successfully in the Philadelphia market only if its per-ton cost of production were substantially lower than that incurred at forges on the east side of the Susquehanna or when the wholesale market price for bar iron in Philadelphia was particularly high. Of these two possible prerequisites for entering the Philadelphia market, the latter was undoubtedly the more realistic, since production costs, like production technology, seem to have been fairly standardized in southeastern Pennsylvania. However, bar iron usually sold at well under £25 wholesale in Philadelphia, rising above that price only during a forty-month period from January 1772 through April 1775.[43] Consequently, Philadelphia could have been an advantageous market for the forge in the western counties only when prices in markets closer to home were significantly lower than the metropolitan market price. This was almost certainly the line of reasoning followed by the owners of the Carlisle Iron Works when they instructed their manager to sell 1.5 tons of bar iron, "sending so much to Philadelphia or Yorktown [York], as the Latter will be a more advantageous place to sell it."[44]

Clearly, the technology of transportation had a significant impact on the entire regional system of producers and market centers. In fact, distance and all that it implied — transportation costs, travel time, and accessibility — seem to have been the primary factors deciding the extent of a producer's activities in the region's various markets — with the exception of Philadelphia. That city was unique as an iron market for a number of reasons. Most important of these were its role as a clearing house and export center for the economic activity of Pennsylvania and the adjacent areas of New Jersey, Delaware, and even Maryland, and its highly concentrated population and consequently its large demand for goods and services.[45] Thus, as an iron market, Philadelphia was the exception to the rule that determined the importance of the hinterland towns — Lancaster, Reading, York, and Carlisle — as iron markets. The relative accessibility of these places and the demand for iron in their respective environs determined their attractiveness as markets.

The hinterland market centers probably competed for iron not so much with Philadelphia as among themselves. This was recognized by the owners of the Carlisle Iron Works, who gave explicit expression of the principle in their written instructions to the company's manager regarding the suspension of operations at the forge. The owners directed him to attempt a liquidation of the firm's debts to various people in Cumberland County by settling the outstanding amounts in bar iron rather than in cash. The hope was that the creditors could be "induced to take Bar Iron at an advanced price," that is, at a higher price than usual, by virtue of the logical argument that they would soon "be under the necessity of going a great distance for a supply." The alternative source of supply was Lancaster, and the

TABLE 16

Transportation Costs for Bar Iron from Hopewell Forge to Philadelphia and Hinterland Market Centers, c. 1768

| Market Center | Distance (Miles) | Transportation Cost (£ Pa.) | | | |
|---|---|---|---|---|---|
| | | Per Ton | Per Ton-Mile | As Percentage of Price | per Ton[a] |
| Lancaster | 15 | 0.6 | 0.045 | 2.7 | (22 [1768]) |
| Reading[b] | 30 | 1.5[c] | 0.050[c] | — | — |
| York | 39 | 1.6 | 0.041 | 6.4 | (25 [1772]) |
| Philadelphia | 75 | 3.1 | 0.041 | 12.9 | (24 [1768–72]) |

Sources: John Flexer Walzer, "Transportation in the Philadelphia Trading Area, 1740–1775" (Ph.D. diss., University of Wisconsin, 1968), pp. 315–17; "Scull's Map"; Hopewell Forge Ledgers B–F, 1767–74; Hopewell Forge Coal, Iron & Time Book, Etc., 1768–75; Bezanson, Gray, and Hussey, Prices, pp. 408–12.

[a] Figures in parentheses indicate the price per ton and the year(s) when this price existed.

[b] Data are for Elizabeth Furnace, which was less than five miles from Hopewell Forge.

[c] The cost probably does not include the cost of crossing the narrow upper reaches of the Schuylkill River.

manager was encouraged to stress to the firm's creditors the inconvenience of having to go there for iron. If swayed by this argument, they might be persuaded "to give at least the price of a ton of Iron in Philadelphia."[46]

For the most part, this was a well-considered argument, and it may have carried the day for the Carlisle Iron Works. In two important respects, however, it also represented wishful thinking. First, the firm's creditors did not have to cross the Susquehanna to Lancaster County for bar iron, since substantial quantities of that commodity were hauled and ferried from there for sale in York.[47] Second, the owners assumed that they might receive a price per ton as high or higher than that given in Philadelphia. But bar iron prices in Philadelphia tended to be higher than those in the hinterland markets. This was the case not only because the aggregate demand for the commodity was so much greater in the city than in the country but probably also because the many producers who had their bar iron hauled to Philadelphia generally sent smaller quantities at a time to that market than to the other centers. For example, although Hopewell Forge commonly sold bar iron in lots of ten tons to Lancaster and York merchants, its shipments to Philadelphia were usually considerably smaller, of about two to five tons.[48] The producers' reasoning in this matter was sound. As was demonstrated earlier, the transportation costs incurred in long-distance hauling were a part of the total per-ton cost of bar iron by the time it reached Philadelphia (see table 16). Consequently, that market was singularly attractive to distant producers only when the price was unusually high or when prices in other markets were particularly depressed. Also, as figure 8 suggests, individual transactions involving small quantities of bar iron generally brought a higher price per ton than did the larger transactions.[49] In this area of operations, as in many others, the owners of the firms demonstrated a sound business sense, using the

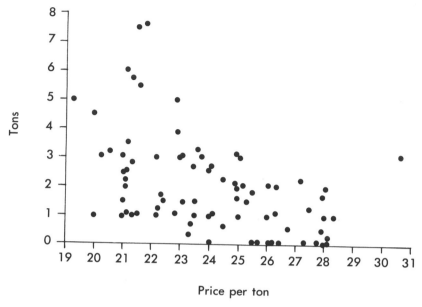

FIGURE 8

BAR-IRON TRANSACTION SIZE BY PRICE PER TON (IN £ PA.) AT HOPEWELL FORGE IN 1768
Number of transactions = 92. Correlation coefficient (product moment) = −0.4689
and is significant at better than the 0.01 confidence level; i.e., there is less than 1 chance
in 100 that the relationship is random. Data from Hopewell Forge Ledgers B and C,
1767–69.

technique of differential pricing. There was nothing novel about its application by Hopewell Forge in 1768; in one form or another, in commerce as
well as in iron production, the technique had long been known and used
successfully. For example, in 1740 Robert Ellis, of the Durham Company,
informed a correspondent that when the company sold iron to smiths "at
35/, we Allow them 7d. [per 112] lb. + if at 40/. 7 1/2 [d]." [50] This company clearly gained an advantage when it sold iron by the hundredweight
at forty shillings because although the real price increased by 14.4 percent,
the discount to the smiths rose by only 6.1 percent.

    The application of differential pricing by the Baltimore Company's Bar-
rister Carroll was perhaps somewhat more straightforward when he
informed an Eastern Shore buyer of his flour that "I fancy you mistook me
in the Price I have not sold yet under 15/ But will Let you have this at 14/6
[per] Cent as you take a Quantity." [51] Irrespective of the commodity, differential pricing meant the same thing: selling a large quantity at a lower
than normal price per unit. If the technique were used optimally, the result
was a maximization of sales revenue and a minimization of the number of
individual transactions and of their attendant costs. Therefore, this technique could be used most effectively in those markets that were most acces-

sible to a producer. For most iron producers, this condition probably lessened the allure of Philadelphia and made the hinterland towns more attractive.

These towns, though located in the countryside, were more than mere villages or hamlets. Even before the close of the colonial period they were thriving centers of population and economic activity, providing goods and services for the far-flung populations of their surrounding areas.[52] Agricultural products, as well as iron, converged on them over an intricate network of roads that radiated from each town like spokes on a wheel (see map 2). A comparison of the four major hinterland towns provides a useful perspective from which to evaluate their roles as iron markets. The first impression of the centrality of York, given by map 2, is amply confirmed; all roads seem to have terminated or started there, particularly those roads leading to the western reaches of Pennsylvania and into northern Maryland. York's importance arose largely from its high degree of accessibility; the road network around the town was very dense. Thus, although York's population was only two-thirds that of Lancaster, its inhabitants were serviced by more than three times the road mileage available to their neighbors across the Susquehanna.

Lancaster, on the other hand, had other, compensating virtues as a market. Lancaster's roads led to Philadelphia, while the roads of York went to the river or to the south and west. Moreover, the population of Lancaster County in 1760 was 20 percent larger than the combined populations of York and Cumberland counties for that year. In 1770 Lancaster itself had about 82 percent as many inhabitants as did the two counties west of the Susquehanna.[53] Finally, Lancaster's relatively concentrated and fairly accessible population was also one of the wealthiest groups in southeastern Pennsylvania.[54] These factors combined to make Lancaster the major hinterland market for iron.

The hinterland and Philadelphia together constituted a significant and growing market. Although it is impossible here to make even an educated guess as to the region's overall demand, one can nevertheless get a general idea of the scale of that demand by examining the use of iron in one of the more ubiquitous things in southeastern Pennsylvania — the wagon. The amount of iron that went into the construction of a wagon varied with the vehicle's purpose. For example, wagons used for handling heavy loads to or from market centers were usually more strongly built and contained more iron parts in their bodies that did farm wagons.[55] Almost all wagons, however, had one thing in common: each of their four wheels rode on wrought iron tires, the combined weight of which was about 145 pounds.[56]

Although this is not a particularly impressive quantity of iron, it quickly becomes so when it is multiplied by the 200 or so wagons in Northampton County to yield a total of 29,000 pounds, or almost 13 long tons, of bar iron.[57] More impressive still is the number of tons of bar iron that went into the tires of all of the wagons in southeastern Pennsylvania. A rough but cautious estimate of this total can be had by assuming that the total number of wagons in the region was 2,000.[58] Multiplying this figure by 145 pounds, we arrive at a total of some 290,000 pounds, or approximately 130 long tons of bar iron. This amount is only about 35 tons less than the average annual number of tons sold by Hopewell Forge from 1767 through 1775.[59] Obviously, the demand in the domestic market for iron was quite impressive. Additional products, such as other wagon parts, tools, and housewares, including stoves and kitchen implements and a variety of other castings, were routinely turned out by furnaces and forges of Pennsylvania, New Jersey, and, to some extent, Maryland.[60] They, too, found local markets.

More sophisticated and more technologically advanced products were also manufactured by specialized production facilities, such as steel furnaces, slitting mills, and forges designed for a particular type of output.[61] Not surprisingly, most of these facilities, were to be found in close proximity to the major market, Philadelphia (see table 17).[62] Eleven of the thirteen special facilities were within forty miles of the city, and slightly more than half were less than twenty miles distant, or within a day's travel by wagon. Philadelphia's premier position as the region's population and commercial center probably guaranteed to these few specialized producers both sufficiently large supplies of pig and bar iron and an adequate level of demand for their more advanced products. Finally, the location of most of these facilities within a day or a day and a half's travel of Philadelphia had the effect of reducing the overall impact of transportation costs. This was so because the ratio of the cost of transporting a ton of iron to the cost of producing it decreased as the iron became more refined, that is, as it passed from pig iron to bar iron to wagon tires.[63]

The owners of these facilities well understood these economic considerations and their relationship to the market.[64] They understood the importance of having adequate access to supplies and markets, and it was no coincidence that almost all iron production facilities, whatever the type, were located on sites convenient to the main wagon roads (see maps 1, 2, and 3).[65] Similarly, there was nothing casual about the attempts by iron producers and others to convince the colonial government to improve the region's roads, and petitions from hinterland inhabitants to the governor and the provincial council were frequent throughout the century.[66] The petition of "sundry [of] the Inhabitants of the County of Lancaster" in 1736 is particularly interesting. The petitioners began their argument by observing that

> the gentlemen in Company concerned in the Ironworks in Coventry
> on the French Creek [in Chester County] by their great Expence Care

TABLE 17

Distribution of Iron Production Facilities by County and Type, 1720–75

| County[a] | Number of | | | | | Special Facilities as Percentage of Total |
|---|---|---|---|---|---|---|
| | Furnaces | Forges | Ironworks[b] | Special Facilities | Total Facilities | |
| Philadelphia | 0 | 0 | 0 | 5 | 5 | 100.0% |
| Delaware | 0 | 2 | 0 | 2 | 4 | 50.0 |
| Montgomery | 0 | 4 | 0 | 1 | 5 | 20.0 |
| Chester | 4 | 2 | 0 | 1 | 7 | 14.3 |
| Bucks | 0 | 1 | 1 | 0 | 2 | 0 |
| Berks | 7 | 15 | 0 | 3 | 25 | 12.0 |
| Lancaster[c] | 4 | 3 | 0 | 0 | 7 | 0 |
| York | 1 | 1 | 1 | 1 | 4 | 25.0 |
| Cumberland | 1 | 2 | 2 | 0 | 5 | 0 |
| Total | 17 | 30 | 4 | 13 | 64 | |

Source: Bining, *Pennsylvania Iron Manufacture*, pp.171–73; "Scull's Map."

[a] With the exception of Bucks County, the counties are arranged in order by their closest distance from the city of Philadelphia. Because of Bucks County's configuration and the fact that its iron production facilities were located along its northeastern side, Bucks has been considered more distant than Chester County.

[b] Includes both furnace and forge.

[c] Lancaster County includes present day Lebanon and Dauphin counties.

& Industry have carried on the said works to such perfection that they are not only of great Benefit to themselves but also very Advantageous to the Province & more Particularly to the Inhabitants of this Country whose Distance from Philadelphia requires large Quantities of Iron to fit out their Waggons & Appurtinances, with which we have been in General very well & Serviceably supply'd from the said works these many years.[67]

They then claimed that they themselves had suffered "for want of Passable Roads in Carriage of the said Iron & such Commodities for Provision as are received in Barter for the same," finally asking that a "Passable Waggon Road from the Town of Lancaster to the Ironworks in Coventry" and also to "Redding Furnace [sic]," then under construction, be laid out.[68] Significantly, and perhaps tactfully, the names of the owners of Coventry Ironworks and Reading Furnace were not listed among the petition's signers.

Other iron producers were less subtle about their needs. In March 1745 Robert Ellis, of the Durham Company in Bucks County, asked that a road be built for the benefit of the company from "Tohickon to Durham." The request was granted.[69] The concern of Peter Grubb for transportation improvements was expressed in a petition "of divers Inhabitants of the County of Lancaster" for a new road "from the Middle-Ferry on Schuylkill . . . as far as the Village of Strasberg [about ten miles from the town of Lancaster]."[70] The petitioners, who included the wealthy Lancaster merchant Edward Shippen and the ironmaster James Old, began by noting that the existing road between Philadelphia and Lancaster was "by constant use of it with heavy Loaded Carriages, and by its being laid in many places over very bad ground, now rendered almost impassable." A thinly veiled threat that "the want of a good Road" might divert "the valuable Trade of this County, or some parts of it, to other places," that is, Maryland, was the linchpin of the argument.[71] Enough of these threats and demands were successful to bring about significant improvements in road transportation by the second half of the eighteenth century. These improvements in turn helped to make the domestic market, especially that of the hinterland, of much greater importance to the Pennsylvania iron producers.

By the end of the colonial period the domestic market was far more important than the overseas trade to all but the very largest iron producers. The relentless logic of geography and the technology of transportation made this choice for these early industrial capitalists. The risks of dealing in distant markets were too great; the costs of transportation were too important to allow the average iron producer to look to London instead of Philadelphia — or better, Lancaster. There, in the prosaic business of wagon tires and axe heads, skillets and stoves, he found a more reliable and growing market, one to which he was close enough to understand better and sooner than his rivals in other colonies or overseas. By the end of the colonial period the iron industry in Pennsylvania was turning inward on the domestic market — an orientation that has remained essentially unchanged to the present day.

# The Response to the Market: The Quest for Control

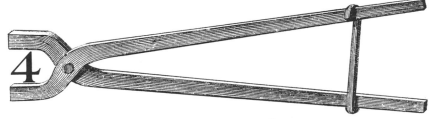

*No Person Can have any Dependence on a Trade or Customers that seem to be actuated by Caprice or Whim only.*

Charles Carroll, barrister

Even though an iron producer might sell his goods close to home, be the master of quality control, and cut his labor costs to the bone, there was much in his business that was beyond his control and frequently beyond his understanding. A sudden drop in prices often defied his attempts at explanation, leaving him perplexed and frustrated. Thus, when Dr. Charles Carroll learned from his correspondents in Bristol that the price of pig iron had dropped in that market even as bar iron sold at a "top price in London," he could only observe that the disparity in prices was "a mistery." [1] Even when the cause of a momentary decline in the price of iron or sluggish sales in a particular market could be readily identified by the producer or his mercantile agent, there was often nothing the iron producer could do about his past shipments. Such was the case during mid-April 1768, when the average price of a ton of bar iron in the Philadelphia market fell suddenly from twenty-four pounds to twenty-three. It was no solace to Peter Grubb to learn from a correspondent in the city that "there is now avast Quantity of Iron on hand in town the Consequence is that it is low + dull Sale." [2]

Although excess supply was the most commonly cited cause of low prices, both iron producers and those merchants who handled the commodity were well aware that inadequate demand could bring about the same results. Moreover, their understanding of this aspect of the market

61

mechanism was not entirely parochial; the influence of even remote factors often caught their attention. The Philadelphia merchant John Wall was particularly astute when he explained to his uncle, Peter Grubb, that the high price of flour in Philadelphia was responsible for the depressed price of iron there. High flour prices, Wall pointed out, had discouraged "the New Ingland vesels" from calling in Philadelphia for either flour or iron. However, Wall assured Grubb, once these ships arrived, iron would be "in great Demand." [3]

Unfortunately, three weeks later, in August 1772, Wall had to write to Grubb that he had "Not Sold but 1½ tunn of Iron yeat the New England vesels is Not yet Come But are Expected Evrey Day." Upon their arrival, he reassured his uncle, "I Shall be [able] to Sell all off." [4] Wall's error was really rather small, considering that the time lag in public communications between Philadelphia and Boston was probably about two weeks. [5] At least that much time would have elapsed before New England merchants and shippers could receive and react to the news of a decrease in the price of flour. Still, in cases of this sort an impotent understanding of the causes of a dull market was not very much better than impotent ignorance.

Of course, when iron prices were high and sales were brisk, producers and merchants spent little time analyzing the source of their prosperity. Instead, they calmly accepted the fact that all things were as they should be. At such times the correspondence between a producer and the merchants who sold his iron in the various markets assumed its most satisfying and useful form. The producer was then at his most optimistic, and the information supplied by his correspondents concerning prices, current and expected demand, shipping space, and political developments that might affect the market was received with a view to applying it in the immediate future. Thus, it was with confidence that Barrister Carroll could, in 1756, predict to his London correspondent that the demand for pig iron in England would certainly increase because of the outbreak of hostilities marking the start of the Seven Years' War. Carroll hoped that "as there must be a demand for it . . . it will fetch me a Good Price." [6] However, almost ten months later Carroll wrote to this same correspondent saying that although he naturally hoped that pig iron would soon bring a better price, he had decided that "if it Dos not it will be Hardly worth Shipping Considering the Great Expence." [7]

Carroll's problem was one that he shared with every other colonial iron producer, wherever his market. While they were well aware of the several individual factors that could move the market in one direction or the other, their understanding of the interplay of these factors was inadequate to the task of integrating these bits and pieces into a coherent and consistent explanation of the market mechanism. [8] Thus, while a producer might with some accuracy attribute a glutted market to the excessive number of sellers in it, he could not be expected to pursue the matter further and consider why so much iron had simultaneously converged there. Nor could he normally afford to take the risk of anticipating when, exactly, these conditions might change. Thus, in 1753, when Dr. Charles Carroll was warned of a glut by a London merchant, he replied that he could have shipped iron the year before to pay the merchant, "but as you complained of low markets and I had no account [of] Sales of what I shipt I thought Glutting the marketts with an unsaleable Commodity was to no purpose."[9] Like Carroll, most merchants were far behind the fast-moving markets of that era, and belated although sincere warnings could do them little good.[10]

Even though iron producers and merchants recognized that the amount of time required to sell a quantity of pig or bar iron varied from one market to another, they seem to have made only a tenuous connection between a particular market's transaction time, or turnover rate, and its levels of demand and supply.[11] For example, despite the awareness of the Baltimore Company's owners that the average transaction time for their iron in London during the early 1750s was about six times that in Bristol, they not only continued to ship most of their iron to London but even complained of the transaction time encountered there.[12] What they failed to see was that the English market centers, like those in Pennsylvania, catered to a rather localized demand that could absorb iron only discontinuously. With the qualified exception of the English ironware manufactures, there was no sector in either the English or Pennsylvania economies that had the constant, voracious demand for iron that would characterize the railroad industry in the nineteenth century and the automobile industry in the twentieth.[13] Consequently, an eighteenth-century iron market was always susceptible to becoming glutted simply through a lengthening of its transaction time.

A producer's decision to sell his iron in an English market was generally based on the reports that he had received about conditions there. Because of the considerable time required for a message to cross the Atlantic Ocean, however, these reports were often outdated by the time they reached him. In such instances, he made his decision on the basis of market conditions that no longer prevailed.

Although the position of a producer in the markets of Pennsylvania was generally not so exposed as that of the Maryland producer in the English markets, their situations were somewhat comparable. The shorter distances between producers and markets in Pennsylvania were of course an advantage, permitting a producer to react more quickly to news of favorable market conditions. However, this very advantage sometimes contributed to glutting the colony's markets. Because it enabled all producers to react quickly to news of a market with high prices and little iron, that market might soon become oversupplied, forcing down prices.[14]

Iron producers and their agents in England, as well as in Pennsylvania, recognized these aspects of their market. In their attempts to minimize the damage, they engaged in the widely practiced techniques of consignment sales and sales by credit. Actually, there was no realistic alternative to these practices; the geography and technology of eighteenth-century markets made them unavoidable. When an iron producer shipped his iron on consignment to a merchant, he had, in effect, entrusted to the merchant a substantial amount of embodied capital. Because the requirements for operating capital in iron production were substantial and unceasing, the producer was often compelled to seek credit advances from the merchants to whom he consigned his iron. These advances did not constitute investments by the merchants; rather, they were designed to carry the producer until his iron was sold.[15] This was all the more necessary since the iron itself was often sold on credit in the markets, and a producer could have no firm idea of when remittance would be made.[16]

All of these factors, but especially slow communication and transportation, precluded any long-range planning by a producer with respect to his participation in the market. Necessarily, then, his approach to that arena was tactical rather than strategic. He was, in short, the compleat opportunist, taking what prices were offered for his iron and hoping that high prices would persist and that low prices would rise. Consequently, those aspects of the iron business to which forethought could be given and planning could be applied were, for the most part, on the production end of the business: land acquisition; the purchase, maintenance, and replacement of capital equipment; and the iron production process itself. Even here, there was no certainty about his efforts, but the number of variables involved was smaller, and more of them were under the owner's control.

The contrasts between the characteristics of these two systems — the commercial network and the production system — provide one measure of the difficulty and complexity of the iron producer's task. He had moved a substantial amount of his interest and money into a system that offered regularity and profits to be gained from ceaseless attention to the small details of production. But he was still highly vulnerable to the uncontrollable changes taking place in the commercial system; iron and iron products had to be sold as well as manufactured. All that he could do was focus on those markets in the hinterland that were least susceptible to sudden change and least vulnerable to glutting by competitors. Otherwise, he could try to anticipate shifts in demand and, through quality control, to protect his share of the demand that did exist. But none of these recourses could change completely his vulnerable position in a system with slow and sporadic information flows and distant markets too large to control and too small to relieve the constant threat of oversupply.

The tension between these two systems, while intrinsic to the industry, affected iron firms in different ways, depending on their maturity. The overriding concern at the beginning of a firm's existence, once the obligations and prerogatives of its owners had been codified, seems to have been the mechanics of production. As a firm gained some experience, however, the most important consideration became regulating the inflow and outflow of revenue and the maintenance of the firm's position in the markets it normally served. Of course even a young firm had to be concerned with its marketing, but the degree of concern differed greatly between the neophytes and the more established enterprises.

Moreover, the companies founded before 1750 and those established during the second half of the century differed in their initial approach to the markets. Firms, such as the Baltimore and Principio companies, that had begun operations in the halcyon days when competitors were few and easily identified seem to have taken the existence of the markets and their access to them as matters of course. Latecomers, such as the Carlisle and American companies, could not afford such complacent optimism. They faced an abundance of competitors many of whom enjoyed a favorable reputation for their products; some of these were firms whose very size must have been impressive, if not intimidating, to the managers of a young business.

Before 1750, however, when costs of entry into the industry were still relatively low, it was possible for a young firm to mount, within a few years of its formation, an effective challenge to an older and larger firm. In 1736, less than five years after the establishment of the Baltimore Company, the English owners of the Principio Company were sufficiently impressed by the younger firm's success in the English markets to regard it with a good deal of circumspection. They communicated their uneasiness to their manager in America, observing that since "the Baltimore Iron [has] acquired a pretty good reputation for toughness and [as] the proprietors are residents in y^e Country, we question whether they would not be competitors with us in freight provided we built on Pertapsco." They were in fact sufficiently disturbed to direct him to make "an inspection into the influence these Gent or Snowdons [sic] parterners may have with Cap^ts" so that the Principio Company would be in a position "to prevent and hinder any ill Consequence" that might result "by retarding our Piggs when made, from a ready Conveyance to this market [London]."[17] Evidently, both firms were quite prepared to compete head-to-head, and both continued to do so matter-of-factly until 1750.

In March of that year John Price, a member of the Principio Company and a London correspondent of the Baltimore Company's Charles Carroll of Carrollton, proposed to the American that their two companies form a cartel "as a means of keeping up prices of pig Iron, of keeping down Coasting Fr[ts] [keeping] the Markets at a Stated settlem[t] and avoid other interferences.[18] Price had broached the subject skillfully, observing to Carroll that "your Baltimore pig Iron having been reduced in price so low as [£5.5 per] ton occasioned us to drop our pigs from [£6.5] to [6.25] + 6£ [per] ton." Even worse, he said, was the fact that his company had "had a difficult matter to keep up to that [price] while you had any on the Market."[19] Price was not engaging in idle flattery, nor was he being indiscreet with a competitor. He knew that the "tough" pig iron made by his company and by the Baltimore Company was not in great demand in the London market and that while his own firm found itself in an unfavorable position, the Baltimore Company shared the misfortune.[20] In the short run a cartel seemed therefore to be the only reasonable means by which to resolve their mutual difficulties.

Ultimately, the success of the plan would depend on the information that could be collected through a "General Correspondence with all the Forgemasters" in England. This was to be accomplished by "having the Chief body of the pig mettal from the plantations imported here [London]" pass through "one or two hands."[21] If this pooling arrangement proved practicable, it would enable them to monopolize the sale of American pig iron to English refiners.[22] Whether the plan would have worked is a moot question; although Price apparently convinced his partners of the desirability of a cartel agreement, the Baltimore Company failed to pursue the matter. A plausible reason for the younger firm's lack of interest might be that its rapid growth had convinced its members that they had more to lose than to gain by agreeing to a fixed share of the English market. In any event, we can be reasonably certain that the proposal was not rejected out of hand by the Baltimore Company because of the business scruples of its members.

Ironically, two of the company's members — Dr. Charles Carroll and, later, his son, Barrister Carroll — were quite vociferous in their condemnations of what they contended were unfair practices by English iron producers and merchants.[23] Barrister Carroll was particularly insistent on this point, and having endured low prices for his iron in English markets for what he considered to have been an unreasonably long time, he was not disposed to take seriously the conventional wisdom about dull markets. Instead, he insisted to his English correspondents that "every method [was] Taken to Lower the value of what Comes from the Colonys."[24] A year later, in 1759, he made this same point more explicitly to a London merchant, advising him that a careful investigation would prove that the English iron producers did not make as much pig iron as they claimed and that these claims were "only a scheme to Beat Down our Price."[25]

In reality, there was probably some truth to Carroll's accusations. English iron producers made frequent attempts during the period 1730–50 to convince Parliament to find *"some Means . . . to support our Ironworks at home"* and to put those *"in the Plantations . . . under some proper Restraints."* [26] There was also some justice in the position taken by the English producers who feared the competition from American pig and bar iron. Nevertheless, a balanced view of the contest leads one to conclude that more than a little self-generated hysteria seasoned each party's perception of the other. [27]

Bitterness of this sort was not unique to the English markets nor to those Americans who sold their iron in them. During the latter part of 1773 and, especially, the first months of 1774 Pennsylvania's iron producers began to organize themselves against what many of them perceived to be a conspiracy of the colony's merchants, especially those in Philadelphia, to depress bar-iron prices. Prices had in fact fluctuated wildly as they fell from a high of twenty-eight pounds per ton in January 1773 to twenty-five pounds a year later. [28] Despite the producers' firm conviction that the source of the decline lay in the machinations of the merchants, a more likely explanation is that the markets were merely signaling an overabundance of iron and a satiated local demand. Still, the producers felt that the evidence of the merchants' perfidy was plain to anyone who cared to look. Paul Zantzinger, a Lancaster merchant and iron producer, became slightly paranoid about the situation. In January 1774 he wrote an almost incoherent letter, in a hurried hand, to Peter Grubb in which he began by saying that he had "just time to inform you that the Iron is Lower'd again to £25 what to do [about] Those Damned fellows I do not [know]." "Those Damned fellows" were the iron merchants; later in the letter Zantzinger proposed to Grubb that the two of them meet with Grubb's brother, Curttis, and another forge owner to discuss "what Measures to take to hinder those fellows." He stated his own aim unambiguously: "For [my] part I have to much Ambition + Spirit to have any to do with them I am determined to do all in My Power to knock [them] out of the Trade & get it up to £28." [29]

The reaction of Curttis Grubb to proposals such as that made by Zantzinger was one of matter-of-fact acceptance. A little more than two weeks after Zantzinger had sent his letter, Curttis Grubb sent a letter to his brother in which he advised him that by "Keeping up the Price of barr Iron , . . . we Could dispense with a Great deal Att £28." [30] Of course all such hopes rested on the concerted action of Pennsylvania's iron producers, since one producer could exert no influence on the market by himself. The producers' recognition of this fact prompted them to meet in March 1774 at Philadelphia, where they set production quotas for each of their furnaces and forges and arranged to ship out of Philadelphia, by 1 May, the iron each had produced. Once their allocations had been shipped, they would raise the price of bar iron in the Philadelphia market to twenty-seven pounds.[31]

As a reaction to a perceived conspiracy, the cartel of Pennsylvania iron producers had more than a little irony to it. Although the plan was similar to the proposed cartel of the Principio and Baltimore companies, the great difference between the two cartel schemes was that the Pennsylvania effort was implemented and bore fruit. While bar-iron prices never again attained the high level that they had reached in 1772 and did not even reach the projected twenty-seven pounds per ton, Pennsylvania producers nevertheless enjoyed almost a year of price stability at twenty-six pounds per ton. This more than satisfactory state of affairs lasted until the outbreak of fighting in April 1775.[32]

The cartel represented the first known successful attempt by eighteenth-century American iron producers to shape their markets rather than merely to respond to them. Their demonstrated ability to coordinate the iron production process at each of their separate facilities and their equally impressive capacity for long-range planning had made them price-makers; before, they had always been price-takers. This very considerable accomplishment would not have been possible had not there been a high degree of standardization in the industry's production facilities. As was pointed out in chapter 2, the use of charcoal fuel imposed a definite limitation on the height and width of blast furnaces. Similarly, the forges of the region were built to accommodate pig iron of the size that could be conveniently hauled in wagons. Moreover, the physiographic and climatic features of the natural environment were primary determinants of the seasonal rhythm of production. The result was a uniformity in the size of the region's production facilities, a uniformity that worked in the favor of the cartel.[33]

The cartel of the iron producers of Pennsylvania did not last long (the common fate of such agreements), but it was an important departure in the industry's behavior. It is doubtful that such an arrangement could have been realized fifty or even twenty-five years earlier; the markets were different then, as were the producers. The perception of the markets by the ironworks owners of Pennsylvania, like that of their counterparts in Maryland, had been transformed. After years of passively drifting along with the prevailing currents of the markets but at the same time learning to coordinate complex industrial enterprises, they finally felt confident enough to steer their own course. Like the colonists who would shortly take their political fate in their own hands, the iron producers were now certain enough of themselves and their erstwhile competitors to seek to control their markets. They had sailed too long on an ocean of uncertainty. They wanted in their market relationships some of the same regularity they had achieved in the production system. In this regard, the cartel was a measure of the maturity of the iron producers of the late colonial period.

With the outbreak of fighting in April 1775, the Pennsylvania ironmasters' cartel quickly dissolved. The uncertainty in the Philadelphia market and the standing to the colors by many of the cartel's organizers contributed much to the scheme's collapse. Just as important, if not more so, however, was the fact that from its beginning the cartel had depended upon sales in British iron markets to drain off excess supply in the domestic market. Hostilities severed this connection and flooded the Philadelphia market with iron formerly destined for Great Britain. The consequences of this sudden overabundance of iron are evident from the behavior of prices for bar iron in Philadelphia. In March 1775 bar iron sold at an average of £26 per ton — the prevailing price during the twelve preceding months when the cartel had held sway. One month later the price had declined to £25.7, and over the next eight months it pursued a somewhat erratic course down to £22.5 in December, a level not seen since 1757.[34]

By the beginning of 1776 the excess supply in the Philadelphia market had dissipated. The price of bar iron was twenty-six pounds again in January, and after a few months of hovering slightly above that, it quickly climbed to almost forty pounds by December.[35] The dramatic decline in prices after Lexington and Concord and their still more startling recovery beginning in January 1776 suggests that the prolonged slump after April 1775 in part reflected the slow reaction time of the metropolitan market as it adjusted to the beginnings of a wartime economy.[36] This impression is reinforced by the behavior of prices at New Pine Forge in Berks County.

The price of bar iron at New Pine, as at other forges prior to the Revolution, had generally been two or three pounds lower than that charged in Philadelphia because prices in the city included a number of additional costs, especially the cost of transportation. The war quickly distorted this price differential.[37] This was undoubtedly largely because the immediate source of demand for iron to meet the needs of the war effort was in the hinterland around the forge and not in Philadelphia. This is not to say that the *ultimate* source of demand was not in the city, where the Continental Congress initiated war orders and purchased supplies. However, the blacksmiths and gunsmiths who filled these orders were themselves hinterland manufacturers who bought skelps — strips of bar iron — which they then bored to make musket and rifle barrels. The common quantity of skelp iron per order seems to have been two hundred pounds, enough to make the barrels of eight rifles or ten muskets.[38]

The demand for iron for firearms, cannon, and other tools of war undoubtedly helped to propel iron prices to hyperinflated levels. Bar iron, which sold for £70 per ton in mid-1777, ultimately reached its highest price in April 1781, when a ton sold for £3,818, or almost 14,800 percent above its prewar price.[39] A debased currency and the concomitant rapid rises in the prices of food and clothing and in the wages paid by the iron producers helped push prices to this level.[40] The records of New Pine Forge for 1776–78 offer a graphic illustration of how this sort of "supply-push" inflation occurred. From May 1776 to May 1778 the price charged by New Pine Forge for its bar iron increased by 540 percent, while the price paid by the forge for pig iron rose by 160 percent, from £8.2 to £21.2 per ton.[41] Although, at first sight this hardly supports the assertion made above about supply-push inflation, the forge's accounts and the general record of wholesale prices in the period reveal the nature of the forge's predicament. Further, they suggest that New Pine did not initiate price increases for its bar iron but, instead, passed along its rising costs to buyers. For example, the price paid by the forge for cordwood doubled during the two years between May 1776 and May 1778, from £0.125 to £0.25 per cord. Worse, the cost of hauling pig iron to the forge had increased by 360 percent in just seven months, from July 1775 through February 1776.[42]

Had such increases in the cost of raw materials and labor been the extent of the inflation confronted by the forge, bar-iron prices would never have climbed so sharply as they did. New Pine Forge, like most forges and furnaces of the time, paid its workers in kind as well as in cash. The workers bought their food and clothing from the forge's store, which had first to purchase these articles from merchants, millers, farmers, and artisans in Philadelphia and in the neighborhood.[43] It was this connection between the forge as buyer and the market that lay at bottom of the inflation in bar-iron prices. The increase in the price of almost every commodity purchased by the forge store easily outstripped the rise in bar iron, in some cases (beef, molasses, and rum) by better than two times and in one case (pepper) by almost three times.[44] Moreover, the chronology of the price movements of twenty-four commodities and of bar iron makes clear that price increases for bar iron generally followed rather than led those for other goods.[45]

Caught as it was between rising prices for its bar iron and even more rapidly increasing costs, did New Pine Forge make a profit during the Revolution? The forge's records are too fragmentary to provide a definite answer. Its volume of business, as measured in its balance sheets, suggests that it did, but the welter of currencies — Pennsylvania pounds, Continental money, and specie — and the significant use of barter in the forge's dealings preclude certainty on this point. A clue to the fortunes of New Pine Forge may lie in the unfortunately truncated record of its bar-iron sales, the volume of which (measured in tons) fluctuated considerably from May

1775 through March 1778, the last month for which complete data exist.[46] Although some of this fluctuation was very likely the result of the seasonality of iron-making and marketing (discussed in chapter 3), other sources were probably the disruption of normal transportation services by the war and the chaotic monetary conditions.[47] In any event, the fluctuation in sales necessarily affected the forge's gross revenue, which, while increasing by 130 percent from April 1776 to April 1777, nevertheless lagged behind the rates of price increases for most other commodities. Thus, if New Pine Forge made a profit during those years, it could not have been a large one. Moreover, the forge's records indicate, as do those of Hopewell Forge, that most revenue came, not from production for war, but from the sale of iron of the same description and in the same quantities as during the war years.[48]

This historical record argues for a more modest appraisal of the iron industry's contribution to the nation's war effort than has generally been made. While the evidence is far from extensive, that which we have suggests that the war's impact on the industry was of far greater consequence than that of the industry on the war. The hyperinflation, the draining away of skilled and unskilled labor, the disruption of the always delicate technology of the market, and the general climate of uncertainty all had a profound effect on the iron industry in Pennsylvania — an effect quite different from that of subsequent wars. It may well have been the stimulation of the metals industries provided by the Civil War and World War I that led students of the Revolution to conclude that that war, too, must have stimulated the iron industry.[49] Data on production at Cornwall Furnace and on the number of iron firms established during the eighteenth century suggest the contrary: the Revolution did less to stimulate the industry than it did to disrupt and retard its growth.

Figure 9 charts the production efficiency — measured in tons of pig iron and castings produced per cubic foot of furnace volume — of Cornwall Furnace from 1766 to 1800. The decline during the years preceding the outbreak of fighting, when output fell from 946 tons in 1766 / 67 to 744 tons in 1773 / 74, may well have resulted from a greater emphasis on the production of time-consuming castings. The more pronounced decline during the Revolution (when annual output averaged about 230 tons) may also have reflected this, but the more likely explanation, in view of the extremely low output for the war years, is that production was disrupted by the war and by the service in the Lancaster County militia of the furnace's owner manager, Curttis Grubb, during 1775-77. The almost continuous increase in output after 1782 (from 362 tons to 1,458 tons by 1800) also supports this conclusion.

The war sharply reduced the formation of new iron firms (see table 18). Not only did the number of firms formed during the Revolution not

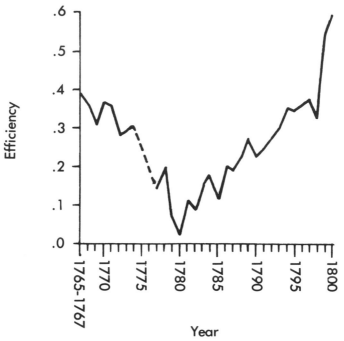

FIGURE 9

PRODUCTION EFFICIENCY AT CORNWALL FURNACE, 1766–1800
Efficiency is measured here in terms of tons of output per cubic foot of furnace
volume. Tons of output are from Bining, *Pennsylvania Iron Manufacture,* pp. 177–78.
The volume of Cornwall Furnace has been computed from the dimensions of its stack
(30 ft.) and bosh (9 ft.) (ibid., p. 177). I have considered the interior of Cornwall Furnace to have been a rectangular box. Thus, its volume is equal to its stack multiplied by
its cross-sectional area, or $V = 30 \times 9 \times 9 = 2,430$ cu. ft.

increase over the total for the eight years preceding the war but the rate of
formation of new firms actually declined from the prewar levels. In this
regard, as in others, however, the effect of the war proved not to be
damaging over the long run, and the return of peace brought a rapid
recovery to the industry.

Peacetime conditions stimulated rapid growth in the iron industry. The
expansion began during the six years under the Articles of Confederation
and continued at a much more rapid pace during the next twelve years
under the Constitution. The adoption of the Constitution was clearly a
watershed in the eighteenth-century history of the Pennsylvania iron
industry. The stability, uniform currency, and the removal of impediments
to interstate commerce that followed quickly upon adoption greatly
improved the business climate. The sharp increase in the total number of

TABLE 18

Formation of Iron Firms in Pennsylvania, 1716–1800

| Period | Number of Years | Number of Firms | | | Mean Annual Rate (Total) |
| | | Eastern Pa.[a] | Western Pa. | Total | |
|---|---|---|---|---|---|
| 1716–66 | 51 | 55 | 6 | 61 | 1.2 |
| 1767–74 | 8 | 6 | 3 | 9 | 1.1 |
| 1775–82[b] | 8 | 7 | 1 | 8[c] | 1.0 |
| 1783–88 | 6 | 12 | 2 | 14 | 2.3 |
| 1789–1800 | 12 | 28 | 42 | 70 | 5.8 |

Source: Derived from Bining, Pennsylvania Iron Manufacture, pp. 171–76.

[a] Defined here as those counties lying east of the Susquehanna River.

[b] The Revolutionary War ended officially with the signing of the Peace of Paris on February 3, 1783, but a preliminary peace treaty providing for an armistice was signed on November 30, 1782. News of this treaty arrived in America on March 12, 1783. For the purposes of this table, then, 1782 is considered as the last year of the war (see Samuel Eliot Morison, The Oxford History of the American People [New York: Oxford University Press, 1965], pp. 267–68).

[c] This total does not include facilities built before 1775 that failed before 1775 and were revived during the war. Such facilities are included in the total for the period in which they were built.

firms formed and the large number of firms formed west of the Susquehanna, particularly in the far western part of the state, indicate that investors in the iron industry had quickly noted the improvement.

In the eighteen years following the end of the fighting, eighty-four firms were founded, slightly more than half in the central and western counties. Most of these firms probably catered, as did Pine Forge in Berks County, to buyers in their immediate neighborhoods and to one of the state's two large urban markets — Philadelphia for eastern and central firms and a rapidly growing Pittsburgh for those in the west.[50] By 1810 the iron industry had grown considerably in size and geographical extent. The westward movement across the Susquehanna River that had begun in earnest in the last decade of the eighteenth century continued, but at a greater rate (see table 19). As the state's population pushed inland over improved roads, iron producers found new local markets, new transportation services, and a new source of labor. Even as early as 1792 Pittsburgh and the surrounding area had boasted of fourteen blacksmiths, three gunsmiths, and two nailers. By 1815 the city styled itself "The Birmingham of America" (more a town booster's wish than a fact) because of the rapid growth of the city's iron industry. By that time Pittsburgh had two foundries, a rolling mill, a wire mill, and a steam-engine works.[51] At the same time, the surrounding area in Allegheny County held six furnaces and six naileries.[52] Pittsburgh's impressive growth as a population, commercial, and industrial center before and especially during and immediately following the War of 1812 ensured a market for the pig and bar iron and iron manufactures produced by the expanding western branch of the Pennsylvania iron industry.[53] Fortunately for the eastern branch of the industry, the popula-

TABLE 19

Status of the Pennsylvania Iron Industry, 1716–1800 and 1810,
by Type of Facility and Region

| Type of Facility | 1716–1800[a] | | | | | 1810[b] | | | | |
| | | Eastern Region[c] | | Western Region[c] | | | Eastern Region[c] | | Western Region[c] | |
| | Total | No. | % | No. | % | Total | No. | % | No. | % |
|---|---|---|---|---|---|---|---|---|---|---|
| Furnace | 41 | 24 | 59 | 17 | 41 | 50 | 20 | 40 | 30 | 60 |
| Forge and bloomery | 83 | 60 | 72 | 23 | 28 | 82 | 54 | 66 | 28 | 34 |
| Rolling and slitting mills | 12 | 9 | 75 | 3 | 25 | 18 | 12 | 67 | 6 | 33 |
| Ironworks | 12 | 3 | 25 | 9 | 75 | – | – | – | – | – |
| Total | 148 | 96 | 65 | 52 | 35 | 150 | 86 | 57 | 64 | 43 |

Sources: Figures for 1716–1800 are derived from Bining, Pennsylvania Iron Manufacture, pp. 171–76; figures for 1810 are derived from Tench Coxe, A Statement of the Arts and Manufactures of the United States of America for the Year 1810 (Philadelphia, 1814), pp. 49–52.

[a] To ensure comparability, one wire mill is not included.

[b] To ensure comparability, 170 naileries – of which 113, or 66 percent, were in eastern Pennsylvania and 1 wire mill was in western Pennsylvania – are not inlcuded.

[c] The Eastern region is defined as those counties east of the Susquehanna River. This rule does some violence to the political and economic geography of the state in 1810, by which time a number of counties subsumed under "Western Region" were, strictly speaking, in the central part of the state.

tion and demand for iron in its region were also growing rapidly, probably more so than was supply.[54]

Estimates of aggregate output of iron for the eighteenth and early nineteenth centuries are unavoidably rough approximations because of the fragmentary data from which they must be constructed. Still, these estimates provide a useful basis for cautiously assessing the early growth of the iron industry's production. Such data for furnaces in Pennsylvania for 1800–1850 are presented in table 20. Although a detailed explanation of the figures is included in the notes to the table, two points concerning the table's construction require emphasis. First, the number of furnaces and their respective outputs in 1828 and 1830 are far lower than their proper totals during those years and have been listed primarily to provide a basis for the calculation of the much more accurate figures for output per furnace. Second, the values of output and output per furnace for 1840–50 and their fluctuation reflect, in great part, events in the iron economy and in the larger economy. A writer in Hunt's Merchants' Magazine put the matter in the proper light when he observed that "every Pennsylvanian is familiar with the great embarrassments to the business of the country, checking commercial enterprise, disasterous to every branch of industry, and fatal to public and private credit, during the period from 1838 to 1842."[55] He was referring to the economic dislocation that followed the Panic of 1837.

TABLE 20

Estimates of Aggregate Furnace Output in Pennsylvania,
1800–1850, Selected Years

| Year | Number of Furnaces | Output (tn.) | Output per Furnace (tn.) |
|------|--------------------|--------------|--------------------------|
| 1800 | 41[a] | 21,730[b] | 530 |
| 1810 | 50 | 26,879 | 538 |
| 1818 | 44 | 23,672[c] | 538 |
| 1828[d] | 44 | 28,515 | 648 |
| 1830[d] | 45 | 31,056 | 690 |
| 1840 | 213 | 151,885[e] | 713 |
| 1842 | 210 | 194,580[e] | 927 |
| 1846 | 316 | 368,056[e] | 1,165 |
| 1847 | 298 | 388,805[e] | 1,305 |
| 1849 | 294 | 253,035[e] | 861 |
| 1850 | 294 | 198,533 | 675 |

*Sources:* The number of furnaces in 1800 is derived from Bining, *Pennsylvania Iron Manufacture,* pp. 171–76. The mean output per furnace for 1800 is derived from the mean annual production of Elizabeth Furnace during the period 1780–90, in ibid., p. 178. Figures for 1810 are computed from Coxe, *Statement of the Arts and Manufactures,* pp. 49–52. The numbers of furnaces in 1818, 1828, and 1830 are from C. G. Childs, "The Iron Trade of Europe and the United States: With Special Reference to the Iron Trade of Pennsylvania," *Hunt's Merchants' Magazine* 16 (June 1847): 584–85. Data for 1840 are drawn from "Iron and Coal Statistics: Being Extracts from the Report of a Committee to the Iron and Coal Association of the State of Pennsylvania." *Journal of the Franklin Institute,* 3d ser., 12 (August 1846): 124–28. Data for 1842 and 1846 are from *Hunt's Merchants' Magazine* 16 (June 1847): 587, 590. Data for 1847, 1849, and 1850 are from Charles E. Smith, "The Manufacture of Iron in Pennsylvania," *Hunt's Merchants' Magazine* 25 (November 1851): 576.

[a] This figure is probably too high. It represents the total number of furnaces built between 1716 and 1800, as listed in the source, and the working assumption made here is that all survived, which is unlikely.

[b] This figure is probably too high and is based on a mean output per furnace of 530 tons (see Bining, *Pennsylvania Iron Manufacture,* p. 178).

[c] This figure was computed by multiplying the number of furnaces reported in Coxe, *Statement of the Arts and Manufacture* (pp. 49–52) by the output per furnace for 1810. The justification for repeating it is the absence of significant changes in furnace size from 1810 to 1818 (see table 7).

[d] The numbers of furnaces listed for these years are much lower than the numbers of furnaces that were then in operation. Childs, "Iron Trade," notes that the totals are not complete (p. 585).

[e] For alternative estimates of output see Robert William Fogel, *Railroads and American Economic Growth: Essays in Econometric History* (Baltimore: The Johns Hopkins Press, 1964), p. 154.

Prior to the panic, however, the national economy had experienced a long period of rapid growth (some of the results can be seen in the data in table 20). The Pennsylvania iron industry expanded rapidly in the 1830s. While the figures overstate the case, the growth in the number of firms and in the total output was nonetheless impressive. By the end of the decade output was considerably greater than it had been in 1830; in the seven years following 1840 it more than doubled. Between 1840 and 1847 the number of firms increased by about 40 percent, an impressive growth rate for any industry. Even this sort of success did not, however, keep a number of the industry's leaders from calling for more tariff protection. Their demands for protection and the opposition they aroused made the tariff, after the controversy over slavery, the most fiercely contested political issue of the ante-bellum period.

Few subjects in American economic history have received as much attention as has the tariff. And yet, for all this attention, we remain unsure of the tariff's precise effects on the growth of the particular industries that came under its protection. More certain is our understanding of the political origins and ramifications of the various tariffs of the ante-bellum period, particularly of the Compromise Tariff of 1833. There is no small amount of irony in the fact that the political aspects of the tariff, involving, as they did, the motives and maneuverings of men and parties, should be more thoroughly understood by us than the tariff's economic import. Still, we can use the tariff's history as a means of examining the structure of the Pennsylvania iron industry.

By the early 1820s the industry had already matured to the point where it embraced two distinct sectors, each with a fairly well-defined notion of its own interests. The producers of primary iron products were, sometimes literally but more often figuratively, the heirs of the eighteenth-century furnace and forge owners and continued to turn out iron in many, but not all, of the same forms as had their predecessors. While the latter had produced pig and bar iron, they had also worked these generic goods up into pots, stoves, wire, and other hardware items. Many of their descendants had, in accordance with the broadening and deepening of the market, become far more specialized in their product lines, largely confining themselves to pig, bar, and rolled iron.[56] Firmly lodged in the space left by the primary producers when they began to abandon consumer goods were the iron manufacturers, or as they styled themselves in an 1828 memorial to Congress, the "Manufacturers of Hardware, Smiths and Iron-Founders."[57] The dichotomy noted by M. W. Flinn between producers and manufacturers within the eighteenth-century English iron industry had at last arisen in America.[58]

This difference between the two parts of the Pennsylvania iron industry was more than simply a difference of function; it was also a matter of distinct practical ideology. For producers, no amount of protection from imported British iron could ever be too much protection; for the manufacturers, who purchased foreign as well as domestic pig and bar iron, rates in excess of *pro forma* levels were "an excessive burden."[59] In a series of memorials and petitions to Congress between 1820 and 1850 each of the two increasingly antagonistic branches of the industry attempted to persuade the House and Senate of the wisdom, justice, and public-spiritedness of its position and of the base and groundless character of its opposition, which had only its own interests, and not those of the nation, at heart.[60] While both sides acknowledged that a major purpose for any tariff was the raising of a revenue for the federal government, the producers, understandably enough, stressed a tariff's other inherent purpose — protection. Manufacturers, for their part, railed against the unfair advantages conferred by the tariff on a privileged few.

That the iron industry in Pennsylvania, like that in New England and in

New York, should have reached this level of specialization and, with it, internecine warfare is hardly surprising in view of the rapid urbanization and population growth that occurred following the War of 1812.[61] Demand for iron of all descriptions had grown faster than had the population, in part because of the widespread introduction of nails and screws for construction in the cities. At the same time, aggregate domestic production of pig and bar iron in the United States may well have grown at a far more modest rate, barely keeping pace with population growth.[62] Obviously, the difference between aggregate national demand for iron and domestically produced supply represented foreign — especially British — iron. This does not mean that American productive capacity was inadequate; rather, American producers often were not competitive in a number of product lines, such as those of rolled bar iron and, later, rails, and they admitted as much when they campaigned for the tariff.[63]

Attempts to ascertain the size of the domestically produced national supply of pig, bar, and rolled iron have not been particularly successful and are clouded with uncertainty. In part, this failure has been due to defects — deliberate and inadvertent — in the reports the iron producers made at various times, but especially in 1832 and 1849.[64] Another difficulty arises from the fact that a part of each year's output undoubtedly never passed through the hands of wholesale buyers and consequently never showed up on their books or in the Treasury Department estimates of aggregate national iron output. Instead, this "missing" portion of any year's iron production probably passed from producers to buyers in the hinterland. That this was almost certainly the case in Pennsylvania, especially before the 1840s, is suggested by the producers' records, which show a significant number of local transactions.[65]

These obstacles to the calculation of the domestic supply of iron contribute in large part to the difficulty of determining the economic costs and benefits of protection to the iron industry under the various tariffs. But the possible costs and benefits were not limited in their effects to price competition. Students of the subject have pointed out that the tariff discouraged technological change in America by artificially sustaining antiquated, less efficient domestic operations in the face of competition from the more advanced British technology.[66] The proofs for the validity of this assertion were generally taken to be the lower cost per ton of British iron, exclusive of the duty; the early adoption in Great Britain of smelting with coke in place of charcoal, while American producers persisted in using the latter fuel alone until the early 1840s; and the domination of the American market for railroad iron by British rails and related products.[67]

British bar iron — hammered and rolled — often did undersell American bar iron in the Philadelphia market prior to the 1840s. In great part, this was due to the lower wage rates paid by British ironmasters and also the more widespread use of the hot-blast furnace and coke fuel in Britain, again until the 1840s.[68] Another reason cited by Pennsylvania's producers for the lower price of imported iron was the practice by British producers of dumping iron on American markets, that is, selling iron in the United States at or below cost. According to the New England producers who made this accusation in 1850, "when iron is low in England, the manufacturers there will always export to this country, even without profit, rather than diminish the prices upon the much larger quantity reserved for home consumption. As the low price at home compels them to seek our market, they will not be deterred by high duties."[69] There was possibly some truth in this. In any case, the iron producers had long believed it to be so and had based their appeals for protection, at least in part, on the conviction that British iron competed unfairly with their own.[70]

Less ambiguous is the point about railroad iron. British rails often undersold the American-produced rail in American markets, including Philadelphia. But even when the price differential was negligible or swung in the favor of American rolling mills, buyers preferred the British product, which enjoyed a better reputation. This was no doubt in part the result of the superior quality of British railroad iron during the 1830s and 1840s.[71] Another reason, however, was probably the early and commanding lead established in the American markets by British rail producers.[72] In 1840 American rails accounted for only 12 percent of the market, and although the American product occasionally overtook its British competition during the next few years, by 1850 the American producers' share of their own market was only about 14 percent. Having achieved this comfortable position, British producers enjoyed the advantage arising from the inertia of the market: unless compelled by significant differences in quality or price, buyers tended to stick with a familiar make. The tariff was the means by which American rail producers hoped to create that compelling difference. That they largely failed to realize this objective is perhaps less important for our purposes than the fact that here, too, the efforts by American iron producers to secure protection were tenaciously and often successfully fought by industrial consumers of iron products.

Particularly strenuous opposition to duties on railroad iron came, predictably enough, from the railroads, especially in the first few months of 1844, during the boom in railroad construction that followed the Panic of 1837 and the depression of the early forties.[73] Early in 1844 the first session of the Twenty-eighth Congress convened and took up what by then had become an American perennial — the tariff. Under the Compromise of 1833 tariff rates in that year, essentially those of the tariff of 1832, were to decline from their 1832 levels to 20 percent by 1842. The hard times that had overtaken a number of industries after 1837 and especially after 1839 had revived protectionist sentiment in the North and had lent an added urgency to the calls in Congress for higher duties. The tariff act of 1842, hastily passed, offered something in the way of real relief but, as John C. Calhoun, hardly a protectionist by that time, pointed out, it had little to do with political economy and much to do with politics.[74] By 1844 the economic dislocation had run its course, and with its passing, housing construction and railroad construction began once again to expand.

The general improvement of the economy carried the Pennsylvania iron industry along in a rapid recovery from the business slump of the preceding three years. Yet, while the strident calls from the textile industry for strenuous protection had been muted by a return of prosperity, the iron producers of Pennsylvania, if anything, raised the volume of their own campaign for higher duties.[75] Nothing came of this until 1846, when the Walker Tariff, so called for Secretary of the Treasury Robert J. Walker, was passed. The Walker Tariff's rate structure made its passage a hollow victory for protectionist forces in Congress and particularly for the Pennsylvania iron producers. Iron imports were subject to an ad valorem duty of 30 percent, about the same ratio as under the 1842 act.[76] Within only a few years, opposition to the Walker Tariff among iron producers was both widespread and articulate. A lengthy memorial to Congress by the "Iron Manufacturers of New England" in 1850 urged a revision of the act, pointing out that it "is said that a duty of 30 per cent. ad valorem, with the cost of transportation, ought to be a sufficient protection. But the fact shows that it is not. The present ad valorem duty is no protection, either to the producer or consumer, against the extraordinary fluctuations in the prices of iron abroad."[77] The memorialists made a number of telling, well-documented points in support of their position, all to no effect. The Walker Tariff stood until 1857.

The stubborn protests by the iron producers on behalf of protection should not be confused with an unwillingness on their part to concede the validity of each of the three proofs of their technological backwardness vis-à-vis the British competition. In fact their petitions and memorials have a somewhat desperate tone precisely because the producers acknowledged British technological and marketing superiority and saw no reasonable way of surmounting it without the aid of government. What galled the Americans most was that British iron undersold and outsold their own despite their conviction that "the superiority of American over British iron is unquestionable."[78]

While they recognized that "the manufacturers of iron in this country have often been charged with making slower progress than other manufacturers," they attributed their slower progress, not (as Frank Taussig later did) to inefficient and outmoded operations subsidized by too much protection, but to the problems occasioned by too little protection.[79] Adequate protection, they said, would "let the manufacturer have fair profits and remunerating prices," with the result that "improvements will rapidly take place, for there is no industry which is so much improved by prosperity." [80] Hyperbolic and self-serving prose aside, how can these two seemingly mutually contradictory points in the producers' argument be reconciled? How could they have asserted, in almost the same breath, the superiority of their iron and the inferiority of their technology? The perceived contradiction is only an apparent one and arises from the ways in which the producers used the term "improvements," or what we call "technological change."

Iron producers recognized the desirability of adopting the more advanced techniques of production practiced in Great Britain, especially those that promised increased labor productivity and increasing returns to scale, generally. But, as they were quick to point out, massive new machinery and experiments with new techniques and improvements required "a large capital," much more than "in any other branch of manufactures." Technological change on such a grand scale in the American iron industry would, of necessity, require the sort of geographical and organizational concentration of the industry that had occurred in Great Britain, especially in Scotland. There, "where all the material is taken from the same mine any number of furnaces and rolling mills can be included in one gigantic establishment, and the costs of superintendence and administration, which are borne by each one of the many works required in this country, to produce the same quantity of iron, are there limited to one." A consistent, adequate policy of protection would, the producers argued, encourage the "development of iron establishments upon the coal-fields [as in Scotland] instead of upon their margins; situations which possess, in a great degree the advantages above described." [81]

It was on a far more modest physical scale that the ironmasters could and did claim to have made improvements in their operations, improvements that resulted in the production of iron superior to the cheaper British iron that flooded American markets. American producers, Pennsylvanians among them, had long insisted that among the unfair practices used by British iron producers and merchants when selling their iron was the shipping to the United States of inferior grades of iron, which they represented as being of the higher grades. [82] This misrepresented inferior iron commanded a higher price in American markets than it would have if it had been honestly marked, and because of the excellent reputation enjoyed by the finest British iron, the deceit permitted inferior foreign iron to outsell the superior American product and to dominate the trade.

In support of their claims for superior iron, American producers usually invoked the unhappy "experience of American citizens" with foreign iron. [83] Such claims, however, had been easily countered in the past by antiprotectionist forces among the iron manufacturers, who, like the protectionist producers, made the market the arbiter of quality. The "Manufacturers of Hardware, Smiths and Iron-Founders of the City of Philadelphia" did just that in their March 1828 memorial to the House of Representatives. They argued that the preference of the founders among them for foreign pig iron at "50 to 70 dollars per ton . . . whilst they could buy domestic at 30 to 45 dollars per ton . . . shows a difference in quality, and is not a matter of competition." [84] Subjective evidence of this sort, used by pro- and antiprotectionist groups within the iron industry, obviously was not definitive because for every affidavit affirming the superiority of American over imported British iron another could be had attesting to the inferiority of the American product.

What American iron producers needed to press their case more convincingly were results of tests of their iron conducted by recognized authorities. Such testing for strength and density had become increasingly common in Great Britain, France, and the United States during the 1830s and 1840s, probably largely due to the interest of those nations' respective armies and navies and to the high standards for iron required by the railroads. [85] In their 1850 memorial to Congress the "Iron Manufactures of New England" included a table of results from strength tests of what was probably the best American chain cable iron conducted at the Washington, D.C., navy yard from 1830 through 1843. These results, according to the memorial, clearly demonstrated "the superiority of American iron, and the improvement in its quality within a few years." [86]

The figures reported in the memorial are probably reliable; at the very least, they are consistent with results reported elsewhere of similar tests conducted during the same period and justify the producers' contention that the quality of American iron was improving. [87] The improvement in this case — about eighteen pounds per year — occurred, not because of the adoption of large-scale technological innovations such as coke, but because of enhancements and modifications of the traditional charcoal-iron technology. [88] The producers, for their part, confidently assured Congress, and presumably one another, that such improvements in the quality of iron produced, like the quantity of iron to be had from large-scale improvements in production technology, would increase under a strongly protectionist tariff. They were substantially wrong.

Frank Taussig's conviction that the tariff subsidized inefficiency and technological stagnation in the American iron industry, although overstated, was well-founded with respect to technological change on the grand scale. So long as a high rate of duty reduced the otherwise significant price differential between British iron made with coke and American charcoal iron, consumers had little reason not to indulge their sound preference for the latter. A lower rate structure exposed the charcoal-pig-iron producers to what often proved fatal competition by British coke-

TABLE 21

Status of the Pennsylvania Iron Industry, 1849, by Type of Facility

| Type of Facility | Intact | | Sold | | Failed | | Total Number |
|---|---|---|---|---|---|---|---|
| | % | No. | % | No. | % | No. | |
| Cold-blast charcoal furnace | 56.9% | 82 | 34.7% | 50 | 8.3% | 12 | 144 |
| Hot-blast charcoal furnace | 50.0 | 42 | 40.5 | 34 | 9.5 | 8 | 84 |
| Anthracite blast furnace | 74.1 | 40 | 22.2 | 12 | 3.7 | 2 | 54 |
| Charcoal forge and bloomery[a] | 68.0 | 83 | 24.6 | 30 | 7.4 | 9 | 122 |
| Rolling mill | 82.0 | 64 | 12.8 | 10 | 5.1 | 4 | 78 |
| Total[b] | 64.5% | 311 | 28.2% | 136 | 7.3% | 35 | 482 |

Source: "Documents Relating to the Manufacture of Iron in Pennsylvania," tables following p. 72.
[a] Four charcoal bloomeries were listed.
[b] Not included are 7 hot-blast bituminous furnaces, 4 hot-blast coke furnaces, and 1 rolling mill under construction.

smelted iron. The degree of such exposure for a Pennsylvania firm seems to have depended in great part on two things: (1) its level of technology; and, to a lesser degree, (2) whether it was located in the eastern or western part of the state.

The iron producers complained bitterly that British competition had forced many of them to declare bankruptcy or to surrender their property and stock to the sheriff for sale. An analysis of data provided by them bears out their claims.[89] More than a third of all iron production facilities statewide had failed or had been sold by 1849 (see table 21). The casualties, however, did not fall into any uniform pattern. Instead, those branches of the industry characterized by the more advanced technologies of production — that is, the anthracite-fueled blast furnaces and rolling mills — suffered least, while cold-blast and hot-blast charcoal-furnace operators suffered most. This suggests that American producers could effectively compete with British iron when they made iron with a similar process, on a similarly large scale, and at a comparable cost. As early as 1832 some Pennsylvania producers recognized this. One, Henry Moore, of Delaware County, noted in his response to a question concerning tariff reduction in the McLane questionnaire that "until anthracite coal be introduced in the smelting of iron ore, our iron masters cannot meet English competition if the duty were reduced to 12¼ p.ct."[90] Most producers sensed as much in 1850 and bemoaned the fate of the predominant means of making pig iron — the charcoal blast furnace — saying "that the ruin of the charcoal establishments, if the present revenue system is continued, is inevitable."[91]

Although unduly funereal in the light of subsequent events, the alarm sounded by the New England memorial captured the distress of the charcoal-furnace operators in Pennsylvania, east and west. The extent to which producers in both parts of the state shared the misfortune that had overtaken their branch of the iron industry is made plain in tables 22 and 23. What these tables also show, however, is the degree to which the distress differed from one region to the other. With the exceptions of forges and hot-blast charcoal-furnace firms, the western firms had a higher survival rate than did those in the east. Moreover, when we consider the actual numbers of charcoal furnaces in blast — that is, those furnaces in operation — and out of blast, or shut down, the regional disparity is even more pronounced, and it is clear that the western branch of the industry fared far better than did the eastern branch.

This situation had to do partly with the particular product mix of each region's facilities, a subject examined in detail in the following chapter. Another reason for the lower morbidity of firms in the west was the partial insulation from the effects of British competition afforded them by distance, distance not yet completely overcome by the state's railroads and canals. Even as early as 1832 producers in the east and in the west recognized that Pennsylvania's rapid progress in internal improvements promised to nullify the natural tariff geography imposed on imported iron. The matter was of sufficient importance to merit a question concerning it in Secretary of the Treasury McLane's detailed questionnaire of that year: "Are not the manufacturers of salt and iron remote from the points of importation, out of foreign competition within a certain circle around them, and what is the extent of that circle?" From the many responses to this question, two — one from the east and one from the west — will suffice to illustrate the point made above. M. & H. Coate, owners of a rolling mill in Chester County, dismissed the idea that distance would protect western producers for long and predicted that "canals and railroads would convey imported articles everywhere." In a similar vein, A. McCalmont, owner of Franklin Forge, in Venango County, West Pennsylvania, noted that while iron producers had once been beyond the reach of foreign competition, "the improvements by canal, which are now being made, is [sic] drawing them nearer to a foreign competition: any change that will affect the Pittsburgh market will be immediately felt in this country."[92]

The Coate brothers and particularly McCalmont worried about what the future would bring — and they had reason to be anxious: both firms were out of business by 1849.[93] Their demise was not exceptional. Only about one in four firms throughout the state survived from 1832 until 1850 (see table 24). And of course while some types of firms — notably furnaces, integrated rolling mills (mills associated with forges, which fed the mills bar iron and blooms), and specialized facilities such as nail and wire works — did better than the average for the industry, the mortality rates for all types of firms are impressively high. A regional breakdown of these

TABLE 22
Status of the Pennsylvania Iron Industry, 1849, by Type of Facility and Region

| | Eastern Region | | | | | | | | Western Region[a] | | | | | | | |
| | Intact | | Sold | | Failed | | No. Sold and Failed as % of Total | | Intact | | Sold | | Failed | | No. Sold and Failed as % of Total | |
| Type of Facility | % | No. | % | No. | % | No. | % | No. | % | No. | % | No. | % | No. | % | No. |
|---|---|---|---|---|---|---|---|---|---|---|---|---|---|---|---|---|
| Cold-blast charcoal furnace | 52.5% | 31 | 44.1% | 26 | 3.4% | 2 | 47.5% | 59 | 60.0% | 51 | 28.2% | 24 | 11.8% | 10 | 40.0% | 85 |
| Hot-blast charcoal furnace | 51.5 | 34 | 39.4 | 26 | 9.1 | 6 | 38.5 | 66 | 44.4 | 8 | 44.4 | 8 | 11.1 | 2 | 55.5 | 18 |
| Anthracite blast furnace | 74.1 | 40 | 22.2 | 12 | 3.7 | 2 | 25.9 | 54 | – | – | – | – | – | – | – | – |
| Charcoal forge and bloomery | 68.9 | 82 | 23.5 | 28 | 7.6 | 9 | 31.1 | 119 | 33.3 | 1 | 66.7 | 2 | – | – | 66.7 | 3 |
| Rolling mill | 78.2 | 43 | 14.5 | 8 | 9.3 | 4 | 23.8 | 55 | 91.3 | 21 | 8.7 | 2 | – | – | 8.7 | 23 |
| Total facilities | 65.1% | 230 | 28.3% | 100 | 6.5% | 23 | 99.9% | 353 | 63.0% | 81 | 27.9% | 36 | 9.3% | 12 | 100.2% | 129 |

Source: "Documents Relating to the Manufacture of Iron in Pennsylvania," tables following p. 72.

Note: Percentages may not equal 100 due to rounding.

[a] The western region consisted of the following counties: Allegheny, Armstrong, Beaver, Butler, Cambria, Clarion, Crawford, Elk, Erie, Fayette, Forest, Greene, Indiana, Jefferson, Lawrence, McKean, Mercer, Venango, Warren, Washington, and Westmoreland.

TABLE 23

Furnaces In and Out of Blast in Pennsylvania, 1849, by Type of Facility and Region

| Type of Facility | Eastern Region | | | Western Region | | | Statewide % Out |
|---|---|---|---|---|---|---|---|
| | In | Out | Total | In | Out | Total | |
| Cold-blast charcoal furnace | | | | | | | |
| No. | 27 | 33 | 60 | 49 | 36 | 85 | |
| % | | 55.0% | | | 42.4% | | 47.6% |
| Hot-blast charcoal furnace | | | | | | | |
| No. | 31 | 36 | 67 | 10 | 8 | 18 | |
| % | | 53.7% | | | 44.4% | | 51.8% |
| Anthracite blast furnace | | | | | | | |
| No. | 29 | 23 | 52 | | | | |
| % | | 44.2% | | | | | |
| Total | | | | | | | |
| No. | 87 | 92 | 179 | 59 | 44 | 103 | |
| % | | 51.4% | | | 42.4% | | 48.2% |

Source: "Documents Relating to the Manufacture of Iron in Pennsylvania," tables following p. 72.

persistence, or survival, data (presented in table 25) suggests that firms in the eastern part of the state had a better chance overall of surviving the 1830s and 1840s — which may or may not have been true. The eastern branch of the industry was certainly the more highly developed of the two in the 1830s and might therefore have stood a better chance of surviving the effects of economic crises and British competition. But it was also more exposed to this competition. The uncertainty on these points arises from the imperfections in the 1832 data, which are sadly incomplete for both regions, but especially for the east, where many of those queried by representatives of Secretary McLane simply refused to respond.[94] Nevertheless, the results presented in tables 24 and 25 probably would change little, if at all, if the missing data could be added. Even were the missing data to double the statewide survival rate for the industry as a whole, the revised estimate would still mean that almost 50 percent of all firms active in 1832 were no longer in business by 1850.

The reasons for this high mortality rate have been alluded to above: the economic crises of 1837, following the Bank War; the depression of 1839–43; and of course the consequences of an erratic tariff policy. Data on the operations of individual iron firms for an extensive period during those eventful years are scarce, and prudence dictates that we not make too much of those sets of data that we have. Still, when used with restraint and in conjunction with the published compilations for 1832 and 1850, they offer an especially close view of the economic conditions that confronted the industry. The production records of Speedwell Forge, in Berks

TABLE 24

Survival in the Pennsylvania Iron Industry, 1832–50, by Type of Facility

| Type of Facility | Number of Firms Listed in | | Total Number | Rate of Survival (%) |
|---|---|---|---|---|
| | 1832 | 1832 and 1850 | | |
| Furnace | 15 | 11 | 26 | 42% |
| Forge | 18 | 8 | 26 | 31 |
| Rolling mill | 4 | 0 | 4 | 0 |
| Foundry | 17 | 0 | 17 | 0 |
| Hardware[a] | 3 | 0 | 3 | 0 |
| Engine[b] | 10 | 1 | 11 | 9 |
| Furnace and forge | 11 | 4 | 15 | 36 |
| Rolling mill and forge | 2 | 4 | 6 | 67 |
| Wire and nailworks[c] | 1 | 1 | 2 | 50 |
| Total | 81 | 29 | 110 | 26% |

Sources: For 1832, Louis McLane, Documents Relative to the Manufactures of the United States, 4 vols. in 1 (1833; reprint [4 vols. in 3], New York: Burt Franklin, 1969), vol. 2, docs. 13 and 14 (hereafter cited as McLane Report); for 1850, "Documents Relating to the Manufacture of Iron in Pennsylvania," tables following p. 72.

Note: Of the firms listed in the source for 1832, those that were also listed in the source for 1850 are considered to have survived.

[a] Includes tool- and lock-making establishments and one manufacturer of plate ware.
[b] Steam-engine-making establishment.
[c] Includes 1 rolling mill that was an adjunct to a nailworks, the firm of M. & H. Coate.

TABLE 25

Survival in the Pennsylvania Iron Industry, 1832–50,
by Type of Facility and Region

| Type of Facility | Eastern Region | | | | Western Region | | | |
|---|---|---|---|---|---|---|---|---|
| | Number of Firms Listed in | | | | Number of Firms Listed in | | | |
| | 1832 | 1832 and 1850 | Total Number | Rate of Survival (%) | 1832 | 1832 and 1850 | Total Number | Rate of Survival (%) |
| Furnace | 6 | 7 | 13 | 54% | 9 | 4 | 13 | 31% |
| Forge | 13 | 8 | 21 | 38 | 5 | 0 | 5 | 0 |
| Rolling mill | – | – | – | – | 4 | 0 | 4 | 0 |
| Foundry | 5 | 0 | 5 | 0 | 12 | 0 | 12 | 0 |
| Hardware[a] | 1 | 0 | 1 | 0 | 2 | 0 | 2 | 0 |
| Engine[b] | – | – | – | – | 10 | 1 | 11 | 9 |
| Furnace and forge | 10 | 4 | 14 | 29 | 1 | 0 | 1 | 0 |
| Rolling mill and forge | 1 | 0 | 1 | 0 | 1 | 4 | 5 | 80 |
| Wire and nailworks[c] | 0 | 1 | 1 | 100 | 1 | 0 | 1 | 0 |
| Total | 36 | 20 | 56 | 36% | 45 | 9 | 54 | 17% |

Sources: See table 24.

Note: Of the firms listed in the source for 1832, those that were also listed in the source for 1850 are considered to have survived.

[a] Includes tool- and lock-making establishments and one manufacturer of plate ware.
[b] Steam-engine-making establishment.
[c] Includes 1 rolling mill that was an adjunct to a nailworks, the firm of M. & H. Coate.

County, for 1832–48 are particularly extensive and detailed; they fairly reflect the short-term cyclical movement of the economy of Pennsylvania and that of the Middle Atlantic region generally.

Except for its having survived the 1830s and 1840s, Speedwell Forge was typical of forges in Berks County and throughout eastern Pennsylvania during these years. Water-powered, charcoal-fueled, and owned by an individual, it usually employed between ten and fourteen men and produced about 260 tons of blooms and bar iron over the course of a year.[95] And as its records indicate, Speedwell's annual rate of production fluctuated considerably during the years 1833–47.

During this period the Pennsylvania economy and most of the regional economies outside the cotton South were now stimulated, now depressed, by alternating episodes of boom and bust. Of the latter, the Panic of 1837 — the effects of which lasted through most of 1838 — and the depression of 1839–43 were certainly the most severe. Similarly, the expansions in overall business activity and the inflation associated with the sudden easing of credit controls in early 1835, the rise of cotton prices in late 1838, and the sharp and sustained increase in railroad construction that began in early 1843 were particularly pronounced. Through it all, the movement of prices of iron products more or less mirrored that of the wholesale price index for Philadelphia and of the railroad stock index for eight companies — including the Philadelphia and Reading — in the region (see fig. 10). Moreover, Speedwell Forge's annual bar-iron production and inventory levels echoed these price movements, the one directly, the other inversely.

As iron prices fell by 15 percent from 1839 to 1840, Speedwell's output of bar iron plummeted by 40 percent to its lowest level in this period — about 186 tons. At the same time, the forge's inventory — bar iron unsold from the preceding year — began to rise. By 1843, when prices reached their lowest point, production of bar iron was only slightly above the 1840 low, and an inventory of a staggering 77 tons, or one-third of the year's output, had accumulated. If not already in serious difficulty, the forge soon would be unless prices began to rise once again or unless the management took immediate steps to cut operating costs in the face of a sharp decline in gross revenue.

Speedwell's owner apparently had no consistent strategy for meeting the crisis of the early 1840s. The forge's production records suggest instead that he reduced the monthly rate of production from a mean of about 26 tons in 1839 to less than 17 tons for the years 1840–43. Also, some of the forge's skilled workers — the finers and chaffers — began in 1840 to devote increasing amounts of their labor time to Speedwell's bloomery, where wrought iron was made directly from iron ore.[96] Bloomery wrought iron, or blooms, an inferior form of bar iron best suited for use by rolling mills,

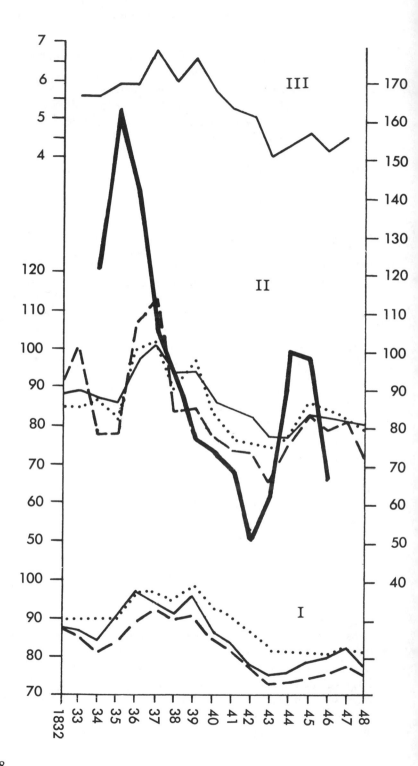

sold for less than did the refined bar made of pig iron.[97] Although sufficient accounts and memoranda do not survive for conclusive verification, it seems that the decision to make blooms in lieu of returning to the pre-1837 bar-iron production levels may have been an attempt to sustain revenue by producing for a more specialized market. In any event, by midsummer 1843 the owner evidently felt that the additional revenue generated by the sale of blooms was not great enough to sustain the forge. On 1 July he recorded a memorandum to the effect that because of a 4.5-ton inventory of 72 anconies, "the time Reduction in Hammermans wages commences."[98] The circumstances must have been extreme for him to cut the wages of a skilled worker.[99]

Of course the reduction of wages and the desultory, on again–off again production of blooms represented at best only a short-term response to the problems signaled at this time by price movements. Ultimately, the owner of Speedwell Forge could do little to affect prices and was, like producers before the Revolution, a passive participant in the iron economy. As a price-taker, he could do fairly well when prices were high; when they fell sharply, he was hard-pressed just to survive.

As the precarious success of Speedwell Forge illustrates, the Pennsylvania industry of the 1840s was far from having a firm control over its

FIGURE   10 *(opposite page)*
MOVEMENT OF IRON PRICES AND OTHER ECONOMIC INDICATORS, 1832–48

*Group I*
Wholesale price index (WPI) for 157 commodities: _____
Index of prices of raw industrial commodities: ........
Index of prices of consumption industrial commodities: . ____ . ____ .

*Group II*
Price index of 8 railroad stocks: ▬▬▬▬
Index of prices of ferrous metals: _____
Index of pig-iron prices: . __ . __ .
Index of bar-iron prices: ..........

*Group III*
Price of nails in cents per pound: _____

All commodity price indices are from Anne Bezanson, Robert D. Gray, and Miriam Hussey, *Wholesale Prices in Philadelphia, 1787–1861*, 2 vols. (Philadelphia: University of Pennsylvania Press, 1937), as follows: WPI for 157 commodities, table 41 (p. 392); raw and consumption industrial goods prices, table 42 (p. 393); ferrous metals, table 42 (p. 395); bar- and pig-iron values as averages of monthly values, tables 90 and 97 (pp. 103 and 110, respectively). The prices of nails are annual averages derived from the monthly prices in Arthur Harrison Cole, *Wholesale Commodity Prices in the United States, 1700–1861: Statistical Supplement; Actual Wholesale Prices of Various Commodities* (Cambridge, Mass.: Harvard University Press, 1938), pp. 244–310. The index of the price of eight railroad stocks is from Walter Buckingham Smith and Arthur Harrison Cole, *Fluctuations in American Business, 1790–1860* (Cambridge, Mass.: Harvard University Press, 1935), pp. 179–80.

own fate. Despite the higher degree of specialization achieved, the growth in output since 1830, and the modest technological advances of the past two decades, iron-making was still a very risky undertaking. The failure rate was high, and even enterprises such as Speedwell Forge suffered acutely on the downturn of the business cycle. Pennsylvania firms did not yet have a tight grip on the national market. Their pleas for tariff protection had not been answered. Lagging behind their technologically advanced rivals in Britain, they could still not compete in terms of either quality or price with the foreign product.

Still there were reasons for optimism in 1850. The domestic market was growing very rapidly, and the future looked brighter as the rails pushed into the West. Within the Pennsylvania industry, moreover, there was already developing an advanced set of producers ready to take full advantage of these conditions.

# Organization, Structure, and Technology, 1800–1850

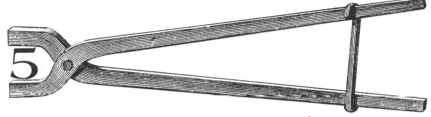

*First commencement of these works about 1800, since improved and enlarged. Owned only by the subscriber.*

P. Benner, ironmaster

By mid-century the Pennsylvania iron industry was quite different from what it had been a century earlier. The industry of 1850 operated in most parts of the state, with four concentrations of activity: in the anthracite coal fields; in the southeastern counties; in the centrally located Juniata Valley; and in the western counties that had strong commercial ties to Pittsburgh.[1] Not only was the industry more geographically dispersed by 1850 but it was also more diverse in terms of its technology and markets. These profound differences, however, tend to obscure the considerable continuity that characterized the industry's development, especially with respect to forms of business organization.

Rapid as was the pace of technological change, especially after 1830, the traditional forms of business organization common in the eighteenth century—that is, firms owned by individuals or by share partnerships of two or three men—persisted well into the nineteenth century in almost every branch of the iron industry and in virtually every part of the state. This form of organization was compatible with technological change, and indeed firms organized along such traditional lines were often among the first to adopt innovations.

This point assumes a special significance when we consider that the adoption of technological innovations by industrial firms during the first half of the nineteenth century is generally thought to have been associated with the appearance of increasing numbers of newer, more formal and complex forms of business organization, that is, the joint-stock company and the state-chartered corporation. These more sophisticated entities, so the argument goes, were necessary for the technological transformation of industry because they provided the most suitable means for raising the large amounts of capital required to finance production with the new technologies.[2] A related assumption about the role of these more advanced forms of organization is that by virtue of their embrace of more advanced technologies and accounting methods, they necessarily enjoyed higher levels of labor productivity and, presumably, higher total factor productivity than did firms owned by individuals or small partnerships.[3] By testing these assumptions against a considerable body of evidence, we can arrive at a clearer understanding of the relationship between organizational structure and technological change in the Pennsylvania iron industry.

The bulk of this evidence consists of data on the formation and operation of 146 firms active in the eighteenth century; 110 firms — for the most part in western Pennsylvania — that responded to a U.S. Treasury Department questionnaire in 1832; 103 firms covered in the federal census taken in 1840, reported in 1842; and 350 firms operating 490 facilities about which they supplied information for a statistical report compiled by a convention of ironmasters in Philadelphia in 1849.[4] Some ambiguity in the distinction between large partnerships and companies during the eighteenth century is unavoidable. No doubt some firms called companies by their owners were in fact partnerships. In such cases, however, the organization was a formal one, embracing several shareholders, and the distinction between these firms and joint-stock companies was generally one without essential difference. This problem of taxonomy is much less vexing with respect to the nineteenth century, when government and industry questionnaires asked owners of iron firms to indicate whether their business was a joint-stock company.

The rough statistical outlines of the changing organizational structure of the industry are evident in the figures given in table 26. While the relative number of production facilities owned by individuals fell from 68 percent in the eighteenth century to 43 percent in the middle of the nineteenth century, partnerships and joint-stock companies gradually increased their respective shares of the industry from less than 20 percent to almost 30 percent. Although the pattern seems clear enough, the figures require some explanation.

As is so often the case with statistical findings, the accuracy of the figures in table 26 suffers to the extent that the sources from which they spring are incomplete. This is not a particularly serious problem with respect to the results for the eighteenth century and for 1849. The 1832

TABLE 26

Business Organization of Production Facilities, 1716–1800, 1832, and 1849

| Type of Facility | 1716–1800 | | | 1832 | | | 1849 | | |
|---|---|---|---|---|---|---|---|---|---|
| | I | P | Co. | I | P | Co. | I | P | Co. |
| Furnace | 51% | 16% | 33% | 58% | 15% | 27% | 40% | 29% | 31% |
| Forge | 81 | 9 | 10 | 46 | 27 | 27 | 61 | 27 | 12 |
| Ironworks[a] | 62 | 8 | 31 | 60 | 33 | 7 | — | — | — |
| Rolling mill | 69 | 31 | 0 | 17 | 33 | 50 | 24 | 35 | 41 |
| Other[a] | 67 | 11 | 22 | 52 | 26 | 23 | — | — | — |
| Total | 68% | 13% | 18% | 49% | 25% | 25% | 43% | 29% | 28% |

Sources: Eighteenth-century figures are derived from Bining, Pennsylvania Iron Manufacture, pp. 171–76; 1832 figures are computed from McLane Report, vol. 2, docs. 13 and 14; 1849 figures are computed from "Documents Relating to the Manufacture of Iron in Pennsylvania," tables following p. 72.

Note: Due to rounding off, totals may not equal 100 percent.

I = individual; P = partnership; and Co. = company.

[a] No figures were listed for 1849.

figures, however, drawn from the *McLane Report* of 1832, faithfully reflect the report's most glaring imperfection concerning the Pennsylvania iron industry: very few firms in the eastern part of the state cooperated with the Treasury Department's questionnaire, thereby lending undue weight to the industry in the west.[5] Most of the state's forges and many of its furnaces owned by individuals were located in the southeastern counties that made no return. Consequently, the percentage figures for 1832 considerably understate the presence of individually owned firms and overstate the importance of joint-stock companies and multi-member share partnerships. This is not to say that the 1830 data are without value; rather, we should take more than a grain of salt to digest them.

With that caveat in mind, we can proceed with an examination of the assumptions that underlie the conventional view of the role of the large-scale–partnership, joint-stock company and chartered corporation in American industrialization prior to the Civil War. If these more formal, more advanced forms of business organization were more significant than other forms in facilitating American industrialization, then we should expect to find that (1) they were at the technological cutting edge of the iron industry; (2) they operated with greater efficiency than did firms owned by individuals and small partnerships, for example, with a higher rate of labor productivity; and (3) their higher levels of capitalization reflected their use of advanced technology and operation on a large scale.

Before determining whether companies and corporations were in the forefront of technological innovation, we must first identify which of the various types of furnaces and other installations, such as forges and rolling mills, were more technologically advanced than others. Of the furnaces, the cold-blast charcoal type was the oldest, operating at relatively low temperatures and using the traditional fuel. More advanced by virtue of the heating of the blast by waste gases was the hot-blast charcoal furnace, which operated at higher temperatures and with greater fuel efficiency.[6] Of the still more advanced types of furnaces in operation by 1850 in Pennsylvania — those fueled with anthracite coal, bituminous coal, or coke — only the anthracite furnaces operated in sufficient numbers to make them significant.

A clear-cut technological hierarchy is more difficult to construct for the other types of production facilities — forges, ironworks, and rolling mills — because they frequently bore little or no similarity to one another. A fairly sound rule of thumb, however, is that forges were generally older and less advanced in design than rolling mills. Ironworks present a unique problem in that they were often compound facilities — that is, consisting of a furnace and a forge. It was therefore possible for an ironworks to have a fairly advanced furnace and a forge of antiquated design and even of considerable vintage.

During the eighteenth century, a period of remarkable technological stability within the Pennsylvania iron industry, the relationship between organizational form and level of technology was of less moment than in the following half-century. Even so, the eighteenth-century figures suggest that except for a strong interest in furnaces, companies played an insignificant role in the iron industry's more specialized branches (rolling mills, naileries, and slitting mills).

The data for 1832 confuse rather than clarify matters because, as was mentioned above, they are heavily biased in favor of western facilities and are also incomplete. Thus, only twelve rolling mills are listed in the *McLane Report,* despite the fact that fifteen rolling mills constructed from 1801 through 1832 survived to be listed in the ironmasters' statistical report of 1849. Of these fifteen rolling mills, ten were located in eastern Pennsylvania, compared with only four of the twelve listed by McLane.[7] More to the point, none of the ten eastern mills was owned by a joint-stock company in 1849, the bulk — seven — being in the hands of partnerships. Of the five western rolling mills, four were company-owned, only one was owned by a partnership, and none by individuals, which suggests, however obliquely, the existence in 1832 of the regional differentiation in the organizational form of rolling mills that is so apparent in the 1849 figures. The 1832 data, presented in table 27, indicate that companies then played an important, but by no means the predominant, role in the iron industry, accounting for about 25 percent of all facilities and from 30 percent to 32 percent of total output, measured in tons and dollars, respectively.

For firms in 1849 the relationship between form of business organization and level of technological advancement is quite clear. Even without disaggregating beyond the three major classes of facilities then in opera-

TABLE 27

Output and Organizational Form in the Pennsylvania Iron Industry, 1832

| Variable | Organizational Form | | | |
|---|---|---|---|---|
| | Individual | Partnership | Joint-Stock Company | All Forms |
| | Facilities Reporting Their Output in Dollars | | | |
| Number of Facilities | 55 | 27 | 28 | 110 |
| Output | $1,205,852 | $1,255,365 | $1,173,222 | $3,634,439 |
| Mean Output | $ 21,925 | $ 46,495 | $ 41,901 | $ 33,040 |
| % facilities | 50.0% | 24.5% | 25.5% | 100% |
| % dollars | 33.2% | 34.5% | 32.3% | 100% |
| | Facilities Reporting Their Output in Tons | | | |
| Number of facilities | 36 | 20 | 17 | 73 |
| Output | 19,937 tn. | 15,680 tn. | 14,912 tn. | 50,529 tn. |
| Mean output | 554 tn. | 784 tn. | 877 tn. | 692 tn. |
| % facilities | 49.3% | 27.4% | 23.3% | 100% |
| % tons | 39.5% | 31.0% | 29.5% | 100% |

Source: McLane Report, vol. 2, doc. 14, no. 323.
Note: Primarily central and western counties are covered.

TABLE 28

Regional Differentiation of Production Facilities and Forms of Business Organization, 1849

| Type of Facility | Eastern Region | | | Western Region | | | Total | | |
|---|---|---|---|---|---|---|---|---|---|
| | I | P | Co. | I | P | Co. | I | P | Co. |
| Cold-blast charcoal furnace | 60% | 19% | 21% | 39% | 34% | 27% | 48% | 28% | 24% |
| Hot-blast charcoal furnace | 44 | 25 | 31 | 28 | 33 | 39 | 40 | 27 | 33 |
| Anthracite blast furnace | 25 | 30 | 45 | 0 | 0 | 0 | 25 | 30 | 45 |
| Forge | 62 | 27 | 11 | 33 | 33 | 33 | 61 | 27 | 12 |
| Rolling mill | 34 | 41 | 25 | 4 | 22 | 74 | 24 | 35 | 41 |
| Total | 48% | 28% | 24% | 30% | 33% | 37% | 43% | 29% | 28% |

Source: "Documents Relating to the Manufacture of Iron in Pennsylvania," tables following p. 72.
Note: I = individual; P = partnership; and Co. = company.

tion — furnaces, forges, and rolling mills — it is apparent that for the state as a whole, companies accounted for about the same proportions of furnaces and forges in 1849 as in the eighteenth century.

A different picture emerges, however, if we distinguish among cold-blast and hot-blast charcoal furnaces and anthracite furnaces (see table 28). It is apparent that as we move up the technological hierarchy, the company form of organization assumes an increasingly important role. Moreover, as we move up this hierarchy, we also move to higher levels of output per furnace, as well as significantly higher levels of capitalization. Thus, while the average cold-blast charcoal furnace was capitalized at about $35,700, and the average hot-blast charcoal furnace at almost $41,000, the mean capitalization of anthracite furnaces was $56,500.[8] Although capitalization figures for individual firms were not included in the 1849 compilation, output levels were listed, and these indicate that although scale of operation consistently increased with the level of technological sophistication, the same was not true with respect to the level of organization within a particular furnace type. For example, while mean output for cold-blast charcoal furnaces increased from the 491 tons for those owned by individuals to 739 tons for companies, hot-blast furnaces owned by partnerships had a higher mean output level (1,018 tons), than did companies (858 tons) or installations owned by individuals (542 tons). The anthracite furnaces present an equally curious situation. Although company-owned furnaces had by far the largest mean output — 2,480 tons — the mean output of furnaces owned by individuals exceeded that of furnaces owned by partnerships, 1,735 tons as compared with 1,641 tons. These variations notwithstanding, it is apparent that the company form of organization became more important within the pig-iron sector of the industry with each step up the technological hierarchy.

Companies also had extensive interests in the rolled-iron sector of the industry, accounting for about 41 percent of all rolling mills, compared with 50 percent of those listed in the less reliable 1832 compilation and none of the thirteen rolling mills included in the eighteenth-century list. The role of the companies in the ownership of rolling mills is even more pronounced in a regional breakdown of the data. Companies owned 74 percent of the twenty-three rolling mills in western Pennsylvania but only 25 percent of the fifty-six mills in the east.

This regional pattern of business organization reflects primarily the regional differences in the structure of demand for iron products. In both eastern and western Pennsylvania, rolling mills turned out a variety of products, including both generic and specific goods (see table 29). A decomposition of the output of rolling mills with respect to form of business organization reveals a pronounced relationship between the two. Of fifty-four eastern Pennsylvania rolling mills for which complete data exist, eleven of the sixteen mills owned by individuals produced boiler and flue iron exclusively, while mills owned by partnerships and companies produced rods, bar iron, nails, plate and sheet metal, and rails. The differences in the levels of labor intensity and fuel consumption help to explain the distribution. Boiler and flue iron, the major products of rolling mills owned by individuals, required less fuel and fewer workers per ton of output than did the products turned out by mills owned by partnerships and especially by companies (see figure 11). Moreover, the mills that pro-

TABLE 29

Distribution of Rolling-Mill Products in Pennsylvania, 1849, by Region

| No. | Product | Eastern Region | | | Western Region | | |
|---|---|---|---|---|---|---|---|
| | | I | P | Co. | I | P | Co. |
| 1 | Sheet iron | 2 | 2 | 1 | 1 | 3 | 15 |
| 2 | Nails | 1 | 4 | 2 | 1 | 3 | 14 |
| 3 | Boiler iron | 11 | 8 | 2 | 0 | 2 | 11 |
| 4 | Rod iron | 2 | 6 | 7 | 1 | 3 | 16 |
| 5 | Bar iron | 5 | 11 | 7 | 1 | 4 | 14 |
| 6 | Plate | 0 | 3 | 2 | 1 | 1 | 4 |
| 7 | Axles | 0 | 0 | 0 | 0 | 0 | 2 |
| 8 | Wire | 0 | 1 | 0 | 0 | 0 | 0 |
| 9 | Flue | 8 | 5 | 4 | 0 | 0 | 0 |
| 10 | Spring steel | 0 | 2 | 1 | 0 | 0 | 0 |
| 11 | Steel | 1 | 0 | 0 | 0 | 1 | 0 |
| 12 | Rails | 1 | 2 | 4 | 0 | 1 | 0 |

Sources: "A Detailed Statement of All the Rolling Mills in Eastern Pennsylvania in the Year 1850" and "A Detailed Statement of All the Rolling Mills in Western Pennsylvania in the Year 1850," both in "Documents Relating to the Manufacture of Iron in Pennsylvania," tables following p. 72.

Notes: A particular rolling mill often made several of these products.

I = individual; P = partnership; and Co. = company.

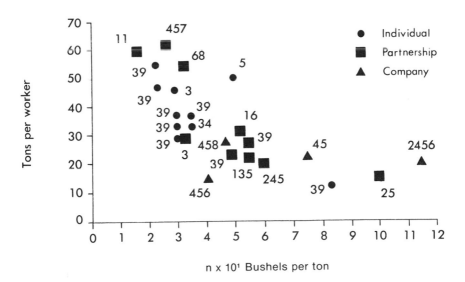

FIGURE 11

BITUMINOUS ROLLING MILLS IN EASTERN PENNSYLVANIA, 1849: OUTPUT BY FUEL CONSUMPTION

Output = total tons of product per worker. Fuel consumption = bushels of bituminous coal consumed per ton of output. Product numbers in figure identify specific products and correspond to those in table 29. Data sources are the same as for table 29.

duced boiler and flue iron exclusively were generally capitalized at a level considerably below that of mills owned by either partnerships or companies (see table 30).[9] Thus rolling mills intended for the production of boiler and flue iron operated on a scale that was sufficiently small to be within the reach of individual capitalists.[10] This explains the near absence of rolling mills owned by individuals in the western part of the state, where little boiler or flue iron was produced in rolling mills (the supply of these products coming from foundries).[11]

Rolling mills owned by partnerships and companies accounted for most of the iron produced statewide in such facilities — about 33,600 and 68,700 tons, respectively, of a total of about 108,400 tons — while the balance of 6,060 tons came from mills owned by individuals. But here, again, the product type explains much of the disparity. Boiler iron and flue iron were products often turned out in relatively small lots for sale in small lots, while bar iron, rod iron, nails, and particularly rails were products made in large quantities, especially by companies.[12] The differences in scale among the forms of organization are even more evident in a comparison of mean output levels: 356 tons for mills owned by individuals; 1,243 tons for partnerships; and 2,217 tons for companies. An important point, however, should be borne in mind: rolling mills owned by partnerships and those owned by companies that made the same products — including rails — operated on a similar scale and, as will be shown below, with comparable efficiency.[13] Once again, a regional pattern clearly existed.

In western Pennsylvania company-owned mills produced the lion's share of output — 80 percent — but suffered slightly in a comparison of mean output levels with mills owned by partnerships. The east, however, was quite different. There mills owned by companies accounted for about 48 percent of the output, as opposed to a 43 percent share for partnerships. Moreover, the mean output of company mills was 1,858 tons, while mills owned by partnerships turned out only about 1,000 tons. These differences between eastern and western rolling mills are readily understood when we recall the distinctly regional character of the product mix already discussed: in the east the output of rolling mills was far more heterogeneous than in the west. The mean output levels and shares of total output of mills owned by partnerships and those owned by companies simply reflect this heterogeneity.

Although a technological hierarchy defined according to process type is useful in determining the relative importance of various forms of business organization, it is not comprehensive. The development of furnace design from charcoal blast to hot blast to anthracite blast was a gradual process that, in the case of the shift from cold- to hot-blast charcoal types, involved a significant number of conversions of furnaces initially built as cold-blast installations into hot-blast ones. All told, twenty-five cold-blast

TABLE 30

Size of Rolling Mills in Eastern Pennsylvania, 1849, by Type of Product

| Type of Product | Number of Mills | Mean Largest Output[a] | Mean Number of Workers[b] | Mean Output per Worker[c] | Mean Number of | | | % Total Mills Owned by an Individual |
|---|---|---|---|---|---|---|---|---|
| | | | | | Puddling Furnaces[d] | Heating Furnaces[e] | Rollers[f] | |
| Boiler and flue iron | 12[g] | 691 | 20.27 | 43.07 | 0.50 | 2.67 | 1.25 | 67% |
| All other products | 44 | 1,953 | 79.42 | 24.56 | 5.60 | 3.07 | 2.12 | 25 |
| All products | 56 | 1,728 | 66.33 | 25.18 | 4.49 | 2.98 | 1.93 | 34% |

*Sources:* See table 29.

[a] Output figures were not listed for 2 mills, one of which produced boiler and flue iron. Thus, mean largest output for mills producing only boiler and flue iron is computed on the basis of 11 mills. Similarly, mean largest output for mills producing all other products and for those producing all products is computed using 43 mills and 54 mills, respectively.

[b] One mill, unfinished but geared to produce bars, reported no workers. Thus the mean number of workers per mill for mills producing products other than boiler and flue iron and for those producing all products, is computed using 43 and 55 mills, respectively.

[c] Mean output per worker for mills producing only boiler and flue iron is computed using the total work force at 11 mills.

[d] A puddling furnace was, in some respects, a more advanced design in which the iron and fuel were segregated into two compartments divided by a low wall. The flames from the blast, but not the fuel itself, touched the iron, thereby avoiding contamination (Peter Temin, *Iron and Steel in Nineteenth-Century America: An Economic Injury* [Cambridge, Mass.: M.I.T. Press, 1964], p. 17).

[e] A heating furnace was one built along more or less conventional lines.

[f] Rollers, as opposed to forge hammers, turned blooms into bar-iron products.

[g] Mills that made boiler and flue iron exclusively.

furnaces built before 1830 were converted to hot-blast furnaces between 1830 and 1849, and of these, nine were owned by individuals, eight by partnerships, and seven by companies. As this indicates, companies were active in upgrading their production plants, but they were hardly alone in doing so.[14]

Still another consideration in constructing a technological hierarchy for the iron industry is the type of power used — water or steam — by specific kinds of facilities, as well as the regional and organizational patterns of power use. Here again, the data for 1832 are not all that we could wish them to be, but they nevertheless permit some useful comparisons with later, better-documented periods. For example, of ninety-six facilities of all types active in 1832 about 30 percent were powered by either steam alone or a combination of steam and water, depending upon the season. By 1849 the proportion of facilities using steam power had increased to 34 percent. The shift to steam appears to have been even more pronounced when we examine power use with respect to organizational form in 1832 and 1849. Fifty-one percent of all facilities operated by companies in the latter year used steam, compared with only 31 percent in 1832. While the proportion of steam-powered facilities owned by individuals barely changed over the twenty-year period, the use of steam in works owned by partnerships declined from 42 percent to 38 percent. In this instance, the imperfections in the 1832 data are probably responsible for the anomalous behavior of the figures. These same imperfections, especially the western bias of the data, no doubt overemphasize the importance of steampower in the iron industry of 1832. A relative dearth of accessible waterpower sites in the west had early made steam an attractive, almost essential source of power for iron making. The iron industry in the east, by contrast, had long exploited that region's abundant waterpower sites and, consequently, to the extent that eastern ironworks are inadequately represented in the 1832 data, the role of steampower in the industry is exaggerated.

Despite the shortcomings of the 1832 data, it is clear that the incidence of steampower increased as technological sophistication increased.[15] That there was a similar strong relationship between steampower usage and level of technology in 1849 is evident from the figures given in table 31. The relationship, however, is more complex than it appears to be at first glance, and predictably enough, the matter of regional variation in the distribution of steampower intrudes and assumes considerable importance.

With the exception of the anthracite furnaces, all but one of which were in the east, the use of steam in the east never approached the levels achieved in the west (where roughly 45 percent of the cold- and hot-blast charcoal furnaces were steampowered). The regional disparity was even greater with regard to rolling mills. Fifty percent of the fifty-six eastern

TABLE 31
Steam Use in 1849 (in Percent)

| Type of Facility | Form of Organization | | | All Forms |
| | Individual | Partnership | Company | |
|---|---|---|---|---|
| Cold-blast charcoal furnace | 25% | 37% | 37% | 31% |
| Hot-blast charcoal furnace | 26 | 24 | 26 | 25 |
| Anthracite blast furnace | 77 | 80 | 72 | 75 |
| Forge | 6 | 6 | 14 | 7 |
| Rolling mill | 33 | 61 | 84 | 64 |
| All types | 23% | 38% | 50% | 35% |

Source: "Documents Relating to the Manufacture of Iron in Pennsylvania," tables following p. 72.
Note: Both facilities using steam and those using steam and water are included.

mills used steam, compared with 96 percent of the twenty-three mills in the west. Moreover, the use of steampower by firms of various types in each region varied greatly. For example, although firms owned by individuals accounted for 18 percent of the steam-powered rolling mills in the east, the corresponding figure in the west was only 4 percent. Similarly, partnerships and companies in the east owned 43 percent and 39 percent, respectively, of the mills powered by steam, while their respective western counterparts accounted for about 22 percent and 74 percent of the steam-powered mills. Much of this regional variation in the relationship between business organization and the use of the steampower arose from the distinct regional differences in the availability of waterpower sites and in the scale of operations, the latter having much to do with the product mixes of rolling mills in each region.

The weight of the evidence presented here warrants giving the company an important but only a supporting role in the technological transformation of the Pennsylvania iron industry prior to 1850. Companies were seldom if ever first in the introduction of new production processes, including the smelting of ore with anthracite coal. The other major innovation in furnace design — the hot-blast process — was adopted first by firms owned by individuals in the early 1830s. And except in the western rolling mills, almost all of which were company-owned, companies followed rather than led firms owned by individuals and partnerships in the introduction of steampower.[16]

Moreover, companies generally did not erect furnaces, irrespective of type, with an annual capacity larger than that of furnaces built by individuals or partnerships. The exceptions of course were the anthracite blast furnaces, which had an average capacity much larger than that of either cold-blast or hot-blast charcoal furnaces. For example, thirty-three anthracite furnaces had been erected or were near completion by 1846. Of these, eleven with a mean rated capacity of 3,050 tons were owned by individuals; ten with a mean capacity of 2,950 tons were owned by partnerships; and twelve having a 3,646-ton mean capacity were owned by companies. Although the company-owned furnaces were on average 20 percent larger than the furnaces owned by individuals and partnerships, this was due entirely to the fact that two company-owned furnaces were behemoths with a 13,000-ton capacity between them, or an average capacity of 6,500 tons. The next largest furnace size was 5,000 tons, and one of this size, owned by an individual, was already built; the only other one, then under construction, was owned by a company.[17]

Charcoal-furnace sizes varied virtually not at all with respect to form of business organization. The average capacity of sixty-six furnaces built between 1840 and 1846 was 1,048 tons. Of these, twenty-one were built by individuals and had a mean capacity of 1,060 tons; twenty-seven with a mean capacity of 1,048 tons were owned by partnerships. The remaining eighteen furnaces were owned by companies and had an average capacity of 1,033 tons.[18] The same near uniformity of furnace size irrespective of organizational form is evident from an examination of the data for fifty-seven cold-blast and sixty-four hot-blast charcoal furnaces built between 1736 and 1849. The former range in mean capacity from 1,145 tons for facilities owned by individuals to 1,276 tons for those owned by companies. The hot-blast furnaces had somewhat larger capacities, averaging 1,566 tons for those owned by individuals and 1,501 tons for those owned by companies.[19]

Nor did companies operate their facilities at higher levels of efficiency — measured in terms of labor productivity and fuel consumption rates — than those achieved by firms owned by individuals and partnerships. An examination of the annual output (in tons) and number of workers employed in 1842 at each of sixty-seven furnaces reveals that although the shares of the total number of furnaces and the total output of 70,075 tons were fairly evenly distributed among the three organizational forms, the average furnace owned by an individual employed fewer workers, produced more, and achieved a higher rate of output per worker — 20.5 tons — than did the average furnace owned by a partnership or company.[20]

Unlike furnaces, whose output is measured here only in tons of pig iron, forges made two distinct products — bar iron and boiler plate — and ten of the forty-two eastern forges operating in 1842 made both.[21] Thus, no single figure for output per worker can possibly be an accurate measure of the performance of the average forge, or even of the average forge owned by each form of business organization. Instead, measures of output per worker inevitably reflect the type of product made at each forge. At the aggregate level of analysis a breakdown of mean output per worker by organizational form suggests that forges owned by individuals were substantially less productive than those owned by partnerships — the mean output per worker at the former being 9.7 tons, as compared with 11.1 tons at the latter — and that both were grossly inferior to company-owned forges, which achieved a mean output per worker of 23.8 tons. These results are quite misleading, for an examination of forge-production data, disaggregated according to product and type of firm, leads to the almost opposite conclusion.

As noted above, three major product groupings comprised forge output in 1842. Forges apparently specialized in one or two of these groupings, according to their form of organization and therefore probably according to scale as well. Thus, although about half of the forges owned by individuals produced only bar iron, the other half made boiler plate almost exclusively. By contrast, almost all forges owned by partnerships and companies produced more bar iron than anything else. A comparison of the mean output per worker within each product grouping for forges of each organizational type reveals that of twenty-three forges making only bar iron, those owned by partnerships achieved the highest rate (18.5 tons), followed by those owned by companies (15.7 tons) and then those owned by individuals (13.3 tons). Forges owned by partnerships were also more efficient on average than those owned by individuals in the making of boiler plate, a product not made at all by companies. Finally, of the ten forges that turned out both bar iron and boiler plate, little difference in output rates distinguished one type of firm from the others.[22]

Many of the points just made concerning forges were made above with respect to rolling mills and furnaces, and led to virtually the same conclusion: installations owned by companies were often less efficient and generally no more efficient than those owned by partnerships and individuals. The obvious question, then, is, Why were the firms with the most advanced form of organization so often less efficient in the operation of facilities at almost all levels of technology? One obvious possibility to be rejected out of hand is that the company form of organization suffered from the crippling effects of a cumbersome bureaucratic structure. As should be apparent, most of these companies were not very large, and fewer than twenty of the companies active between 1800 and 1850 were chartered corporations.[23] Moreover, all three types of firms made use of hired ironmasters, managers, and foreman. With the exception of the few incorporated companies, many of which after 1830 had allied coal and railroad interests, little backward integration of advanced operations occurred within the iron industry.[24] Of the 350 firms listed in the 1849 compilation, only twenty, or less than 6 percent, owned one or more furnaces and a rolling mill, and of these twenty, nine were companies, eight

TABLE 32

Organizational Form and Furnace Performance: Output in 1849 as a Percentage of Rated Capacity

| Type of Furnace | Percentage Capacity[a] for Firms Owned by | | | |
| | Individuals | Partnerships | Companies | All Firms[b] |
| --- | --- | --- | --- | --- |
| Cold-blast charcoal furnace | 37% | 38% | 59% | 42% |
| Hot-blast charcoal furnace | 33 | 63 | 51 | 47 |
| Anthracite blast furnace | 51 | 46 | 53 | 49 |
| All furnaces[c] | 39% | 46% | 54% | 47% |

Source: "Documents Relating to the Manufacture of Iron in Pennsylvania," tables following p. 72.
[a] Rounded off to nearest whole number.
[b] Excluded are firms owned by banks and heirs to estates.
[c] Excluded are 11 furnaces: 7 bituminous and 4 hot-blast coke furnaces. Included are 283 furnaces: 144 cold-blast charcoal furnaces, 84 hot-blast charcoal furnaces, and 55 anthracite blast furnaces.

were partnerships, and three were owned by individuals.[25] In view of the demonstrably small size and modest levels of capitalization of all firms of whatever organizational type, the explanation for the lackluster performance of company-owned facilities must lie elsewhere.

The cause of the companies' poor showing was their probable inability to push their facilities to their operating limits — that is, to realize the economies of scale that many of the technological innovations had made possible. Because company-owned facilities of most types were generally the most heavily capitalized and also somewhat larger than those owned by partnerships or individuals, their fixed costs were comparatively high. Moreover, variable-cost inputs such as labor at some types of facilities were not very susceptible to manipulation within specific product groupings. Thus, at rolling mills that made bar and rod iron — specialties of company-owned mills — output per worker was almost completely inelastic with respect to changes in the size of the labor force. Boiler- and flue-iron mills, on the other hand, commonly owned by individuals, enjoyed a fairly elastic inverse relationship between the two.

Ultimately, the level of demand for iron products was the greatest single influence on the performance of all of the iron firms, company-owned and others alike. The differences in the effect of the level of demand on the three types of firms arose from their different scales of operation. Because iron-making was still a labor-intensive activity in all its processes, and because the capital equipment required a rather large number of workers to produce any output at all, the larger, company-owned facilities suffered acutely when they ran at levels substantially below capacity (see table 32). At such times, fixed-cost and normally variable-cost factors of production frustrated attempts to realize greater efficiency. The available advanced technology, adopted by firms of all organizational types, carried with it the potential for realizing increasing returns to scale. Aggregate demand for iron products, however, was still insufficiently developed in 1850 to enable these firms to reap the full benefits of this technology.

The rapid growth of the industry in the 1830s and 1840s had thus taken place without a sharp, revolutionary break with the past. Firms using the new technology existed alongside those using far older modes of production. The older styles of organization were yet to be pushed aside by the large companies. Individuals and small partnerships could still cope with the capital demands of iron-making and were at least as innovative as the companies. The day of the corporation was just faint light on the horizon as late as 1850.

The light was there, however, and the continued expansion of the domestic economy would shortly launch a new phase in the industry's development. Already one could see what was coming in the form of the great company-owned furnaces and rolling mills in the west. Other even more startling changes in technology and scale would follow shortly, as the first signs of the modern iron industry emerged in the next decade.

# A Wheel Within a Wheel: Growth and Continuity, 1850–60

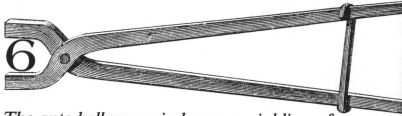

*The ante-bellum period gave an inkling of what was to come rather than fully accomplishing the ultimate revolution.*

Albert Fishlow

By the end of the 1840s there were, in effect, two iron industries in Pennsylvania: one looked to the past and the industry's traditional technology, mode of organization, and patterns of growth; the other looked to the future, to new technologies, forms of business organization, and patterns of development. Both of these industries had little reason to regret the passing of the 1840s. The decade had begun and ended in depression. The political gyrations over the protective tariff had left large segments of the iron industry confused and vulnerable to devastating British competition. Even firms in the modern branches of the industry had suffered during the decade. Of twenty-six firms that had begun to produce anthracite pig iron between 1840 and 1847 more than a third were no longer in business in 1850. The survival rate for rolling mills was worse: of the twenty firms in business in 1846 only 55 percent were still in business four years later.[1]

Nevertheless, the modern sectors had responded to these adverse conditions in a manner significantly different from that of the traditional sectors of the industry. The forces of competition destroyed the weaker firms in both sectors, but in the former the losses were more than offset by new firms entering the industry. Thus the anthracite furnaces and the rolling mills emerged from the 1840s in larger numbers and in robust health. Here, destructive competition had the sort of healthy, cleansing effect that

TABLE 33

Regional Distribution of Production Facilities and Forms of Business Organization, 1849 and 1859 (in Percent)

| Type of Facility | Eastern Region | | | Western Region | | | Whole State | | |
|---|---|---|---|---|---|---|---|---|---|
| | I | P | Co. | I | P | Co. | I | P | Co. |
| *Cold-blast charcoal furnace* | | | | | | | | | |
| 1849 | 60% | 19% | 21% | 39% | 34% | 27% | 48% | 28% | 24% |
| 1859 | 33 | 30 | 37 | 44 | 25 | 31 | 37 | 28 | 35 |
| *Hot-blast charcoal furnace* | | | | | | | | | |
| 1849 | 44 | 25 | 31 | 28 | 33 | 29 | 40 | 27 | 33 |
| 1859 | 42 | 29 | 29 | 20 | 55 | 25 | 32 | 41 | 27 |
| *Anthracite blast furnace* | | | | | | | | | |
| 1849[a] | 25 | 30 | 45 | — | — | — | 25 | 30 | 45 |
| 1859[a] | 23 | 27 | 50 | — | — | — | 23 | 27 | 50 |
| *All furnaces* | | | | | | | | | |
| 1849 | 44 | 24 | 32 | 37 | 34 | 29 | 42 | 27 | 31 |
| 1859 | 28 | 28 | 44 | 31 | 42 | 28 | 30 | 31 | 39 |
| *Charcoal forge* | | | | | | | | | |
| 1849 | 62 | 27 | 11 | 33 | 33 | 33 | 61 | 27 | 12 |
| 1859[a] | 51 | 28 | 21 | — | — | — | 51 | 28 | 21 |
| *Rolling mill* | | | | | | | | | |
| 1849 | 34 | 41 | 25 | 4 | 22 | 74 | 24 | 35 | 41 |
| 1859 | 33 | 38 | 28 | 17 | 28 | 55 | 28 | 35 | 37 |
| *All facilities* | | | | | | | | | |
| 1849 | 48% | 28% | 24% | 30% | 33% | 37% | 43% | 29% | 28% |
| 1859 | 31% | 30% | 33% | 25% | 35% | 40% | 34% | 31% | 35% |

*Sources:* Figures for 1849 are from table 28; figures for 1859 are from J. P. Lesley, *The Iron Manufacturer's Guide to the Furnaces, Forges and Rolling Mills of the United States* (New York: John Wiley, 1859), passim.
*Note:* I = individual; P = partnership; and Co. = company.
[a] The source lists none for the western region.

Joseph A. Schumpeter described.[2] This was not true of the charcoal-pig-iron sector, in which the effects of the high mortality rate among existing firms — 47 percent of sixty-three firms active in 1842 did not survive until 1850 — were exacerbated by a sharp decline in the number of new firms formed after 1846, the year of the Walker Tariff.[3] By 1850 virtually no one with capital and a desire to make money by producing pig iron was so foolish as to try it by building a charcoal furnace.[4]

In the decade that followed, the gulf between the modern and the traditional sectors widened. The interest in advanced technology intensified. In response to a growth in demand and a more stable, more certain political and business climate, the output of the iron industry as a whole and that of its constituent firms increased rapidly during the 1850s. Enjoying the largest share of this growth were the firms using advanced techniques, and these were the businesses that normally used the company form of organization. By 1859 the organization of the industry had changed in important regards (see table 33). The distinct regional pattern so prominent in the

TABLE 34

Percentage Distribution of Output (Largest Product), 1840s and 1850s, by Form of Business Organization

| Type of Facility | Form of Organization | | | Output of All Firms (gross tons) |
| --- | --- | --- | --- | --- |
| | Individual | Partnership | Company | |
| Cold-blast charcoal furnace | | | | |
| 1840s | 46% | 27% | 27% | 124,355 |
| 1850s | 34 | 23 | 42 | 41,714 |
| Hot-blast charcoal furnace | | | | |
| 1840s | 37 | 30 | 33 | 92,719 |
| 1850s | 25 | 52 | 24 | 54,541 |
| Anthracite blast furnace | | | | |
| 1840s | 21 | 19 | 60 | 145,279 |
| 1850s | 23 | 23 | 54 | 324,222 |
| Raw bituminous coal and coke hot-blast furnaces[a] | | | | |
| 1840s | 11 | 62 | 27 | 17,800 |
| 1850s | 12 | 7 | 81 | 50,230 |
| All furnaces | | | | |
| 1840s | 33 | 26 | 41 | 380,153 |
| 1850s | 23 | 25 | 52 | 470,707 |
| Rail mills | | | | |
| 1840s | 0 | 60 | 40 | 23,642 |
| 1850s | 3 | 10 | 87 | 95,887 |
| Non-rail mills | | | | |
| 1840s | 11 | 26 | 64 | 139,088 |
| 1850s | 19 | 32 | 49 | 166,789 |
| All rolling mills | | | | |
| 1840s | 9 | 31 | 60 | 162,730 |
| 1850s | 14 | 24 | 63 | 262,676 |
| All facilities[b] | | | | |
| 1840s | 26% | 27% | 47% | 542,883 |
| 1850s | 20% | 25% | 56% | 733,383 |

*Sources:* Figures for the 1840s are derived from "Documents Relating to the Manufacture of Iron in Pennsylvania," tables following p. 72; figures for the 1850s are derived from Lesley, *The Iron Manufacturer's Guide, passim.*

*Notes:* The largest product is the largest output recorded for each facility. Due to rounding off, percentage totals may not equal 100.

The pertinent years within the 1840s are 1846–49; within the 1850s, 1854–57.

[a] The dramatic decrease in partnerships' share of total output results from the fact that in 1849 all coke furnaces with a product of 10,000 tons were owned by partnerships, while pig iron from bituminous furnaces totaled only 7,800 tons and was distributed among producers as follows: individuals, 26 percent; partnerships, 13 percent; and companies, 62 percent.

[b] Not including all types of physical plant. Forges and bloomeries are excluded because data are lacking for the 1850s.

1840s was still evident a decade later, but with some new twists, especially in the west, where the organizational distribution of firms had become much less homogeneous. Moreover, although companies still represented far less than half of the industry's firms — except among the anthracite furnaces and the western rolling mills — the company form of organization had made significant inroads in the ten years since 1849, when it had accounted for little more than one-fourth of all firms. By 1859 better than one of every three iron firms in the state was a company.

TABLE 35

Percentage Distribution of Furnace Capacity, 1849 and 1859,
by Form of Business Organization

| Type of Furnace | Form of Organization | | | Capacity of All Firms (gross tons) |
|---|---|---|---|---|
| | Individual | Partnership | Company | |
| *Cold-blast charcoal furnace* | | | | |
| 1849 | 46% | 32% | 22% | 198,384 |
| 1859 | 37 | 34 | 39 | 62,965 |
| *Hot-blast charcoal furnace* | | | | |
| 1849 | 40 | 27 | 33 | 128,125 |
| 1859 | 27 | 49 | 24 | 82,882 |
| *Anthracite blast furnace* | | | | |
| 1849 | 20 | 26 | 54 | 219,400 |
| 1859 | 16 | 20 | 64 | 212,364[a] |
| *Coke hot-blast furnace* | | | | |
| 1849 | 0 | 100 | 0 | 12,000 |
| 1859 | 6 | 5 | 89 | 51,127 |
| *Raw bituminous coal hot-blast furnaces* | | | | |
| 1849 | 32 | 12 | 56 | 12,600 |
| 1859[b] | — | — | — | — |
| *All furnaces*[c] | | | | |
| 1849 | 34% | 30% | 37% | 558,909 |
| 1859 | 20% | 26% | 55% | 409,338 |

*Sources:* See table 34.

*Note:* Capacity for 1849 is explicitly given in the source for that year. Capacity for 1859 must be computed from the following data given in the source: the output of each furnace in a particular year and the number of weeks during that year in which the furnace was in blast. Thus, capacity = 52 (output/weeks in blast).

[a] Capacity is lower than the corresponding value for largest product in table 34 because more furnaces reported largest product.

[b] Data are insufficient for calculation of value.

[c] Bituminous furnaces are not included.

But even this figure understates the increased significance of the company form of organization. All firms within a particular sector of the industry were of course not equal in size or output capacity. Thus, a truer measure of the relative importance of the three forms of business organization is their share of total realized output and total capacity (see tables 34 and 35). What is most striking about the figures is the companies' disproportionately large share of both capacity and actual output in almost every sector of the industry. During the 1850s about half of all pig-iron products and more than 60 percent of all rolled-iron products came from company-owned furnaces and rolling mills. As one would expect, the companies' share of total output was even greater and had grown more rapidly in the larger, more heavily capitalized sectors of the industry, the anthracite and coke furnaces and the rail mills.

By 1859 capital requirements seem to have exceeded the relatively modest resources available to most lone entrepreneurs. This situation had come about in large part as a result of the significant increases in the scale of most production processes since the 1840s. As the figures in tables 36

TABLE 36

Mean Largest Product, 1840s and 1850s, by Facility and Form of Business Organization (in Gross Tons)

| Type of Facility | Form of Organization | | | All Firms |
|---|---|---|---|---|
| | Individual | Partnership | Company | |
| *Furnaces* | | | | |
| *Cold-blast charcoal furnace* | | | | |
| 1840s | 833 (68) | 895 (38) | 971 (35) | 882 (141) |
| 1850s | 899 (16) | 816 (12) | 1,169 (15) | 970 ( 43) |
| % change | + 8% | − 9% | +20% | +10% |
| *Hot-blast charcoal furnace* | | | | |
| 1840s | 1,039 (33) | 1,251 (22) | 1,145 (27) | 1,117 ( 82) |
| 1850s | 955 (14) | 1,573 (18) | 1,072 (12) | 1,240 ( 44) |
| % change | − 8% | +26% | − 6% | +11% |
| *Anthracite blast furnace* | | | | |
| 1840s | 2,830 (11) | 2,122 (13) | 3,935 (22) | 3,158 ( 46) |
| 1850s | 3,955 (19) | 3,484 (21) | 4,754 (37) | 4,210 ( 77) |
| % change | + 40% | +64% | +21% | +33% |
| *Rolling mills* | | | | |
| *Rail mill* | | | | |
| 1840s | ( 0) | 7,100 ( 2) | 7,455 ( 3) | 6,594 ( 5) |
| 1850s | 3,000 ( 1) | 5,259 ( 1) | 10,829 ( 8) | 10,210 ( 10) |
| % change | | −26% | +45% | +55% |
| *Non-rail mill* | | | | |
| 1840s | 689 (17) | 1,442 (25) | 2,600 (29) | 1,735 ( 71) |
| 1850s | 1,414 (24) | 2,117 (27) | 3,124 (25) | 2,247 ( 76) |
| % change | + 105% | +47% | +20% | +30% |

*Sources:* See table 34.
*Note:* Figures in parentheses denote number of facilities. Furnace output was always measured in gross tons (2,240 lb.). Puddled iron and nails, both products of rolling mills, were always measured in double gross tons (2,464 lb.) and net tons (2,000 lb.), respectively. To simplify matters, I have taken all products in gross tons.

and 37 make clear, except in the much diminished charcoal-pig-iron sector of the industry, the output levels of most facilities had grown substantially. Larger output levels or capacities were the result of larger furnaces and rolling mills, the construction of which entailed an increased level of capitalization per facility.

The increase in the scale of production reflected the producers' efforts to press the technological advances made during the 1840s to their limits in response to rapidly growing demand after 1850.[5] Unlike during the prosperous mid-1840s, when most furnaces operated at about two-thirds of capacity (the rate was much lower in 1849 [see table 32]), during the best years of the later decade, 1854–57, most furnaces achieved output levels that were three-quarters of capacity (see table 38). The exceptions were to be found among the charcoal furnaces — particularly the hot-blast installations — which, their numbers sharply reduced from the 1840s, accounted for only 36 percent of total actual output and about 41 percent of all furnace capacity in the mid-1850s. Just ten years earlier they had accounted for about 60 percent of both real output and capacity.[6]

TABLE 37

Mean Furnace Capacity of Pig-Iron Production, 1849 and 1859,
by Form of Business Organization (in Gross Tons)

| Type of Furnace | Form of Organization | | | All Firms |
|---|---|---|---|---|
| | Individual | Partnership | Company | |
| Cold-blast charcoal furnace | | | | |
| 1849 | 1,339 (68) | 1,590 (40) | 1,250 (35) | 1,387 (143) |
| 1859 | 1,459 (16) | 1,278 (12) | 1,619 (15) | 1,465 ( 43) |
| % change | + 9% | − 20% | + 30% | + 6% |
| Hot-blast charcoal furnace | | | | |
| 1849 | 1,571 (33) | 1,568 (22) | 1,547 (27) | 1,563 ( 82) |
| 1859 | 1,589 (14) | 2,248 (18) | 1,681 (12) | 1,884 ( 44) |
| % change | + 1% | + 43% | + 9% | + 21% |
| Anthracite blast furnace | | | | |
| 1849 | 3,427 (13) | 3,588 (16) | 4,698 (25) | 4,100 ( 54) |
| 1859 | 4,132 ( 8) | 3,948 (11) | 5,622 (24) | 4,939 ( 43) |
| % change | + 21% | + 10% | + 21% | + 20% |
| Coke blast furnace | | | | |
| 1849[a] | ( 0) | 3,000 ( 4) | ( 0) | 3,000 ( 4) |
| 1859 | 1,630 ( 3) | 2,718 ( 1) | 3,782 (12) | 3,312 ( 16) |
| % change | | − 9% | | |
| Bituminous coal blast furnace | | | | |
| 1849 | 2,000 ( 2) | 1,500 ( 1) | 1,775 ( 4) | 1,800 ( 7) |
| 1859[a] | − | − | − | − |
| % change | | | | |

Sources: See table 34.
Note: Figures in parentheses denote number of furnaces.
[a] Data are insufficient for calculation of mean value.


TABLE 38

Largest Product Made as a Percentage of Furnace Capacity, 1840s and 1850s,
by Form of Business Organization

| Type of Furnace | % Capacity for Firms Owned by | | | All Firms |
|---|---|---|---|---|
| | Individual | Partnership | Company | |
| Cold-blast charcoal furnace | | | | |
| 1840s | 62% ( 68) | 53% (38) | 77% (35) | 63% (141) |
| 1850s | 62 ( 16) | 64 (12) | 72 (15) | 66 ( 43) |
| Hot-blast charcoal furnace | | | | |
| 1840s | 66 ( 33) | 80 (22) | 74 (27) | 72 ( 82) |
| 1850s | 60 ( 14) | 70 (18) | 64 (12) | 66 ( 44) |
| Anthracite blast furnace | | | | |
| 1840s | 70 ( 11) | 48 (13) | 74 (22) | 66 ( 46) |
| 1850s | 81 ( 19) | 75 (21) | 82 (37) | 80 ( 77) |
| All furnaces | | | | |
| 1840s | 65% (112) | 57% (73) | 74% (84) | 66% (269) |
| 1850s | 69% ( 49) | 71% (51) | 79% (64) | 75% (164) |

Sources: Figures for the 1840s are derived from "Documents Relating to the Manufacture of Iron in Pennsylvania,"
tables following p. 72; figures for the 1850s are derived from Lesley, The Iron Manufacturer's Guide, pp. 6–109.
Note: Figures in parentheses denote number of furnaces. In the case of the 1850s, the reader should note that the
numbers of furnaces denote only those for which complete data are available.

The pig-iron producers who benefited most from the healthier business climate of the mid-1850s were those — particularly companies — who operated anthracite (and to a degree, coke) blast furnaces. As was suggested earlier, the larger capacities of these furnaces and their consequently higher levels of capitalization meant that anthracite-furnace owners did well only when they could operate their facilities at near-capacity levels. This was so because of the more demanding amortization schedule for anthracite furnaces than for the much smaller charcoal furnaces. The major reasons for the ascendancy of the anthracite furnace and the concomitant move away from the charcoal furnace were the greater capacity and cost efficiency of the anthracite model and the growing demand for anthracite pig iron, due to improved quality, by industrial consumers, including rolling mills that made rails.[7]

We might expect to find that the significant increases in the physical scale of production and the proliferation of the company form of business organization were accompanied by a growing degree of concentration of the iron industry into fewer hands. Some increase in concentration did in fact occur, but for the most part it was slight and confined to the rolled-iron sector of the industry (see tables 39 and 40). The increased concentration ratio there was a direct result of the larger size and importance of the rail mills and the pattern of ownership among them. This point can be demonstrated by comparing the position of rail mills within the rolled-iron sector during the 1840s with their position in the 1850s. During the mid-1840s the five largest firms (all of which were rail firms and represented 6.5 percent of all rolling-mill firms) accounted for almost 26 percent of the output of all mills. A decade later the five largest rolling-mill firms (again, all were rail firms and together represented 6.1 percent of all firms) produced 33 percent of all mill output. Thus, not only was there a substantial degree of concentration within the rolled-iron sector of the industry during the 1840s but concentration significantly increased in the 1850s.[8]

Output within the rolled-iron sector was also fairly concentrated among non–rail-producing firms during both decades; about 18 percent of such firms produced slightly less than half of all non-rail output. There was, then, virtually no change in the degree of concentration among these firms from one decade to the next. Much the same situation prevailed within the anthracite-pig-iron sector, where the share of total output produced by the top 10 percent and 25 percent of all firms remained all but constant from one decade to the next, at about 38 percent and 58 percent, respectively (see table 39).

The concentration of so much productive capacity in so relatively few entrepreneurial hands was probably a recent development. Certainly, nothing similar had occurred during the eighteenth century or, probably,

TABLE 39

Concentration of Ownership by Largest 10% and 25% of All Firms within the Anthracite-Pig-Iron Sector, 1849 and 1859

| Year | Total Firms | 10% of Firms | 25% of Firms | Total Anthracite Blast Furnaces | Anthracite Blast Furnaces of | | % Anthracite Blast Furnaces | Total Volume (cu. ft.)[a] | Volume (cu. ft.)[a] of | | % Volume[a] |
|---|---|---|---|---|---|---|---|---|---|---|---|
| | | | | | 10% | 25% | | | 10% | 25% | |
| *Largest 10% of Firms* | | | | | | | | | | | |
| 1849 | 38 | 4 | | 54 | 15 | | 27.8% | 225,097 | 83,807 | | 37.2% |
| 1859 | 61 | 6 | | 91 | 22 | | 24.2 | 531,436 | 206,153 | | 38.8 |
| *Largest 25% of Firms* | | | | | | | | | | | |
| 1849 | 38 | | 10 | 54 | | 26 | 48.1 | 225,097 | | 132,204 | 58.7 |
| 1859 | 61 | | 15 | 91 | | 41 | 45.1 | 531,436 | | 309,579 | 58.3 |

*Sources:* Figures for 1849 are derived from "Documents Relating to the Manufacture of Iron in Pennsylvania," tables following p. 72; those for 1859 are derived from Lesley, *The Iron Manufacturer's Guide,* pp. 6-23.

[a] Volume is taken here to be cylindrical; that is, Volume $= \pi r^2 h$, where $r$ = half the diameter of the furnace bosh and $h$ = the stack, or height, of the furnace.

TABLE 40

Concentration of Ownership by Largest 10% and 25% of All Firms within the Rolled-Iron Sector, 1840s and 1850s

| Year | Total Firms | 10% of Firms | 25% of Firms | Total Mills | Mills of | | % Mills | | Total Output (tn.) | Output (tn.) of | | % Output | |
|---|---|---|---|---|---|---|---|---|---|---|---|---|---|
| | | | | | 10% | 25% | 10% | 25% | | 10% | 25% | 10% | 25% |
| Largest 10% of Firms | | | | | | | | | | | | | |
| 1840s | 77 | 8 | 19 | 79 | 9 | | 11.4% | | 162,730 | 58,249 | | 35.8% | |
| 1850s | 82 | 8 | 20 | 87 | 12 | | 13.8 | | 264,776 | 108,852 | | 41.1 | |
| Largest 25% of Firms | | | | | | | | | | | | | |
| 1840s | 77 | | 19 | 79 | | 20 | | 25.3 | 162,730 | | 98,375 | | 60.5 |
| 1850s | 82 | | 20 | 87 | | 24 | | 27.6 | 264,776 | | 176,011 | | 66.5 |

Sources: Figures for the 1840s are derived from "Documents Relating to the Manufacture of Iron in Pennsylvania," tables following p. 72; those for the 1850s are derived from Lesley, *The Iron Manufacturer's Guide*, pp. 229–40, 247–53.

Notes: No date is specified in the first source for the "largest product," given in tons, for each rolling mill. But because this source also gives the actual output in 1849, and because the tabulation of the Pennsylvania iron industry presented follows one given for 1846 (published in 1847), the pertinent years within the 1840s are 1846–49. The second source specifies the year for the output, presumably the largest product, of each mill. The range of years given is 1854 through 1857.

during the first few decades of the nineteenth.[9] The uncertainty on this point stems from the imperfect historical record for those years. The same must be said of the record for the 1830s and early 1840s. The dearth of complete and reliable evidence for this period is particularly unfortunate because in all likelihood these were the years during which significant concentration of ownership began to occur. We know, for example, that a high degree of concentration existed in the anthracite sector almost from its inception in 1840. Of twenty-six firms that by the end of 1845 had built or were erecting thirty-six anthracite blast furnaces with a combined capacity of 104,800 tons, the seven largest firms — 26.9 percent — owned 44.4 percent of the furnaces, with just over 50 percent of the capacity.[10] These figures, although lower than those for 1849 and 1859 (table 39), are close enough to suggest that the anthracite sector was relatively concentrated from the beginning and changed very little in subsequent years.

Where concentration of ownership within the iron industry did take place after 1844, the primary impetus probably came from a small number of firms in the rolled-iron sector. These businesses, including most rail producers, were the integrated mill firms organized during the 1840s and early 1850s.[11] Integrated mills — mills allied through common ownership with a furnace or forge that supplied them with pig iron or blooms — were generally much larger and, as Peter Temin has observed, more successful than nonintegrated mills.[12] The largest of the integrated mills were those geared for the production of rails, although these mills represented only a fraction of the total number of integrated mills.

Because of the inherent advantage conferred on a rolling-mill firm by integration — that is, greater control over the quantity and quality of inputs — integration probably improved a firm's chances of surviving changes in market conditions.[13] This was as true of the smaller non-rail-makers as it was of the great rail mills. In fact integration rather than sheer size seems to have been the more important factor in assuring a firm's survival. While about 68 percent of the nineteen largest mill firms in 1849 survived until 1859, more than 77 percent of the thirty-one integrated mill firms in 1849 were still in business a decade later.[14] Even among non-rail mill firms, integration was more important to survival than size. Of the thirteen largest non-rail firms active in 1849, about 62 percent were still active ten years later; of twenty-five non-rail integrated firms in 1849, 76 percent were still in business in 1859.

Backward integration clearly improved a rolling-mill firm's chances in the market. The guarantee of sufficient quantities of pigs or blooms of suitable quality to feed the mill's furnaces facilitated the efforts of the firm's owners to respond to changing market conditions. Obviously, firms that could meet most of their requirements for pigs or blooms through their own allied furnaces or forges had more overall control over their

TABLE 41

Production of Integrated and Independent Rolling Mills in Pennsylvania in 1849, by Region

| Mean of | Western Region[a] | | Eastern Region[b] | |
|---|---|---|---|---|
| | Integrated Mills (3) | Independent Mills (3) | Integrated Mills (5) | Independent Mills (6) |
| Tons of output per worker | 14.4 tn. | 8.1 tn. | 33.6 tn. | 26.3 tn. |
| Bushels of coal per ton | 124.5 bu. | 172.0 bu. | 28.8 bu. | 51.3 bu. |
| Number of workers | 113 | 103 | 17.8 | 22.3 |
| % survival to 1859 | 33–67% | 33% | 80% | 67% |

Source: "Documents Relating to the Manufacture of Iron in Pennsylvania," tables following p. 72.
[a] Assorted products: bar, rod, sheet, plate, hoops, nails; fuel: bituminous coal.
[b] Products: boiler and flue iron; fuel: bituminous coal.

operations than did firms dependent upon independent suppliers.[15] We might suspect that greater control over supply would have led to an increase in the efficiency with which rolling mills made their products. Peter Temin concludes otherwise: "There were not yet [by the mid-1850s] any large technical economies from integration."[16] The production data for integrated and independent rolling mills in eastern and western Pennsylvania in 1849, however, indicate that integration was more important than Temin believed (see table 41). Although the number of firms is too small for the results to be considered conclusive, the consistency of the figures for output per worker and fuel consumption per ton argue strongly for a relationship between integration and production efficiency. Generally, the more efficient firms should have had a better chance of surviving the volatile markets of the 1840s and 1850s, a conjecture lent some support by the survival rates in table 41.

The benefits arising from backward integration — greater administrative control and production efficiency — probably encouraged rolling-mill firms able to raise the required additional capital to build or acquire furnaces and forges. By 1849 thirty-one firms (40 percent of all mill firms) had done so. Ten years later thirty-two firms, or 39 percent of the total number, were integrated establishments.[17] One effect of this high degree of integration was a concentration of ownership of the industry's physical plant among integrated mill firms (see table 42). Moreover, the share of ownership in the hands of these firms increased from 1849 to 1859 within every sector of the industry except the anthracite sector. There, despite a small increase in the actual number of furnaces owned by integrated mill firms, the latter's relative share decreased.

Despite this decline, the concentration of ownership by integrated mill firms within the anthracite sector was more important than their holdings

TABLE 42

Concentration of Ownership by Integrated Mill Firms, 1849 and 1859

|  | 1849 | 1859 |
|---|---|---|
| Number of integrated mill firms | 31 | 32 |
| Number of mill firms | 77 | 82 |
| Total number of all firms | 350 | 372 |
| Integrated mill firms as % of all mill firms | 40.3% | 39.0% |
| Integrated mill firms as % of all firms | 8.9% | 8.6% |
| Total number of charcoal furnaces | 228 | 143 |
| % owned | 9.2% | 14.7% |
| Total number of anthracite furnaces | 55 | 91 |
| % owned | 23.6% | 19.8% |
| Total number of other mineral-fuel furnaces | 11 | 16 |
| % owned | 36.4% | 31.3% |
| Total number of forges | 122 | 104 |
| % owned | 19.7% | 22.1% |
| Total number of non-rolling-mill facilities | 416 | 354 |
| % owned | 14.9% | 18.9% |
| Total number of rolling mills | 79 | 87 |
| % owned | 45.6% | 40.2% |
| Total number of all facilities | 495 | 441 |
| % owned | 19.8% | 23.1% |

Sources: Figures for 1849 are derived from "Documents Relating to the Manufacture of Iron in Pennsylvania," tables following p. 72; those for 1859 are derived from Lesley, The Iron Manufacturer's Guide, passim.

within any other part of the industry, apart from the rolled-iron sector itself. The reason was that by the mid-1850s the anthracite furnaces produced by far the majority of all pig iron made in Pennsylvania.[18] Thus, the ownership of a substantial proportion of these furnaces and an even larger proportion of their total capacity had significant ramifications for the integrated mill firms, the pig-iron sector of the industry, and the iron industry as a whole. The degree to which anthracite-furnace capacity was concentrated in the hands of the integrated mill firms, especially the rail producers, is evident in table 43. In addition to capacity, three other measures of furnace output — cubic feet of furnace volume, largest recorded product (tons), and total actual output (tons) in 1849 — are used to compute the degree of concentration of ownership. All four measures of concentration support the conclusion that a sizable share of the anthracite sector was controlled by a numerically small but highly powerful group of integrated firms.

With so much furnace capacity owned by so few integrated firms (which generally built or acquired the largest furnaces), the output of pig iron in any given year was in great part determined by the needs of these mills.

TABLE 43

Share of Anthracite-Blast-Furnace Capacity Owned by Integrated Rolling-Mill Firms, 1840s and 1850s

| Measure | 1840s | 1850s |
|---|---|---|
| | *All Firms* | |
| Capacity, 1849, 1859[a] | 221,400 tn. (55; 100%) | 222,635 tn. (46; 51%) |
| Volume, 1849, 1859[b] | 225,097 cu. ft. (54; 98%) | 531,436 cu. ft. (91; 100%) |
| Largest product[c] | 147,279 tn. (47; 85%) | 324,222 tn. (77; 85%) |
| Total output, 1849, 1856 | 109,168 tn. (53; 96%) | 129,281 tn. (32; 35%) |
| | *All Integrated Mill Firms* | |
| % total capacity | 25.3% | 26.9% |
| % total volume | 26.3 | 24.3 |
| % total largest product | 27.0 | 21.8 |
| % total output, 1849, 1856 | 26.2 | 22.1 |
| | *Integrated Rail Mill Firms* | |
| % total capacity | 20.3% | 18.5% |
| % total volume | 22.2 | 16.8 |
| % total largest product | 22.1 | 14.4 |
| % total output, 1849, 1856 | 19.9 | 9.5 |
| | *Integrated Non-Rail Mill Firms* | |
| % total capacity | 5.0% | 8.4% |
| % total volume | 4.1 | 7.5 |
| % total largest product | 4.8 | 7.3 |
| % total output, 1849, 1856 | 6.3 | 12.6 |

*Sources:* Figures for the 1840s are derived from "Documents Relating to the Manufacture of Iron in Pennsylvania," tables following p. 72; those for the 1850s are derived from Lesley, *The Iron Manufacturer's Guide*, pp. 6–23, 229–40, 247–53.

*Note:* Numbers in parentheses are (1) the number of blast furnaces for which data are available and (2) the percentage of all listed blast furnaces.

[a] Capacity figures for 1849 represent the total of the rated capacities given in the source for the 1840s. Those for 1859 are totals of values computed from, in the source for the 1850s, two numbers given for each of the 46 furnaces: the output in a particular year and the number of weeks during that year in which the furnace was in blast. Thus, Capacity = 52(output / weeks in blast).

[b] Volume is computed as in table 39.

[c] Largest product was the largest output recorded during a period of years within each decade. For the 1840s the period was probably 1846–49; for the 1850s it was 1854–57.

Their interest in the construction of new, larger furnaces during the 1840s and the first half of the 1850s pushed existing furnace technology to its engineering limits, thereby setting the standard and the pace for furnace construction and performance for other anthracite-pig-iron producers.[19] This largely explains the rapidity with which concentration of ownership within the anthracite sector occurred before 1850. It probably also helps to explain the rapidity with which the mean size of newly constructed anthracite blast furnaces increased from 1844 through 1855 and the subsequent decrease in new furnace sizes from 1855 through 1857 (see table 44). Ultimately, the needs of the integrated mill firms for additional furnace capacity were determined by the level of demand for rolled iron. For the

TABLE 44
Mean Size of New Anthracite Blast Furnaces, 1844-57

| Year | Number | Volume (cu. ft.) | Capacity (gross tons) |
|------|--------|------------------|-----------------------|
| 1844 | 3      | 3,154            | 3,333                 |
| 1845 | 10     | 3,993            | 4,015                 |
| 1846 | 7      | 4,776            | 4,457                 |
| 1847 | 6      | 3,678            | 3,883                 |
| 1848 | 5      | 4,758            | 3,900                 |
| 1849 | 3      | 4,454            | 3,600                 |
| 1850 | 7      | 7,858            | 6,612 (6)             |
| 1851 | 1      | 6,154            | 5,054                 |
| 1852 | 2      | 10,626           | 5,832                 |
| 1853 | 9      | 5,705            | 4,343 (6)             |
| 1854 | 11     | 6,326            | 4,407 (8)             |
| 1855 | 11     | 7,479            | 4,536 (8)             |
| 1856 | 5      | 4,538            | 3,712                 |
| 1857 | 3      | 4,245            | 3,661 (2)             |

Sources: Figures for 1844-49 are derived from "Documents Relating to the Manufacture of Iron in Pennsylvania," tables following p. 72; those for 1850-57 are derived from Lesley, The Iron Manufacturer's Guide, pp. 6-23.

Note: Numbers in parentheses indicate the number of furnaces for which capacity data are available. The absence of a number in parentheses indicates that the number of furnaces for which capacity is known is equal to the total number constructed.

rail firms, this meant of course the demand for rails and other forms of railroad iron by the several railroad corporations that undertook massive construction projects to initiate or extend their lines during the 1840s and 1850s.

Because railroad construction consumed substantial quantities of iron, foreign and domestic, the extent of the demand for iron products by the railroad and the significance of that demand for the growth of the American iron industry have figured prominently in the historical debate over the role of the railroad in spurring economic growth in the United States before 1860. The railroad industry was, according to Walt W. Rostow, the "leading sector" of the ante-bellum economy by virtue of its high rate of capital investment, its rapid growth, and its demand for a sizable proportion of the output of heavy industries, particularly the iron industry. Presumably, the railroad's demand was crucial to the iron industry, stimulating its growth to new heights between 1843 and 1860, the period during which the economy entered upon rapid and sustained growth.[20]

Robert Fogel and Albert Fishlow, in their respective studies of the railroad's role in the nineteenth-century American economy, concluded that Rostow had very much overstated his case. The railroad's demand for domestically produced rails and other forms of iron, they said, was not negligible, but it was hardly extensive or decisive in the iron industry's growth before the Civil War. Fogel, who was particularly forceful in rejecting Rostow's claim, concluded that the demand for iron nails was even more important than the demand for rails: "One could just as well argue that nails rather than rails triggered the 1845–49 leap in iron production. Indeed in 1849 the domestic production of nails probably exceeded that of rails by over 100 per cent."[21]

My own findings concerning the importance of railroad-generated demand for iron products in part corroborate and in part contradict those of Fogel and Fishlow. In aggregate, quantitative terms it appears that Rostow's critics were correct. There was, for example, no significant relationship between furnace volume or capacity on the one hand and railroad construction activity or gross investment on the other.[22] Moreover, railroad-derived demand for Pennsylvania iron in 1849 was not especially large, amounting to at most about 12 percent of the total product from the state's furnaces that year (see table 45).[23] No doubt this figure would have been higher had the end of the English railroad boom not occurred in 1848, just in time to permit English rail mills and other railroad-iron producers to take full advantage of the lower rates of the 1846 tariff and dump their iron on the American market.[24] But the railroads' share of the total demand for Pennsylvania's iron in the absence of cheap English iron probably would not have been very much higher than its actual level. Even at the end of the 1850s, aggregate railroad demand for the nation's pig-iron output amounted to about 15–21 percent.[25]

Still, the railroad exerted a significant influence on the industry's development by virtue of having stimulated concentration of ownership and backward integration among the rail mill firms.[26] Whether the railroad stimulated integration and concentration among non-rail mill firms is less certain. There were, as we have seen, definite advantages to integration, and these may well have been sufficient incentive for the non-rail firms to integrate their operations. Additional incentive may have come, however, from the rail mills by way of example and, more to the point, by way of competition. Although almost all rail mills in the 1840s and 1850s produced rails to the exclusion of other products, some were also geared for the production of other forms of railroad iron and non-railroad iron. For example, the integrated rail firm of Reeves, Buck & Company (the Phoenix Iron Company, Inc., as of 1855), of Phoenixville in Chester County, produced rails and other forms of railroad iron but also bar and sheet. The mill geared for bar and sheet produced them very efficiently — in fact, 60 percent more efficiently in terms of output per worker and 47 percent more efficiently in terms of fuel consumption than its most efficient competitor.[27]

Because greater efficiency permitted the charging of lower unit prices, integrated rail firms whose activities spilled over into other product lines could undersell their nonintegrated competitors, and this may have

TABLE 45
Railroad-Derived Demand for Pennsylvania Pig Iron, 1849

| Pig-Iron Production | Based on Largest Product | | Based on 1849 Output |
|---|---|---|---|
| *Output* | | | |
| Total | 374,753 | | 257,996 |
| Of integrated rail mills | 32,604 | | 21,672 |
| Of integrated non-rail mills | 44,595 | | 28,895 |
| Of independent producers | 297,554 | | 207,429 |
| *Gross consumption*[a] | | | |
| By integrated rail mills | | 42,397 | |
| By integrated non-rail mills | | 37,055 | |
| By independent rail mills | | 3,800 | |
| *Net consumption*[b] | | | |
| By integrated rail mills | 9,793 | | 20,725 |
| By integrated non-rail mills | 7,540 | | 8,160 |
| By all rail mills | 13,593 | | 24,525 |
| *Rail-mill net consumption as* | | | |
| % of total output | 6.5% | | 9.5% |
| % of output of non-rail-mills and independent furnaces | 4.0% | | 10.4% |
| % of independent-furnace output | 4.6% | | 11.8% |

*Source:* Derived from "Documents Relating to the Manufacture of Iron in Pennsylvania," tables following p. 72.
*Note:* All quantities are in gross, or long, tons: 1 ton = 2,240 lbs.
[a] The source is not clear concerning the dating of gross consumption, i.e., whether the tons of pig iron consumed refer to output in 1849 or to largest product.
[b] Net consumption of integrated rolling-mill firms is equal to their gross consumption *minus* the production of pig iron at their allied furnaces.

induced some of the latter to integrate. It seems likely that some of the integration among non-rail firms came about in this fashion — that is, as a response, however indirect, to the influence of the railroad. In any case, we know that in 1859, of twenty-two integrated non-rail mill firms that had existed as either integrated or independent establishments in 1849 six had been independent concerns at the earlier date.[28]

On balance, the verdict on the railroad's influence on the growth of the Pennsylvania iron industry before 1860 rests on the standard — qualitative or quantitative — one employs. To limit the search for the effects of the railroad's demand for iron to the realm of the purely quantitative is to miss the important structural and technological changes that the railroad induced within the iron industry. The integrated mill firms, particularly the rail firms among them, of the ante-bellum years emerged from the Civil War as the major element of a highly concentrated and integrated iron and steel industry. As such, they were, in Harold Livesay's words, "the precursors, indeed, often the direct antecedents of the modern, giant, integrated iron and steel firms." [29] These were the companies that came to dominate the industry during the postwar decades, when iron and steel played a central role in America's industrialization.

Yet, we must obviously look beyond the railroad for an explanation of *most* of the iron industry's growth in output and capacity, especially if we wish to understand the behavior of the pig-iron sector, including the fluctuations in the number and size of anthracite blast furnaces during the 1840s and 1850s. As was suggested before, the interests of the integrated mill firms in anthracite-furnace construction accounted for only some of this fluctuation, and other factors were primarily responsible. We can now pursue this point, looking in particular at the influence of the availability of capital and the general business climate. Although these two and the health of the iron industry were often intimately related, there were times, notably at the end of the 1840s, when depressed business conditions within the iron industry did not reflect conditions within the larger economy and therefore were unrelated to the overall demand for and supply of capital.

What we first need to explore is the manner in which the annual fluctuation in the mean size (and therefore in the level of capitalization) of newly constructed anthracite blast furnaces was related to the health of the regional or national economy; that is, were furnaces constructed during upswings in the economy larger than those constructed during downswings? Put more narrowly, did fluctuations in furnace size reflect conditions in the capital markets, and did furnace size increase with the demand for money, as indicated by interest rates? The primary assumption made here is that anthracite-furnace construction was financed largely with borrowed funds. Although direct evidence for this assumption is scarce, the level of capitalization necessary to construct an anthracite furnace — an average of fifty-five thousand dollars in 1850 — suggests that few if any furnace owners could have had any alternative to substantial borrowing. [30] While we lack an extensive set of data on interest rates charged for loan money in this period, we can use as a proxy the monthly record of the discount rate on commercial paper in New York and Boston. [31]

Generally, a moderate rise in the discount rate within its average range of between 5 percent and 10 percent during the 1840s and 1850s meant that the demand for money and specifically credit had increased. Such rises were an indication of more vigorous business activity. [32] To meet a heightened demand for short-term credit, New York banks (then the nation's most important financial institutions) normally expanded their issuance of notes, using as collateral not only their deposits of specie but also securities. The use of the latter to collateralize commercial paper had been sanctioned in 1838 by the New York State free banking law. [33]

So long as the level of business activity and foreign investment in the

United States increased, banks that had issued large amounts of notes — always well in excess of their specie reserves — were in no danger. However, a sharp decline in securities prices, which in those volatile decades could have any number of causes, could leave these banks in a dangerously exposed position. Moreover, a downturn in the business cycle could result in a rush by holders of the notes to convert them into specie. At such times the banks raised the discount rate on their notes sharply in an attempt to preserve their specie holdings.[34] The resultant soaring of the discount rate to "crisis" levels, such as occurred in 1848 and in the fall of the panic year of 1857, reflected a loss of confidence in bank-issued commercial paper and, fundamentally, in the business outlook for the immediate future. Although we do not need to concern ourselves here with the sources of each rise and fall in the discount rate, the general pattern of its fluctuation and the instances of exceptionally high rates should be borne in mind as we examine the relationship between these rates and furnace size.

The discount rate on commercial paper was of course related to the general health of the economy. It was usually the last indicator of the direction of business activity, after stock prices and commodity prices, to signal either recession or recovery.[35] Because all three indicators moved in the same direction, the plunge of the economy into a depression was indicated, belatedly (after a lag of from one to two months), by a collapse of the discount rate. Thus, although credit was considerably cheaper when the discount rate plunged and remained abnormally low (below 5 percent or 6 percent), those should have been precisely the times when someone who planned to build a furnace had the least reason to borrow the substantial sums necessary to construct a large one. Looking to the short term, there would have been little point — and much risk — in the construction of a furnace of six thousand cubic feet if, because of slack demand, its owner could operate it at only 50 percent or 60 percent of capacity. The more prudent course would have been to borrow a lesser sum, build a smaller furnace, and operate it at a higher proportion of its capacity, thereby being able to amortize its cost more quickly.

It would be unreasonable to suppose that the decision to build a furnace and the borrowing of money to finance its construction occurred during the same year in which the furnace was completed and put into blast. The erection of a furnace required considerable time, and anthracite furnaces, larger than any other type of furnace, took even longer. Thus, of thirty-six anthracite furnaces reported by the Iron and Coal Association of Pennsylvania in the spring or summer of 1846, eight were listed as "Erecting," that is unfinished. The remaining twenty-eight had been completed between 1842 and mid-1845. Similarly, three of six furnaces reported for 1850 were unfinished at the beginning of the year, and one of the remaining three had not been put into blast.[36] In the absence of information giv-

TABLE 46

Annual Anthracite-Blast-Furnace Construction in Year$_t$ and the Annual
Percentage Discount Rate in Year$_{t-1}$, 1840–57

| Year (t) | Number of Furnaces (t) | Mean Volume (t) | Mean % Rate (t − 1) |
|---|---|---|---|
| 1840 | 3 | 2,597 | 13.22% |
| 1841 | 0 | — [a] | 7.69 |
| 1842 | 4 | 4,427 | 6.77 |
| 1843 | 0 | — [a] | 8.15 |
| 1844 | 3 | 3,154 | 4.43 |
| 1845 | 10 | 3,993 | 4.83 |
| 1846 | 7 | 4,776 | 6.03 |
| 1847 | 6 | 3,678 | 8.35 |
| 1848 | 5 | 4,758 | 9.54 |
| 1849 | 3 | 4,454 | 15.13 |
| 1850 | 7 | 7,858 [b] | 10.08 |
| 1851 | 1 | 6,154 | 8.02 |
| 1852 | 2 | 10,626 | 9.69 |
| 1853 | 9 | 5,705 | 6.42 |
| 1854 | 11 | 6,326 | 10.22 |
| 1855 | 11 | 7,479 | 10.38 |
| 1856 | 5 | 4,538 | 8.96 |
| 1857 | 3 | 4,245 | 8.92 |

Sources: The number of furnaces and their mean annual volume for the period 1840–49 are derived from "Documents Relating to the Manufacture of Iron in Pennsylvania," tables following p. 72; the corresponding data for the period 1850–57 are derived from Lesley, The Iron Manufacturer's Guide, pp. 6–23. The mean annual percentage discount rate is computed from the monthly rates given in Walter Buckingham Smith and Arthur Harrison Cole, Fluctuations in American Business, 1790–1860 (Cambridge, Mass.: Harvard University Press, 1935), pp. 192–94.

[a] No furnace construction was reported in the source, so the years are excluded from the statistical operations.

[b] The ironmasters' report of December 1849 listed 6 furnaces for 1850, of which 2 had not yet been completed, 1 was not in blast, and 3 were in blast. The mean of their volumes is 6,276 cubic feet. This value is not used in the table, however, because the report from which it is derived obviously did not report on furnace construction completed after the first part of the year. The value for 1850 used in the table is probably too high. If anything, this makes the test of the hypothesis even more rigorous.

ing the month and year when construction began and the month of the year of completion, we can only speculate about the actual construction time for an anthracite furnace. A year does not seem an unreasonably long time for construction. To be cautious, however, we will assume that a one-year interval separated the projection and financing of a furnace from the completion of a furnace and its first blast. Thus, in testing the hypothesis outlined above, mean furnace size is lagged one year behind the mean annual discount rate.

The data necessary to test the hypothesis are presented in table 46 and are plotted in figure 12. As is readily apparent from inspection of the data, there are two anomalous years, 1840 and 1849. In each instance mean furnace volume is considerably lower than what might be expected. The underlying reason for the anomaly in 1849 (as discussed above) was the depressed conditions in the iron industry following the reduction of rates by the tariff of 1846 and the subsequent dumping of low-priced English iron on the American market. Although rail firms in the United States

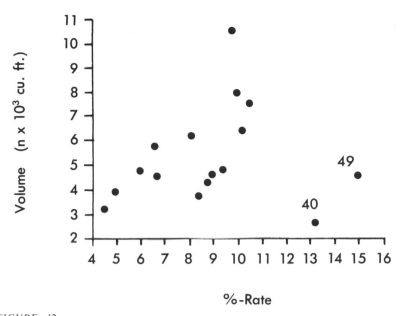

FIGURE  12

MEAN ANNUAL VOLUME$_t$ OF ANTHRACITE BLAST FURNACES, 1840-57, BY MEAN ANNUAL PERCENTAGE RATE$_{t-1}$

The mean annual volume for the period 1840-49 is derived from "Documents Relating to the Manufacture of Iron in Pennsylvania," tables following p. 72; the corresponding data for the period 1850-57 are derived from Lesley, *The Iron Manufacturer's Guide*, pp. 6-23. The mean annual discount rate is computed from the monthly rates given in Smith and Cole, *Fluctuations in American Business*, pp. 192-94.

were very badly hurt by this competition from abroad, pig-iron producers also suffered acutely. The share of imported crude iron (pig and scrap) in the U.S. market increased from 5.3 percent in 1847 to 10.7 percent in 1848. Over the same time, the market share of foreign rails grew from 32 percent to 52 percent.[37] Thus, foreign producers displaced U.S. furnace operators from an increasingly large part of the latter's immediate and ultimate domestic markets. American pig-iron producers, Pennsylvanians among them, who bemoaned the sorry state of their industry in 1848 had sound reasons for pessimism and caution regarding the future.[38]

Compounding their woes of that year was the behavior of the discount rate, which at the end of 1847 had quickly climbed above 15 percent and remained at or near that level for all of 1848. Although this surge may have affected only banks in New York City, the high cost of borrowing money there must have pinched the already depressed Pennsylvania iron industry. While the major reason for the anomalous data for 1849 was doubtless the change in the tariff rate and the ensuing imports, the high discount rate clearly magnified the producers' problems.

The sources of the anomaly in 1840 were quite different from and less ambiguous than those responsible for the events of 1848 and 1849. The most important reason for the small mean size of the furnaces built that year is that the anthracite furnace was first introduced in Pennsylvania in 1840. The initial models were apparently constructed on a scale closer to that of the more familiar hot-blast charcoal furnace, introduced five years earlier. In subsequent years, however, after these experiments had been successful, producers gradually built larger and larger furnaces. Mean volume never again dropped below three thousand cubic feet, not even during the misfortunes of the late forties, which reinforces the conclusion that the value for 1840 reflects the initial phase of trying out a novel furnace design. Again, however, the behavior of the discount rate in 1839 (the year during which the financing of furnace construction for 1840 presumably would have been arranged) could also have contributed to this result. Eighteen-forty was the first full year of a severe general depression that, despite occasional improvements in the economy, lasted until the end of 1843. The discount rate, which had averaged 7.75 percent during the first half of 1839, shot upward (the annual average rate went up to 13.22 percent). With rates hitting 18 percent, 20 percent, and even 36 percent in the fall, few borrowers were going to contract debts for any purpose – including investment.

Thus, the unusual values for mean furnace volume in 1840 and 1849 reflected the influence of readily identifiable and unique factors. After 1840 the anthracite furnace was no longer a novelty. Also, the reduced rates of the tariff of 1846 held sway until 1858. The bubble of the English railway mania burst only once – in 1848. And although after 1848 the discount rate reached "crisis" levels one time, the latter occasion was the panic of 1857, a general economic dislocation.

All of the foregoing argues for special treatment of the data for 1840 and 1849. In principle, sophisticated procedures can be used to adjust them and therefore minimize the influences of the factors identified above. However, the additional data necessary for such an operation do not exist. In any event, a simpler and, admittedly, coarser method can be employed. If a strong relationship between the mean furnace volume of one year and the discount rate of the preceding year exists, the extent to which the anomalous values for 1840 and 1849 obscure it can be determined by their progressive exclusion from a series of correlations. This is the procedure used here; the results are presented in table 47.

On balance, the results in table 47 support the hypothesis of a relationship between furnace size and movements in the capital markets. More generally, however, the relationship identified is between the scale of furnace construction and conditions in the larger economy. Thus, the size of new furnaces tended to increase with upswings of the business cycle and to

TABLE 47

Anthracite-Blast-Furnace Volume and the Percentage Discount Rate, 1840–57

| Run | Values Excluded | Correlation[a] Coefficient, r | $r^2$ | Significance[b] |
|---|---|---|---|---|
| | | *Correlation with Volume as Given in Source* | | |
| 1 | none | 0.1377 | 0.019 | 0.306 |
| 2 | 1840 | 0.3355 | 0.1126 | 0.111 |
| 3 | 1840 & 1849 | 0.6037 | 0.3644 | 0.011 |
| | | *Correlation with Volume Linearized by $\log_{10}$ (volume)[c]* | | |
| 1 | none | 0.0967 | 0.0094 | 0.361 |
| 2 | 1840 | 0.3764 | 0.1412 | 0.083 |
| 3 | 1840 & 1849 | 0.6491 | 0.4213 | 0.006 |

[a] Pearson product moment correlation. The coefficient ranges between $-1.0$ through 0 to $+1.0$. The general form of the equation used to compute $r$ is:

$$r = \frac{n\Sigma xy - \Sigma x \Sigma y}{\{[n\Sigma x^2 - (\Sigma x)^2][n\Sigma y^2 - (\Sigma y)^2]\}^{1/2}},$$

where $n$ = number of pairs of values, or points; $x$ = % discount rate; and $y$ = mean furnace size.

[b] Significance is usually expressed in terms of the level of confidence that one can have that the value of $r$ cannot be equaled or exceeded by a purely random pairing of values. Thus, a value for $r$ significant at the 0.100 level of confidence means that the chances are 1 in 10 that the relationship measured by $r$ is a spurious one. A confidence level of 0.05 indicates that the chances are 1 in 20; at the level of 0.01 the chances are 1 in 100. A confidence level of 0.05 is usually considered a strong indication that a hypothesized relationship between 2 variables does indeed exist.

[c] Because the plot of the points suggests a nonlinear relationship between the variables, and because Pearson's $r$ is a linear coefficient of correlation, $r$ has a lower value than is warranted. By taking the logarithm of mean annual volume, the influence of the nonlinear character of the relationship can be minimized. The linear transformation only slightly alters the equation to compute $r$:

$$r = \frac{n\Sigma x \log y - \Sigma x \Sigma \log y}{\{[n\Sigma x^2 - (\Sigma x)^2][n\Sigma (\log y)^2 - (\Sigma \log y)^2]\}^{1/2}}$$

decrease on the downturn. In this regard, the iron producers were following a well-established course. From the colonial period on, they had navigated deep and often troubled waters, attempting to minimize the risks inherent in their business. They had the good sense to make their decisions about furnace construction and pig-iron production with a careful eye to the changes taking place in the iron markets and in the larger economy. That is what they were doing in the 1840s and 1850s.

These results also help us to see how the rate at which technological innovations spread within the iron industry was related to market forces. Although the larger anthracite furnaces operated on the same principles as the smaller models, the difference in scale between the two was a significant technological distinction. But as the furnace builders realized, the larger furnaces were more efficient in terms of total unit costs (including amortization of capital costs) only when they operated at or near capacity. Their advantage quickly dissipated when the demand for iron was small. At such times operating levels did not approach capacity, and total costs per unit of output rose. While smaller furnaces were not as cost-efficient, they did enjoy a higher level of engineering efficiency, that is, more output per cubic foot of furnace volume (see table 48). During periods of low

TABLE 48

Engineering Efficiency of Anthracite Blast Furnaces, 1840–50, by Volume

| Volume[a] | Number | Total Capacity[b] | Total Volume[a] | Mean Efficiency[c] |
|---|---|---|---|---|
| Under 2,000 | 9 | 19,000 | 11,132 | 1.71 |
| 2,001–3,000 | 6 | 17,700 | 14,288 | 1.24 |
| 3,001–4,000 | 9 | 37,950 | 33,381 | 1.14 |
| 4,001–5,000 | 7 | 28,200 | 30,986 | 0.91 |
| 5,001–6,000 | 14 | 65,000 | 76,225 | 0.85 |
| 6,001–7,000 | 2 | 9,000 | 13,386 | 0.67 |
| 7,001–10,000 | 0 | | | |
| Over 10,000 | 3 | 23,200 | 30,557 | 0.76 |

Source: "Documents Relating to the Manufacture of Iron in Pennsylvania," tables following p. 72.
[a] Volume is given in cubic feet and is computed as $\pi r^2 h$.
[b] Capacity is given in gross tons (2,240 pounds per ton).
[c] Efficiency is measured in terms of tons of capacity per cubic foot of volume.

demand, when average furnace output might be limited to four thousand tons, the furnace with a capacity of five thousand tons might actually do better than one with a six-thousand- or seven-thousand-ton capacity. The five-thousand-ton furnace not only carried lower capital costs but also could achieve a higher level of operating efficiency.[39] Considerations such as these seem to have inhibited the adoption of the very large furnace. In the absence of the assured demand for its tremendous output that would be supplied by the railroad after the Civil War, pig-iron producers chose to minimize their risk and maximize their resources by building smaller furnaces. Much the same point can be made with respect to the construction of charcoal blast furnaces during the 1830s and 1840s.

While, as we have seen, a modern, integrated corporate sector of producers developed in ante-bellum Pennsylvania, it did so within an industry much of which remained wedded to traditional furnace design. As late as 1850 most pig-iron producers were still using a traditional production technology, despite the availability of more efficient new technology — the anthracite, coke, and bituminous furnaces. We can account for the failure of most established pig-iron producers to convert or replace their charcoal blast furnaces by noting the considerable expense involved in conversion and replacement. More difficult to explain, however, is the new construction of cold-blast furnaces after the introduction of the hot-blast design and the continued construction of both cold- and hot-blast charcoal furnaces after 1840, when the anthracite design became available.

The reasons for the behavior of the western branch of the industry in this regard are less obscure than those that governed the behavior of eastern pig-iron producers. Louis C. Hunter first addressed this question in 1929, and Peter Temin further clarified the matter some time later.[40] Hunter attributed the rejection of coke fuel as a substitute for charcoal

TABLE 49

Charcoal-Blast-Furnace Construction and the Percentage Discount Rate, 1832–49

| Year | Cold-Blast Charcoal Furnaces | | Hot-Blast Charcoal Furnaces | | Cold- and Hot-Blast Charcoal Furnaces | | |
|------|--------|--------|--------|--------|--------|--------|--------|
| | Number | Mean Capacity (gross tons) | Number | Mean Capacity (gross tons) | Number | Mean Capacity (gross tons) | Mean Annual Rate (%) |
| 1832 | 4 | 1,158 | 4 | 1,450 | 8 | 1,304 | 6.25% |
| 1833 | 4 | 1,338 | 1 | (1,450) | 5 | 1,360 | 7.83 |
| 1834 | 2 | 1,075 | 2 | 2,030 | 4 | 1,553 | 14.50 |
| 1835 | 9 | 1,167 | 1 | (1,200) | 10 | 1,170 | 7.00 |
| 1836 | 4 | 1,140 | 4 | 1,538 | 8 | 1,339 | 18.42 |
| 1837 | 2 | 900 | 7 | 1,545 | 9 | 1,402 | 14.18 |
| 1838 | 4 | 1,050 | 4 | 1,300 | 8 | 1,175 | 9.03 |
| 1839 | 1 | (1,350) | 3 | 1,600 | 4 | 1,538 | 13.22 |
| 1840 | 2 | 950 | 1 | (1,000) | 3 | 967 | 7.69 |
| 1841 | 2 | 1,225 | 1 | (1,200) | 3 | 1,217 | 6.77 |
| 1842 | 6 | 1,267 | 2 | 2,000 | 8 | 1,450 | 8.15 |
| 1843 | 5 | 1,160 | 0 | – | 5 | 1,160 | 4.43 |
| 1844 | 12 | 1,108 | 1 | (1,800) | 13 | 1,162 | 4.83 |
| 1845 | 13 | 1,302 | 2 | 1,500 | 15 | 1,328 | 6.03 |
| 1846 | 15 | 1,187 | 15 | 1,560 | 30 | 1,373 | 8.35 |
| 1847 | 11 | 1,227 | 1 | (1,800) | 12 | 1,275 | 9.54 |
| 1848 | 3 | 1,200 | 3 | 1,800 | 6 | 1,500 | 15.13 |
| 1849 | 1 | (800) | 1 | (1,800) | 2 | 1,300 | 10.08 |

Sources: Furnace capacities are derived from "Documents Relating to the Manufacture of Iron in Pennsylvania," tables following p. 72; for the discount rate see table 46.

Note: Figures in parentheses are single-furnace values and not means.

(anthracite coal being largely confined to the eastern part of the state) by western furnace operators to their sound understanding of the nature of the demand for their product.[41] Temin considered Hunter's explanation in detail and ultimately found it wanting. For Temin, the most important reason for western pig-iron producers' refusal to abandon charcoal for coke, and therefore smaller furnaces for larger ones (despite the greater efficiency of coke furnaces), was the inferior quality of coke-smelted iron. Pig iron made with anthracite, Temin noted, did not suffer in a comparison with charcoal pig iron.[42] Temin's explanation answers very well for western Pennsylvania, although for reasons explored below, it may not be completely satisfactory.

The producer's decision about furnace design was clearly shaped by considerations other than which fuel to use. He was also making decisions about output rates, decisions made with an awareness of both short- and long-term conditions in the iron markets and in the larger economy as well. Because a furnace's output capacity was a function of its volume, a producer's decision to erect a furnace of a particular size — that is, of a certain width of bosh and height of stack — was also a decision about his future scale of production.[43] He had thus to consider not simply the amount of capital that he could invest but also the prospects for the iron industry and the general economy. This conclusion is supported by the data in table 49 and figure 13, which chart the construction of cold- and hot-blast charcoal furnaces during the 1830s and 1840s in terms of the numbers of furnaces erected and their mean rated capacities in tons. (In the interest of having a sufficient number of furnaces with which to compute mean values, the figures are not disaggregated with respect to region.) The fluctuation in mean capacity is rather striking and is similar to that of Speedwell Forge's output level and those of iron prices and other economic indicators charted in figure 10. Moreover, a correlation of the mean annual capacity with the discount rate on commercial paper indicates a fairly strong relationship ($r^2$

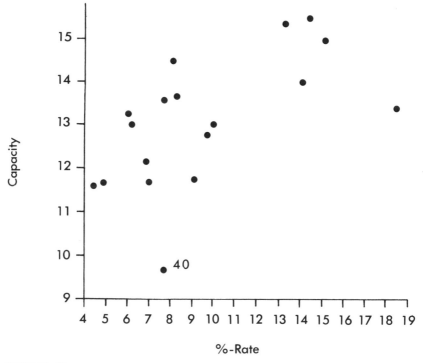

FIGURE  13
MEAN ANNUAL CAPACITY OF CHARCOAL BLAST FURNACES, 1832–49, BY MEAN ANNUAL PERCENTAGE RATE
Capacity is measured in hundreds of tons. The numbers on the vertical scale therefore are to be multiplied by 100. Furnace capacities are derived from "Documents Relating to the Manufacture of Iron in Pennsylvania," tables following p. 72; the discount rate is computed from the monthly rates given in Smith and Cole, *Fluctuations in American Business*, pp. 192–94.

= 0.32, significant at the 0.01 confidence level) between the two, similar to that noted earlier with respect to anthracite furnaces.[44] Variation in the construction size of charcoal furnaces in this period, as in the case of anthracite furnaces during the 1840s and 1850s, was apparently linked closely to short-term movements in the markets.

This relationship helps us to understand the persistence of traditional furnace technology at a time when a newer design — the anthracite furnace — was available. It also helps to account for the persistence of traditional forms of business organization within the iron industry. A charcoal furnace was less expensive to build than an anthracite furnace, and a furnace of whatever type with a fifteen-hundred-ton capacity cost less than one with a capacity of two thousand tons. Thus, the construction of smaller furnaces entailed a level of capitalization well within the reach of an individual or small partnership and did not require the formation of a company. Of fifty-nine furnaces built during the period 1832–49 and in operation in 1850, about 49 percent were owned by individuals, 24 percent by partnerships, and 27 percent by companies.[45] Thus, the persistence of traditional organizational forms probably followed from the persistence of producers in using traditional technologies, a not unreasonable response to a frequently inhospitable economic environment.

# An Industrial Evolution

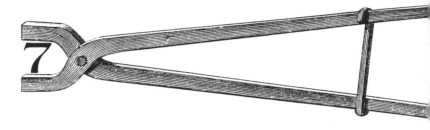

T his book has been about change in a major American industry, but change of a gradual sort. The passage of Pennsylvania iron-making from a small, scattered number of furnace and forge owners to the extensive, complex, and increasingly powerful industry of 1860 was for the most part a transformation by accretion. As we have seen, the technology and business organization of most of the industry in that last ante-bellum year were much as they had been more than a century earlier. Significant changes had of course occurred, notably the rapid growth of output during the 1840s and 1850s that had accompanied the introduction of mineral fuel technology and the appearance of large integrated firms geared to the production of iron for the railroad. But these changes had occurred across a narrow front, and most firms in all branches of the industry continued to trod a long-established path involving only incremental changes in their technology and forms of business organization.

In significant ways, most of the men who owned iron firms in the 1850s were not unlike the businessmen of the 1750s. The markets of 1860, if not quite so mysterious as those of the eighteenth century, still remained essentially beyond the producers' control. Even a cartel like the briefly successful one of 1774–75 would not answer; the rate structure of the tariff and the ever-ready British iron producers guaranteed that a cartel would be a costly and embarrassing failure. And so the market behavior of ante-bellum iron producers in Pennsylvania was such that their fathers and grandfathers would have recognized it as their own. Markets were beasts to be ridden that, like the proverbial tiger, decided when the ride was over. Consequently, the iron producers of nineteenth-century Pennsylvania, unable or at the very least unwilling to confront the problems of demand directly, pursued the only course open to them, that of attempting to

132

improve their individual competitive position by altering the conditions of supply.

During the eighteenth century and in the first decades of the nineteenth the iron industry's static technology effectively prevented significant intensive growth of output — that is, the capital-output ratios in pig- and bar-iron production remained fixed. Increasing competition and a secular decline in prices before the Revolution forced producers to adopt improved management practices with an eye to reducing costs, as at Hopewell Forge, and to maintaining the quality of their products. Despite these pressures on the producers, there was as yet no need for them to expand the scale of their operations by building the bigger furnaces made possible by the introduction of smelting with coke fuel in England. Aggregate demand in Philadelphia and in the hinterland markets was more than adequately met by the industry's extensive growth, that is, by the proliferation in the number of firms and the industry's geographic expansion. Moreover, the technology of the market, especially transportation services, imposed a severe limitation on the geographic range of iron products, thereby confining producers to relatively local, easily satiated centers of demand.

With the growth of Pennsylvania's population and its westward movement across the Susquehanna River and then across the mountains after the Revolution, but especially following the War of 1812, the iron industry continued its extensive growth: aggregate output increased as the number of firms increased, while rates of output per facility remained virtually unchanged from their pre-Revolutionary War levels.

Beginning in the 1820s, aggregate demand and the quality of that demand began to change in response to rapid population growth, improved transportation services — turnpikes and canals — and the introduction of nails and screws for construction. At the same time, except during a brief interregnum from 1825 through 1827, prices for iron products had decreased. Confronted once again by high levels of competition — some of which originated in Great Britain — and falling prices, the drive for intensive growth and increased factor productivity got under way. Thus, the widespread adoption of the hot-blast furnace after 1835 and the subsequent introduction of the anthracite furnace were, in large part, responses by producers to market pressures.

In responding to the new and enlarged character of demand, most producers did not abandon the traditional technology of the industry. They continued to operate aging charcoal furnaces, and until 1850 many firms proceeded to erect new cold- and hot-blast models despite the greater cost-efficiency of the anthracite furnaces. And, as we have seen, even those firms that adopted the innovative anthracite technology during the 1840s and 1850s did not push it to its engineering limits by building the very large furnaces permitted by the design. Instead, most firms that erected anthracite furnaces, like those that had constructed charcoal furnaces during the 1830s and 1840s, built with a sharp eye to the fluctuating condition of the iron markets and of the general economy. This is certainly what we should expect: rational people doing the sensible thing. In doing so, however, the individual iron producers effectively limited the extent to which, before 1860, the iron *industry* adopted the technological innovations that ultimately would transform the industry and in the process temporarily solve the major problems that had plagued it almost from its beginnings, that is, devastating foreign competition for the home market and eroding profit margins.

The decision of many producers to persist in the use of traditional technology and the decision of many others to adopt the newer technologies on a relatively modest scale did more than simply inhibit the technological transformation of the iron industry. These decisions also limited the extent to which the industry's organizational structure would change. As long as the physical scale of production was sufficiently small to be within the financial reach of individual producers and small partnerships, larger and more formal business organizations – joint-stock companies and chartered corporations – were not essential to the industry's existence.

When these large, corporate entities arose, their emergence was in large part a response to the unprecedentedly severe requirements for capital and organizational control over production imposed by the American railroad industry's demand for rolled-iron products, especially rails and boiler iron. Production on the scale necessary to serve the railroad's appetite for large quantities of quality iron at prices competitive with those charged by British producers generally surpassed the capabilities of firms owned by individuals and small partnerships. At the same time, even a company or corporation that hoped to prosper in the fiercely competitive market for railroad iron had only a poor chance of success if an uninterrupted supply of suitable pig iron to its rolling mills was not assured. This assurance was in fact the crucial concern, and the one that impelled the drive for integration in the rolled-iron sector of the industry.

Because the rolling mills' demand for pig iron was voracious, the formation of integrated firms comprising a number of furnaces, as well as the mills themselves, necessarily resulted in a concentration of furnace ownership and capacity and, hence, of investment capital in the hands of a numerically small part of the industry. The tendency toward such concentration, begun in the 1840s, exerted a powerful influence on even the nonintegrated iron producers, furnace owners among them. Thus, even as most firms remained wedded to the industry's traditional technology and forms of business organization, there had arisen in their midst at first merely the presentiment and by the late 1850s the well-defined shape of what the iron industry was to become.

In the decades following 1850 the Pennsylvania iron industry became increasingly concentrated in progressively fewer corporate hands, a development required by the expanded scale of production and made possible by the rapid growth and changing character of demand after 1850, but especially following the Civil War. By 1872, of 262 furnaces in the state, 86 percent used a fuel other than charcoal — usually either coal or coke — and almost two-thirds were owned by joint-stock companies or corporations.[1] In this sense, the Pennsylvania iron industry had come to resemble the British iron industry of a quarter-century earlier, combining advanced technology with an advanced form of business organization. Attempts to join the two before 1850, however, were somewhat premature and for the most part unimpressive in their results. More impressive was the significant transformation of the iron industry in Pennsylvania during the first half of the nineteenth century, brought about through the combination of traditional forms of business organization with new technologies. The aggressive pursuit and adoption on a large scale of the new, more potent production processes by the integrated firms after 1850 was a significant departure from the evolutionary path of the industry's development over the preceding one hundred years. It was also an important endowment for that time after the Civil War when advanced technology and advanced forms of business organization combined to revolutionize the American iron industry.

# Notes

CHAPTER 1

1. Keach Johnson, "The Baltimore Company Seeks English Markets: A Study of the Anglo-American Iron Trade, 1731–1755," *William and Mary Quarterly,* 3d ser., 16 (1959): 37, 41–42.

2. Peter Kalm, *The America of 1750: Peter Kalm's Travels in North America, The English Version of 1770,* ed. and trans. Adolph B. Benson, 2 vols. (1937; reprint, New York: Dover Publications, 1966), 1:87–88.

3. Arthur Cecil Bining, *Pennsylvania Iron Manufacture in the Eighteenth Century,* Publications of the Pennsylvania Historical Commission, vol. 4 (1938; reprint, Harrisburg: Pennsylvania Historical and Museum Commission, 1973), pp. 171–72.

4. Ibid.

5. This estimate of the industry's work force is based upon the verified number of workers at the following facilities: New Pine Forge, thirteen; Mary Ann Furnace, twenty-two; Hopewell Forge, eighteen; and Cornwall Furnace, forty-five. By 1775 a total of seventy-two production facilities are known to have been built: twenty-three furnaces; thirty-five forges; five ironworks (each having at least one furnace and one forge); three bloomeries; and six slitting, plating, and wire mills.

The first step in estimating the total labor force was to assume that all seventy-two facilities survived until 1775. Although this was undoubtedly not true, any error in this direction is probably compensated for by the absence from the total of facilities in operation for which no identification has been made. Next the average number of workers employed at a particular type of facility was determined. Cornwall Furnace, with a mean daily output of 2.8 tons during the period 1767–74, was probably of average size, whereas Mary Ann Furnace was below the average. Using Cornwall's work force as the average and multiplying it by twenty-three (the number of furnaces), the total work force at furnaces is 1,035 workers. Averaging the numbers of workers at New Pine Forge and at Hopewell Forge results in 15 workers. This number multiplied by 35 (the number of forges) is 525 workers. Ironworks were considerably larger than either furnaces or forges. The average work-force size at a furnace added to that of a forge, to give a low estimate of the average number of workers employed at an ironworks, is 60; and this figure multiplied by 5, the number of ironworks, results in a total of 300 workers. Bloomeries, forges where iron ore was directly reduced to wrought iron, probably employed a number of workers comparable to that at forges. Thus the estimated total work force at Pennsylvania's bloomeries is 45. The more specialized facilities — slitting, plating, and wire mills — also were comparable in size to forges; therefore the total work force at these facilities was about 90.

The sum of these individual estimates is 1,995. Not included in this figure are support workers — those who farmed the land of the facilities — and independent blacksmiths.

Sources for data on work-force size are New Pine Forge Time Book, 1760–63, and Mary Ann Furnace Time Book & Miscellaneous, 1765–71, Forges and Furnaces Account Books;

Hopewell Forge Coal, Iron & Time Book, Etc., 1768-75, and Cornwall Furnace Time Book, 1776-85, Grubb Furnace and Forge Account Books, Grubb Collection, all in Historical Society of Pennsylvania. The number of production facilities and the mean daily output are from Bining, *Pennsylvania Iron Manufacture,* pp. 171-172 and 177, respectively. Pennsylvania's population in 1775 was about 250,000 (see James T. Lemon, *The Best Poor Man's Country: A Geographical Study of Early Southeastern Pennsylvania* [Baltimore: The Johns Hopkins Press, 1972], table 7 [p. 23] and fig. 11 [p. 48]).

6. Bining, *Pennsylvania Iron Manufacture,* p. 171.

7. Probably the foremost exponent of the staples thesis has been Douglass C. North; see his *The Economic Growth of the United States, 1790·1860* (Englewood Cliffs, N.J.: Prentice-Hall, 1961), esp. pp. 1-7.

8. Bining, *Pennsylvania Iron Manufacture,* pp. 171-72.

9. Dr. Charles Carroll to Phil Smith, 27 October 1729, "Extracts from Account and Letter Books of Dr. Charles Carroll of Annapolis," *Maryland Historical Magazine* 18 (1923): 336-37.

10. W. Stull Holt, "Charles Carroll, Barrister: The Man," *Maryland Historical Magazine* 31 (1936): 114; Dr. Charles Carroll to William Black, Maryland, 21 January 1746, "Extracts," ibid., 22 (1927): 194; and Frederick B. Tolles, *James Logan and the Culture of Provincial America,* The Library of American Biography, ed. Oscar Handlin (Boston: Little, Brown and Company, 1957), p. 189.

11. Bining, *Pennsylvania Iron Manufacture,* pp. 159, 187-89.

12. James Logan to Thomas Story, Philadelphia, 29 July 1729, Letter Books of James Logan, Logan Papers, Historical Society of Pennsylvania. The role of the Quaker merchants in the financing of the early Pennsylvania iron industry has often been noted; see for example, Frederick B. Tolles, *Meeting House and Counting House: The Quaker Merchants of Colonial Philadelphia, 1682-1763* (New York: W. W. Norton and Company, 1963), pp. 98-99.

13. Two of the twelve partners in the Durham Company — Charles Read and James Logan — were brothers-in-law (B. F. Fackenthal, Jr., comp., *Briefs of Title to Real Estate in Durham and Adjoining Townships in Pennsylvania and the Partition and Allotment of the Durham Iron Company among the Partners as of December 4, 1773 and Its* SUBSEQUENT OWNERS. *Also Briefs of* OTHER LAND *Titles in Springfield Township and Nockamixon Townships in Bucks County and in Williams and Lower Saucon Townships Northampton County together with Other Historical Data* [Riegelsville, Pa.: Historical Society of Pennsylvania, 1936], pp. 47, 685). Two other partners in the Durham Company — Joseph Turner and William Allen — were business partners for fifty years (idem, "The Durham Iron Works in Durham Township," *Papers Read before the Society and Other Historical Papers. The Bucks County* [Pa.] *Historical Society* 7 [1937]: 66. See also Bining, *Pennsylvania Iron Manufacture,* p. 130). The partnership of the brothers Curttis and Peter Grubb in Cornwall Furnace and Hopewell Forge may have been an exception. Although the property and furnace were willed to the Grubbs by their uncle, no document delineating the legal aspects of the partnership exists (see Grubb Collection, Historical Society of Pennsylvania).

14. See "Indenture Tredecupartite of the Durham Company, March 4, 1727," in Fackenthal, *Briefs of Title,* pp. 83-90; and the discussion of the indenture, dated 25 September 1753, which established the Baltimore Company, in Keach Johnson, "The Genesis of the Baltimore Ironworks," *Journal of Southern History* 19 (1953): 170-71. See also Baltimore Company Records, vols. 1 (1703-34) and 2 (1734-35) passim, Maryland Historical Society.

15. The Durham Company's indenture provided that "the whole Company shall have sixteen votes & no more according to the shares that each copartner holds at the time respectively, one full sixteenth part or share to carry one vote" (Fackenthal, *Briefs of Title,* p. 87).

The Baltimore Company's arrangement was similar; see Aubrey C. Land, *The Dulaneys of Maryland: A Biographical Study of Daniel Dulaney, The Elder (1685-1753) and Daniel Dulaney, The Younger (1722-1797)* (Baltimore: The Johns Hopkins Press, 1955), pp. 108-9.

16. Johnson, "The Baltimore Company Seeks English Markets," pp. 52, 56.

17. Richard P. McCormick, *New Jersey from Colony to State, 1609-1789,* The New Jersey Historical Series, vol. 1 (Princeton: D. Van Nostrand Co., 1964), p. 90.

18. Arthur Cecil Bining, "Early Ironmasters of Pennsylvania," *Pennsylvania History* 18 (1951): 97.

19. Quoted in Tolles, *James Logan,* pp. 188-89.

20. James Logan to Thomas Story, 29 July 1729, Letter Books of James Logan.

21. Fackenthal, *Briefs of Title,* p. 83; Clement Plumsted to Dr. Charles Carroll, Philadelphia, 2 January 1731, Baltimore Company Records, vol. 1; Keach Johnson, "The Establishment of the Baltimore Company" (Ph.D. diss., University of Iowa, 1949), p. 364.

22. Robert Erskine to Owners of the American Company in England [probably May 1772], Letter Book of Robert Erskine No. 1, Manuscripts Collection N.J. III 21, New Jersey Historical Society.

23. Fackenthal, *Briefs of Title,* p. 147.

24. Bining argues that the availability of iron ore was the crucial determinant of location, while Fritz Redlich has contended that the supply of wood was the most important consideration (see Bining, *Pennsylvania Iron Manufacture,* p. 49; and Fritz Redlich, "Soderfors in Context: The Production of Iron in the Charcoal Era," introduction to *Soderfors Anchor-Works History,* by Johan Lundstrom, trans. Lars-Erik Hedin [Boston: Baker Library, Harvard Graduate School of Business Administration, 1970], p. 11).

25. See Robert Erskine to Owners of the American Company in England, [? May 1772], Letter Book of Robert Erskine No. 1, p. 5; and Johnson, "Establishment of the Baltimore Company," pp. 403 4.

26. Johnson, "The Genesis of the Baltimore Ironworks," pp. 163-64, 170.

27. See "Lands Bought by the Baltimore Company," Carroll-Maccubbin Papers, 1730-37, Box 1750-56, Maryland Historical Society; and Holt, "Charles Carroll, Barrister," pp. 114-15.

28. See Peter Hasenclever, *The Remarkable Case of Peter Hasenclever, Merchant* (London, 1773), Special Collections, New York Public Library, pp. 6-8, 10, 63, 85-87. In a similar vein, Irene D. Neu has noted that "perhaps Hasenclever's greatest difficulty was that his reach too far exceeded his grasp" ("The Iron Plantations of Colonial New York," *New York History* 33 [1952]: 16).

29. James Logan to Thomas Story, 29 July 1729, Letter Books of James Logan, p. 244. Logan's initial investment of a thousand pounds in 1727 rose to eighteen hundred pounds by 1729.

30. See Tolles, *James Logan,* p. 189. The figures for the Baltimore Company are from Johnson, "The Baltimore Company Seeks English Markets," p. 44, n. 28. In 1764 Peter Hasenclever estimated that the price per ton of bar iron in London — £17.5 — would include a freight charge of £1.5 per ton, or about 8.6 percent of the total price (Hasenclever, *The Remarkable Case of Peter Hasenclever, Merchant,* p. 82).

31. Tolles, *James Logan,* p. 189; Charles Laubach, "The Durham Iron Works," in *A Collection of Papers Read before the Bucks County Historical Society* 1 (1908): 244. The year in which the Durham Company suspended operations is not precisely known, but it was certainly before the spring of 1773 (see a letter of 15 May 1773 from the mercantile firm of James and Drinker to Lancelot Cowper of Bristol, quoted in Anne Bezanson, Robert D. Gray, and Miriam Hussey, *Prices in Colonial Pennsylvania* [Philadelphia: University of

Pennsylvania Press, 1935], p. 161n). With the company's dissolution in December 1773 its holdings were divided among the shareholders (see Fackenthal, "The Durham Iron Works in Durham Township," p. 66n).

32. See Letter Book of Robert Erskine No. 1, pp. 3, 4, 9a, 10, 17.

33. Good descriptive accounts of the types of jobs and working conditions at Pennsylvania ironworks, as well as some specific wage data, can be found in Bining, *Pennsylvania Iron Manufacture,* passim. Similar material of a general nature about Maryland ironworks is contained in Johnson, "Establishment of the Baltimore Company"; and Michael Warren Robbins, "The Principio Company: Iron-Making in Colonial Maryland, 1720-1781" (Ph.D. diss., The George Washington University, 1972).

34. A certain degree of skill was required of a miner to enable him to judge the location of a vein of ore and then to expose it (see Bining, *Pennsylvania Iron Manufacture,* p. 111). The job of those who broke and cleaned the iron ore was to prepare the ore for the furnace by first reducing the size of the chunks of ore and then roasting the ore, usually twice, to expel impurities such as sulfur (see Johnson, "The Genesis of the Baltimore Ironworks," pp. 36-37; see also Account of a Meeting of the Owners, 29 June 1765, Instructions to the Manager, Carlisle Iron Works, Iron Industry and Trade Autograph Collection, Historical Society of Pennsylvania). The furnace fillers "fed the furnace with ore, charcoal and limestone" (see Johnson, "The Genesis of the Baltimore Ironworks," pp. 36-37).

35. See Hopewell Forge Coal, Iron & Time Book, Etc., 1768-75; New Pine Forge Time Book, 1760-63; and New Pine Forge Cole Book, 1744-60, Forges and Furnaces Account Books, Historical Society of Pennsylvania. See also Bining, *Pennsylvania Iron Manufacture,* pp. 106-12. The wages of drivers, or teamsters, woodcutters, colliers, and other unskilled and semiskilled workers at various Pennsylvania ironworks were quite similar. This similarity obtained to some extent for skilled workers such as finers.

Unless otherwise indicated, the wage rates discussed in this chapter are given in Pennsylvania currency. Occasionally, however, wages are expressed in pounds sterling to ensure some measure of uniformity in wages for identical jobs performed at ironworks in various colonies. The procedure has been to use the rates of exchange of the colonial currencies for the English pound sterling.

36. Hopewell Forge Coal, Iron & Time Book, Etc., 1768-75.

37. Ibid., p. 168; see also Account of a Meeting of the Owners, 29 June 1765, Instructions to the Manager, Carlisle Iron Works.

38. In the absence of specific price data for the goods sold at ironworks stores, I have used the Bezanson annual twenty-commodity geometric index of average monthly wholesale prices (base = monthly average, 1741-45) at Philadelphia as a proxy (see Bezanson, Gray, and Hussey, *Prices,* appendix table 19).

39. Bining, *Pennsylvania Iron Manufacture,* p. 162.

40. A precise determination of profits for colonial ironworks is extremely difficult, and it is complicated by eighteenth-century bookkeeping practices, according to which cash flows into and out of a facility's account were recorded as "Balances due to" and "Balances due from," respectively. A positive difference between the two balances did not necessarily represent profits; instead it might represent recorded net cash flow (see for example "Balances Due to the Three Forges and One Furnace of the Baltimore Company for 1772," Carroll-Maccubbin Papers, Box 1770-83, Maryland Historical Society). One contemporary estimate of profits was that of Charles Carroll, of Annapolis, who in 1764 put his annual return from the Baltimore Ironworks at "not less than £400 sterling" (see Johnson, "Establishment of the Baltimore Company," p. 157). Since Carroll owned a one-fifth share in the company, the total return would have been about two thousand pounds sterling; however, this figure may have represented gross profits and not net returns, which would have been considerably less.

A decomposition of estimated production costs per ton of bar iron at Hopewell Forge in 1768 yields a net profit of about £3.28 (Pa.) per ton. Since Hopewell Forge produced slightly more than 173.6 tons of bar iron in 1768, the total net profit for that year was approximately £569.5 (Pa.). Similarly, in 1769 the net profit per ton of bar iron was about £3.24 on an output of 195.9 tons with a wholesale value of £4437 (Pa.). Thus, the net profit was £634.8, or about 14.3 percent of sales — compared with 14.6 percent in 1768. Although the rates of profit per ton in 1768 and 1769 are almost identical — 17.1 percent and 16.7 percent, respectively — the net annual profit for 1769 exceeded that for 1768 by about 11.5 percent because of a larger output. Consequently, the almost 31 percent increase in a finer's wage per ton was easily absorbed despite an increase of less than 1 percent in bar-iron prices at the forge and a 1.5 percent decline in the wholesale price per ton of bar iron in Pennsylvania from 1768 to 1769.

Sources for output tons, production costs, and prices at Hopewell Forge in 1768 and 1769 are Hopewell Forge Coal, Iron & Time Book, Etc., 1768–75; and Hopewell Forge ledgers A–F, 1765–74, Grubb Furnace and Forge Account Books, Grubb Collection, Historical Society of Pennsylvania. Philadelphia wholesale prices for bar iron are from Bezanson, Gray, and Hussey, *Prices,* table 10 (p. 424).

41. Charles Carroll to His Partners in the Baltimore Company, 8 December 1773, Carroll-Maccubbin Papers, Box 1770–83.

42. See Hopewell Forge Coal, Iron & Time Book, Etc., 1768–75, pp. 59–72, 185, 188; New Pine Forge Time Book, 1760–63, back pages; and Bining, *Pennsylvania Iron Manufacture,* p. 101. See also an advertisement of "a Forge and Geared Grist Mill . . . to be sold," which offers "several slaves used to work there, as Finers, Hammermen, and Colliers, and well acquainted with The Business," in *Maryland Gazette,* 21 May 1767.

43. New Pine Forge Time Book, 1760–63, back pages.

44. Bining, *Pennsylvania Iron Manufacture,* p. 102.

45. Ibid., pp. 100, 102. See also an advertisement for "an English Servant Man named William Smith . . . ," who ran away from "Durham Furnace," in *Postscript to the Pennsylvania Chronicle and Universal Advertiser,* 25 May 1767.

46. *Maryland Gazette,* 5 July 1745, under "Advertisements."

47. Letter Book of Robert Erskine No. 1, p. 6.

48. See Hasenclever, *The Remarkable Case of Peter Hasenclever, Merchant,* p. 9.

49. See Curttis Grubb to Peter Grubb, 21 February 1774, Grubb Collection, Box 1, Correspondence, Historical Society of Pennsylvania; see also Bining, *Pennsylvania Iron Manufacture,* pp. 28–30.

50. Curttis Grubb to Peter Grubb, 22 February 1774, Grubb Collection, Box 1.

51. See a report in the *Pennsylvania Chronicle and Universal Advertiser* (hereafter *Pennsylvania Chronicle*), 29 June 1767. The Ringwood Iron-Works referred to was probably that of the American Company.

CHAPTER 2

1. Hopewell Forge Coal, Iron & Time Book, Etc., 1768–75, pp. 1–3; New Pine Forge Cole Book, 1744–60, passim; and Cornwall Furnace Coal and Cordwood Book, 1776–92, Grubb Furnace and Forge Account Books, pp. 1, 3–4, Grubb Collection, Historical Society of Pennsylvania. See also Elk Ridge Company (Caleb Dorsey and Co. Iron Works), 1757–87, Hanson Family Papers, 1737–87, Maryland Historical Society. The percentage is derived from figures in Hopewell Forge Coal, Iron & Time Book, Etc., 1768–75, pp. 1–3, and in Cornwall Furnace Coal and Cordwood Book, 1776–1792, pp. 1, 3–4.

2. The mean distribution of workers by month for Hopewell Forge in 1768–75 is quite different from that for New Pine Forge in 1760–62. Unfortunately, the small amount of

data for the latter facility precludes a rigorous comparison of the two distributions (see New Pine Forge Time Book, 1760–63). The year 1776, the one year for which similar data exist for Cornwall Furnace, owned by the brothers Grubb, suggests a slightly different distribution of the number of workers per month. Cornwall's distribution peaked twice — once in June, at sixty-three workers; and then, after decreasing to forty-three workers in July, once again in August, at sixty workers. However, the Cornwall pattern is quite similar to the distribution at Hopewell for the fall and winter months. It must be emphasized that the distribution at Cornwall Furnace is for only one year and is therefore not a distribution of mean values (see Cornwall Furnace Time Book, 1776–85).

3. Both works were owned and managed by Curttis and Peter Grubb. Consequently, the extent of the coordination between these two facilities, although fairly typical of that between other successful but separately owned furnaces and forges, may have been somewhat greater than was usual. Again, similar records for other ironworks have not survived in sufficient quantities to permit a rigorous analysis. Wherever possible, however, I have attempted to compare the fragmentary data for other ironworks with those of Hopewell Forge and Cornwall Furnace. It should be pointed out that during the period under consideration Hopewell and Cornwall were in a part of Lancaster County that later broke away and became Lebanon County.

4. See Hasenclever, *The Remarkable Case of Peter Hasenclever, Merchant,* pp. 81–82. I have reduced the required quantities of each input by one-half to obtain the appropriate tons and bushels of charcoal to produce one ton of bar iron.

5. In his attempt to explain how his initial cost estimates for making iron were exceeded by the actual costs, Peter Hasenclever pointed to a number of unforeseen difficulties, including the poor quality of his charcoal:

> The difference of the quality of the coal could not be well observed in the beginning: I had bought charcoal with the old decayed work; though my people observed the bad quality, still they attributed it to the charing [sic], and more than a year passed before the real cause was discovered, which was when they had made coal themselves, and then it was first found that it proceeded from the weakness of the wood — an accident which was invisible and irremediable.

(Hasenclever, *The Remarkable Case of Peter Hasenclever, Merchant,* p. 84). Hasenclever also reported that "the woods which had been cut 18 years ago, and now grow up again, were much stronger as to require ¼ to ⅓ less coal than the old wood" (ibid.).

6. The difficulties involving the predicted values based upon pig-iron figures arise in part from the fact that no data on the number of tons of pig iron received from Cornwall Furnace by Hopewell Forge exist for any time before March 1768 (see Hopewell Forge Coal, Iron & Time Book, Etc., 1768–75, p. 59). There are, however, entries in the forge's ledgers that record monthly balances due to Cornwall Furnace, presumably for pig iron (see Hopewell Forge Ledger A, 1765–67, fols. 14, 79, 103, 143).

7. See Account of a Meeting of the Owners, 29 June 1765, Instructions to the Manager, Carlisle Iron Works.

8. Sunday was the single day off for most workers, except those directly involved in the operation of a furnace. For example, one entry in the Cornwall Furnace Time Book reads "Sunday Morng. 23d. [June 1776] Inst. began to heave off Furnace" (see Cornwall Furnace Time Book, 1776–85).

9. The number of man-days worked each month has *not* been derived by multiplying the number of workers by twenty-six days. Rather, the man-days figure for any one month represents the sum of the actual number of days worked by each worker. The bookkeeping technique followed by eighteenth-century ironworks for recording labor time was to mark next to a worker's name each day of a month a "1 [one]," a zero, or a fraction to indicate an entire day of work, a day's absence, or work for part of a day, respectively.

10. See letter to Nathaniel Chapman, new manager of the Principio Company's iron-works, probably from one of the owners, December 1736, Papers Relating to America, 1725–76, Carewe Papers, British Museum Additional Manuscripts 29600, Library of Congress, Washington, D.C. In the same vein, see Charles Carroll, of Carrollton, to his partners in the Baltimore Company, 8 December 1773, Carroll-Maccubbin Papers, Box 1770–83; see also memoranda, Hopewell Forge Coal, Iron & Time Book, Etc., 1768–75.

11. See Walt W. Rostow, *The Process of Economic Growth*, 2d ed. (New York: W. W. Norton, 1962), pp. 83–85; and Douglass C. North, *The Economic Growth of the United States, 1790–1860* (Englewood Cliffs, N.J.: Prentice-Hall, 1961), p. 8.

12. Cornwall Furnace, owned by Curttis and Peter Grubb, may have been an exception. The Grubbs may have substituted blowing tubs for bellows sometime between 1774 and 1780. Blowing tubs provided a more consistent blast at a higher pressure. As of May 1774 Cornwall Furnace still used bellows to generate the blast (see Curttis Grubb to Peter Grubb, 3 May 1774, Grubb Collection, Box 1).

13. Hopewell Forge Coal, Iron & Time Book, Etc., 1768–75; Tench Coxe, *A Statement of the Arts and Manufactures of the United States of America for the Year 1810* (Philadelphia, 1814), pp. 49–52, copy in the Eleutherian Mills Historical Library, Wilmington, Del.

14. Samuel Hazard, ed., *The Register of Pennsylvania. Devoted to the Preservation of Facts and Documents, and every Kind of useful Information Respecting the State of Pennsylvania* 8 (July–December 1831): 397. Calculations based on data extracted from the returns for seventeen forges in operation in Berks County as of 1832 result in a mean output per worker of 8.4 tons and a mean output per forge of 168 tons (see Louis McLane, *Documents Relative to the Manufactures of the United States*, 4 vols. in 1 [1833; reprint (4 vols. in 3), New York: Burt Franklin, 1969], passim; hereafter cited as *McLane Report.*).

15. The mean annual output figures are derived from Bining, *Pennsylvania Iron Manufacture*, pp. 177–78.

16. Ibid., pp. 177–78. Cornwall ran 945.7 tons of pig iron and castings in the 1766–67 blast and 908.75 tons in the 1769–70 blast. Elizabeth Furnace's best year for output of pig iron and castings was 1790 (753.8 tons).

17. The figures are derived from ibid., p. 178.

18. Jeffrey Francis Zabler, "A Microeconomic Study of Iron Manufacture, 1800–1830" (Ph.D. diss., University of Pennsylvania, 1970), p. 212; and Robbins, "The Principio Company," p. 142.

19. The figures are derived from data in "Documents Relating to the Manufacture of Iron in Pennsylvania," *Journal of the Franklin Institute*, 3d ser., 21 (January 1851), tables following p. 72.

20. The percentage figure for pig iron is derived from Hasenclever, *The Remarkable Case of Peter Hasenclever, Merchant*, pp. 81–82. The bar-iron figure is calculated from data in the Hopewell Forge Coal, Iron & Time Book, Etc., 1768–75; and Hopewell Forge Ledgers A–G, 1765–75.

21. Price information is from Bezanson, Gray, and Hussey, *Prices*. For examples of prices charged at the production site see New Pine Forge Ledgers A and B, 1760–63, Forges and Furnaces Account Books, Historical Society of Pennsylvania. Between 1750 and 1775 thirty-eight firms were organized; and from 1716 through 1749, thirty-six (figures derived from Bining, *Pennsylvania Iron Manufacture*, pp. 171–73).

22. The use of charcoal fuel was in large part responsible for the length of time required to prepare an ancony because of the relatively low temperature reached in the hearth. The two-tons-per-week figure represents the mean output per week at Hopewell Forge during 1768–75 (see Hopewell Forge Coal, Iron & Time Book, Etc., 1768–75, pp. 59–75; see also Bining, *Pennsylvania Iron Manufacture*, pp. 74, 109).

23. Hopewell Forge Coal, Iron & Time Book, Etc., 1768-75; and Mary Ann Furnace Time Book & Miscellaneous, 1765-71. Most workers — largely the unskilled and semiskilled such as woodcutters, haulers, and colliers — stayed less than six months. For example, of seventy-four workers employed at Mary Ann Furnace during 1765-66 fifty-six, or more than 75 percent, stayed five months or less.

24. Hazard, *Register of Pennsylvania,* p. 397; and tables in "Documents Relating to the Manufacture of Iron in Pennsylvania."

25. The Pearson correlation coefficient *r* is $-0.74$ for a double log transformation of the variables. The rough form of the regression equation is $Q = 28.25C^{-0.79} + e$, where $Q$ is tons of anconies per worker; $C$ is hundreds of bushels of charcoal consumed per ton of anconies; and $e$ is an error term. This equation is for Hopewell Forge's operations during the period 1768-74.

26. Sources include Hopewell Forge Coal, Iron & Time Book, Etc., 1768-75; New Pine Forge Cole Book, 1744-60; New Pine Forge Time Book, 1760-63; New Pine Forge Ledger A, 1760-62; and Bining, *Pennsylvania Iron Manufacture,* pp. 105-13.

27. Hopewell Forge Ledger B, 1767-68; see also above, n. 22.

28. See also Gary M. Walton and James F. Shepherd, *The Economic Rise of Early America* (Cambridge: At the University Press, 1979), chap. 6, esp. pp. 113-15, 130, 133, 136.

29. Hopewell Forge Coal, Iron & Time Book, Etc., 1768-75, p. 262.

30. New Pine Forge Time Book, 1760-63, back pages.

31. Hopewell Forge Coal, Iron & Time Book, Etc., 1768-75, passim.

32. Letter to Nathaniel Chapman, December 1736, Carewe Papers.

33. Hopewell Forge Coal, Iron & Time Book, Etc., 1768-75, p. 20.

34. See table 9 for data. The 40-50 percent recovery figure is based on the fact that the cost of 1.5 tons of pig iron plus half of the overhead charges — at £1.39 per ton of pig iron — represented about 40 percent of the total production cost per ton of bar iron at Hopewell Forge in 1768. Added to this 40 percent would have been the lower costs of the reduced charcoal requirements for reworking the bar iron.

35. Account of a Meeting of the Owners, 29 June 1765, Instructions to the Manager, Carlisle Iron Works.

36. The articles of agreement between forge managers and forgemen explicitly made the payment of wages conditional on the quality of the anconies or bar iron produced. For example, on 5 November 1768 Peter Grubb, of Hopewell Forge, agreed to pay a finer "twenty Shillings per ton for Every ton of Good and marchantable Anckonys that he Shall make" (see Hopewell Forge Coal, Iron & Time Book, Etc., 1768-75, p. 162). Similarly, on 30 June 1760 the manager of New Pine Forge agreed to pay a hammerman twenty-four shillings "for every Tun of good barr Iron" (see New Pine Forge Time Book, 1760-63, back pages).

37. See Bining, *Pennsylvania Iron Manufacture,* p. 110. This reference is to waste in excess of the permitted limits for making anconies from pig iron, and bar iron from anconies. Bining reports that "less than 300 pounds was permitted as waste from the pig iron stage to that of the ancony, and about 200 pounds from the ancony stage to that of finished bar." See also "Articles of Agreement . . . on this 5th Day of November 1768 . . . ," in Hopewell Forge Coal, Iron & Time Book, Etc., 1768-75, p. 162.

38. Account of a Meeting of the Owners, 29 June 1765, Instructions to the Manager, Carlisle Iron Works.

39. See note by [Dr.?] Charles Carroll, c. 1734 or 1735, in Baltimore Company Records, vol. 1.

40. *Pennsylvania Chronicle,* 14-21 December 1767.

41. Englishmen familiar with the iron trade readily acknowledged the comparative advantage enjoyed by Sweden in the English market (see Mr. Paris to Mr. Penn, "Reasons for Encouraging the Importation of Iron in Barrs from the British Colonys in America . . . ," p. 69, in Papers Relating to American Iron, which past in the Years 1738 & 1739, Penn Manuscripts, Historical Society of Pennsylvania). Swedish bar iron sold for between £17 and £22 per ton in the London market during the years 1762, 1763, and 1764 (see James E. Thorold Rogers, *A History of Agriculture and Prices in England*, vol. 7, pt. 1 [Oxford: Clarendon Press, 1902], pp. 387-89). During the same years, the Philadelphia price of Pennsylvania bar iron was £19.6, £15.6, and £14.8 in sterling equivalents, respectively. The drop in prices may have been a reaction to a reduced demand for iron by the military with the conclusion of the Seven Years' War. In any case, if shipping, insurance, and freight charges are added to the Philadelphia bar-iron price, the resulting total probably would fall within the price range at which Swedish iron sold (cf. Hasenclever, *The Remarkable Case of Peter Hasenclever, Merchant*, p. 82, where Hasenclever gives £17.5 as the 1764 price for one ton of New Jersey bar iron. Of this, £11.63 represented the production cost and other charges of the iron before shipment to England. The charges involved in shipping the iron to England were £2.65, leaving a profit of £3.22 per ton, or 18.4 percent of the selling price in London).

42. See, for example, note by [Dr.?] Charles Carroll, February 1734, in Baltimore Company Records, vol. 1, p. 58. Here, the Baltimore Company's bar iron is described as being "the very Best Iron that can be made and rather better than the best [*illegible*] Iron from Sweden." Michael Robbins describes an instance in which many tons of the Principio Company's pit iron were defective: when the iron "was sold in London in 1765 it nearly destroyed the Principio Company's established reputation" (Robbins, "The Principio Company," p. 58).

43. Lyde & Cooper to Cha. Carroll, Bristol, 8 March 1734, Baltimore Company Records, vol. 1, p. 65.

44. James Gildart to Charles Carroll, Liverpool, 6 June 1751, Carroll-Maccubbin Papers, Box 1750-56.

45. See Instructions Given and Left with Sam'l Hay at the Carlisle Iron Works, 4, 5 May 1769, by the Owners, Carlisle Iron Works.

46. See, for example, the report by "The Committee to whom the Petition of the Merchants & Ironmongers of this Kingdom in behalf of themselves & many others trading to his Matys Plantations in America," in Papers Relating to Iron, Penn Manuscripts. For a detailed account of Parliament's role as a gatherer and publicizer of information about iron see Arthur Cecil Bining, *British Regulation of the Colonial Iron Industry* (Philadelphia: University of Pennsylvania Press, 1933), chap. 3.

47. Robbins, "The Principio Company," p. 198. The first significant tests of colonial iron were made at six navy yards in 1715. These tests established that colonial iron was, at the very least, as good as Swedish iron (see Bining, *British Regulation*, p. 54).

48. See "Reasons for Encouraging the Importation of Iron in Barrs," Penn Manuscripts; and Michael W. Flinn, *Men of Iron: The Crowleys in the Early Iron Industry* (Edinburgh: At the University Press, 1962), chap. 9. The lead sentence of this chapter says: "There was one buyer of wrought ironware in the seventeenth and eighteenth centuries whose purchases dwarfed all others — the Royal Navy."

49. In England there was a sharp distinction between the ironmasters, who made pig and bar iron, and the iron manufacturers, who produced wrought iron and nails (see Flinn, *Men of Iron*, pp. 6-8, 98-99). The same distinction did not apply to the colonial iron industry, in which furnaces cast ironware and forges made plows and other tools (see, for example, "List of Castings for which Patterns are now ready at the Carlisle Iron Works the 29th

June 1765," Carlisle Iron Works. See also Cornwall Furnace Blast and Pig Iron Book, 1776–92, and Hopewell Forge Ledgers A–G, I, K, Grubb Furnace and Forge Account Books, Grubb Collection, Historical Society of Pennsylvania).

50. The Dorseys either were interested in shipping bar iron at the time or, more likely, had already done so (Buchanan to the Dorseys, London, 14 March 175[?], Elk Ridge Company, 1757–87, Hanson Family Papers, 1737–87).

51. Hasenclever, *The Remarkable Case of Peter Hasenclever, Merchant*, p. 10, as quoted in Bining, *Pennsylvania Iron Manufacture*, p. 84. The reader should note that although the quotation in the text is purported to comprise the words of Hasenclever's partners, we have only Hasenclever's word for this. At the time he wrote his apologia, Hasenclever had little affection for his former business associates.

52. Bining, *Pennsylvania Iron Manufacture*, p. 84.

53. Hasenclever, *The Remarkable Case of Peter Hasenclever, Merchant*, p. 80.

54. Charles Carroll, barrister, to James Gildart, 20 August 1758, in W. Stull Holt, ed., "Letters of Charles Carroll, Barrister," *Maryland Historical Magazine* 32 (1937): 189. See also Bining, *Pennsylvania Iron Manufacture*, pp. 60–61, 159.

55. See Thomas S. Ashton, *Iron and Steel in the Industrial Revolution,* University of Manchester Economic History Series, no. 11 (Manchester, 1924), p. 34.

56. See H. J. Habakkuk, *American and British Technology in the Nineteenth Century: The Search for Labour-Saving Inventions* (Cambridge: At the University Press, 1962), pp. 157–58.

57. See Instructions Given and Left with Sam'l Hay at the Carlisle Iron Works, 4, 5 May 1769, by the Owners, Carlisle Iron Works.

58. The figures are presented in Hasenclever, *The Remarkable Case of Peter Hasenclever, Merchant,* pp. 79–82. Unfortunately, no production figures or cost estimates are available for the operations of the Carlisle Iron Works.

59. The decomposition of the production cost of cinder bar iron should be taken with a grain of salt. Cinder-bar-iron production required the crushing of furnace and forge cinders in a stamping mill to remove the iron for processing. Unfortunately, Hasenclever provides no estimate of the construction costs of this plant. However, a stamping mill represented a capital expenditure beyond the standard expenditures for furnace and forge construction. Consequently, the amortization of the mill would have a bearing on the production costs of cinder bar iron.

60. Hasenclever, *The Remarkable Case of Peter Hasenclever, Merchant,* p. 79.

61. Johnson, "The Baltimore Company Seeks English Markets," pp. 37, 41, 42, 47, 48, 50; and Holt, "Letters of Charles Carroll, Barrister," *Maryland Historical Magazine,* 31 (1936) and 38 (1943), passim.

62. Charles Carroll, barrister, to William Anderson, Annapolis, 27 September 1762, in Holt, "Letters of Charles Carroll, Barrister," *Maryland Historical Magazine* 33 (1939): 373.

## CHAPTER 3

1. The useful distinction between private and public information is made by Allan Pred in *Urban Growth and the Circulation of Information: The United States System of Cities, 1790–1840* (Cambridge, Mass.: Harvard University Press, 1973), p. 17.

2. Seymour Dunbar, *A History of Travel in America,* 4 vols. (Indianapolis: Bobbs-Merrill Co., 1915), vol. 1, p. 177, n. 2.

3. For examples of letters accompanying travelers see the correspondence between Edward Shippen, of Lancaster, and Colonel James Burd, contained in Thomas Balch, *Letters and Papers Relating Chiefly to the Provincial History of Pennsylvania, With Some Notes of the Writers* (Philadelphia: Privately printed, 1855), pp. 230, 238, 244.

4. Dunbar, *A History of Travel in America*, vol. 1, p. 143; Pred, *Urban Growth*, p. 178.

5. Pred, *Urban Growth*, pp. 178, 182; Kalm, *Peter Kalm's Travels*, vol. 1, p. 143.

6. *Postscript to the Pennsylvania Chronicle and Universal Advertiser*, 11 May 1767.

7. Ibid.

8. Ibid.

9. Dunbar, *A History of Travel in America*, vol. 1, p. 184; Pred, *Urban Growth*, p. 178.

10. This technique was first used with great effectiveness by Pred, and it and the term "time lag" have been borrowed here. For a detailed explanation of the thinking behind the method see Pred, *Urban Growth*, pp. 35–36. The values listed in table 12 are averages of times throughout the year and only implicitly reflect the seasonal variations in the frequency of arrival and travel times of news carriers. As Pred has observed with regard to the 1820s, "Even in the absence of freezing [of harbors], coastal vessels, which sometimes bore news-worthy information, arrived much less frequently in winter" (p. 36. See also *Pennsylvania Chronicle* and *Maryland Gazette*, 1767, passim).

11. Carl Bridenbaugh, *Cities in Revolt: Urban Life in America, 1743–1776* (New York: Alfred A. Knopf, 1968), p. 96; Lemon, *Best Poor Man's Country*, p. 29.

12. See, for example, letters of 30 July and 23 September 1772 from John Wall, in Philadelphia, to Peter Grubb, at Hopewell Forge, in Grubb Collection, Box 1. See also the draft of a letter from Robert Erskine, manager of the American Company's works in New Jersey, probably May 1772, probably to the owners, in Letter Book of Robert Erskine No. 1.

13. See Pred, *Urban Growth*, pp. 37–39.

14. Lemon, *Best Poor Man's Country*, p. 29.

15. John Flexer Walzer, "Transportation in the Philadelphia Trading Area, 1740–1775" (Ph.D. diss., University of Wisconsin, 1968), p. 279; "Travel Diary of Bishop and Mrs. Reichel and their Company from Lititz to Salem to Wachau (Wachovia) from May 22, to June 15, 1780," in *Travels in the American Colonies*, ed. Newton D. Mereness (New York: The Macmillan Co., 1916), pp. 587, 589; F. Ellis, *History of Northampton County, Pennsylvania* (Philadelphia: P. Fritts, 1877), p. 56.

16. Walzer, "Transportation in the Philadelphia Trading Area," p. 63.

17. Lemon, *Best Poor Man's Country*, pp. 34–36.

18. Ibid., tables 9 (pp. 36–37) and 10 (p. 38).

19. "A Map of Pennsylvania exhibiting not only the improved parts of that Province, but also its extensive frontiers: Laid down from actual surveys, and chiefly from the late Map of W. Scull Published in 1770. Published by Robert Sayer & J. Bennett, 10 June 1775," Milton S. Eisenhower Library, The Johns Hopkins University, Baltimore, Md. (hereafter cited as "Scull's Map"); see also "Minutes of the Provincial Council of Pennsylvania from the Organization to the Termination of the Proprietary Government," in *Colonial Records*, vol. 9 (Harrisburg: Published by the State, 1852), pp. 440, 556–61.

20. John Omwake, with H. C. Frey, H. K. Landis, and Catherine P. Hargrave, *The Conestoga Six-Horse Bell Teams of Eastern Pennsylvania* (Cincinnati: John Omwake, 1930), pp. 35, 39, 10; Walzer, "Transportation in the Philadelphia Trading Area," pp. 256–57, 266.

21. J. L. Ringwalt, *Development of Transportation Systems in the United States* (Philadelphia: J. L. Ringwalt, 1888), p. 39. A rough estimate of the weight of a large Conestoga wagon can be made from information contained in George Shumway, Edward Durell, and Howard C. Frey, *Conestoga Wagon, 1750–1850: Freight Carrier for 100 Years of America's Westward Expansion* (York, Pa.: Early American Industries Association and George Shumway, 1964), p. 195.

22. For Chester County see Lemon, *Best Poor Man's Country*, table 9 (p. 36). Present-day Chester County does not include the area of Delaware County.

23. The description of Berks and Montgomery counties is based on U.S. Department of the Interior, Geological Survey, *State of Pennsylvania Base Map with Highways and Contours* (Washington, D.C.: Department of the Interior, 1955).

24. Quoted in Balch, *Letters and Papers*, pp. 186–87.

25. From "Diary of a Journey of Moravians from Bethlehem, Pennsylvania, to Bethabara in Wachovia, North Carolina, 1753," quoted in *Travels in the American Colonies*, ed. Newton D. Mereness (New York: The Macmillan Co., 1916), p. 328.

26. Kalm, *Peter Kalm's Travels*, vols. 1 and 2, passim and appendix, vol. 2, pp. 738–69.

27. Ibid. Figures have been derived in the following manner. The appendix entitled "Meteorological Observations" lists the year, month, day, and time for each temperature reading and also provides a description of each day's weather, including wind direction and force, as well as a characterization of the type and extent of precipitation, if any. The number of days in each month for which rain or snow was the recorded prevailing weather condition was noted. This done, the readings were then compared with the text of the journal to determine Kalm's location for each day and, consequently, the location from where the meteorological readings were made. Those days that Kalm spent in or about Philadelphia were correlated with the daily record of the weather; the number of inclement days were then divided by the total number of days spent in the Philadelphia area. The observations for June through September 1749 were not made by Kalm but by "Mr. John Bartram, near Philadelphia, During my absence in the Summer of the year 1749" (p. 761).

28. From "Meteorological Observations at Philadelphia," in *Philadelphia Chronicle*, January–June 1767. The percentage in this case was 16.5 percent or 30 inclement days of 181 days overall. The percentages at Williamsburg, Virginia, for the years 1760, 1761, and 1762 were slightly lower: 14.7 percent, 14.6 percent, and 11.7 percent, respectively (Andrew Burnaby, *Travels through the Middle Settlements of North America, 1759–1760*, 3d ed. [1798], reprinted in *Burnaby's Travels through North America*, ed. Rufus Rockwell Wilson [New York: A. Wessels Co., 1904], pp. 215–51).

29. James Lemon successfully used earlier twentieth-century evidence in a comparison of southeastern Pennsylvania's climate — mean monthly and annual temperature and inches of precipitation — with that of northern Europe (*Best Poor Man's Country*, table 8 [p. 33]).

30. Hopewell Forge's bar iron was sold in the Philadelphia, Lancaster, and York markets (see letters in Grubb Collection, Box 1, such as, William Bell to Peter Grubb, Lancaster, 27 April 1770; Peter Grubb to Attmore and Peters in Philadelphia, Hopewell Forge, 16 February 1768; Paul Zantzinger to Peter Grubb, Lancaster, 27 January 1772; White and Caldwell to Peter Grubb, Philadelphia, 4 May 1768; George Stake to [Peter Grubb], York, 22 February 1770; George Stake to Peter Grubb, York, 20 August 1772).

31. Indirect support for this conclusion is contained in a letter to the *Maryland Gazette* dated "Frederick County, March 22, 1767." The writer, who describes himself as a "Dutch Farmer," asked that the paper "let every Body know to send Ships, for we Back People will carry more Wheat to *George-Town* next fall, in case it be a very dry Fall that we can get along the Road with our Waggons."

32. The disadvantages of shipping upstream were several. On the Delaware "about three times as long a period was required for upstream travel as for drifting with the current" (Wheaton J. Lane, *From Indian Trail to Iron Horse: Travel and Transportation in New Jersey, 1620–1860* [Princeton: Princeton University Press, 1939], pp. 69–70). Moreover, although the downstream load of the large Durham boats that carried iron from the Durham ironworks to Philadelphia was fifteen tons, the upstream load was only "about two tons" (for downstream load size see Ringwalt, *Development of Transportation Systems*, p. 13; the upstream figure is from Lane, *From Indian Trail to Iron Horse*, p. 69). Movement upstream was also more expensive than water transport in the opposite direction

or land transport in the upstream direction (see Walzer, "Transportation in the Philadelphia Trading Area," p. 114).

33. Lemon notes that there was little complementarity between overland and river transportation in southeastern Pennsylvania (*Best Poor Man's Country,* pp. 29, 37).

34. Walzer, "Transportation in the Philadelphia Trading Area," pp. 38-39, n. 10; see also Lemon, *Best Poor Man's Country,* p. 37.

35. Lemon, *Best Poor Man's Country,* p. 37.

36. See "Travel Diary of Bishop and Mrs. Reichel," p. 586. The traveler, Johann David Schoepf, noted in 1783 that at Wright's Ferry the Susquehanna was "two miles wide, not deep to be sure, but full of reefs and little islands . . . so that with high winds, strong currents, or ice, travellers are often delayed many days" (*Travels in the Confederation* [1783-84], ed. and trans. from the German edition of 1788 by Alfred J. Morrison [Philadelphia: William J. Campbell, 1911], pp. 19-20. See also Lemon, *Best Poor Man's Country,* p. 37). Lemon describes the Susquehanna as having been "treacherous, rocky, and a mile wide at many ferry points" and "a major obstacle." The cost of a ferry across the Susquehanna was far higher than the cost of one across the Schuylkill River — 7.5 shillings as compared with about 1.63 shillings (Walzer, "Transportation in the Philadelphia Trading Area," pp. 236-38).

37. Copy of a letter to Col. John Armstrong, Lancaster, 1 July 1765, Carlisle Iron Works.

38. Walzer, "Transportation in the Philadelphia Trading Area," p. 238.

39. Ibid., pp. 236-37. A calculation executed with Walzer's data yields an increase of 1.3 percent due to the Schuylkill Ferry.

40. Again, a calculation of the total percentage increase in transport costs due to the Susquehanna and Schuylkill ferries yields a figure of 7.9 percent, within but at the high end of the range given by Walzer. The mean of the values given by him has been used to avoid the danger of overstating the argument presented here. The procedure used in the extrapolation is as follows:

(1) Susquehanna ferriage cost = 7.5 shillings = £0.375
(2) Let $x$ = base transport cost per ton
(3) Solve for $x$ in equations ($a$) and ($b$)
  ($a$) $0.06x = 0.375$; $x = £6.25$
  ($b$) $0.07x = 0.375$; $x = £5.36$
(4) Average the values for $x$ in ($a$) and ($b$) = £5.8
(5) Schuylkill ferriage cost = £0.08
(6) Add: £5.8 + £0.375 + £0.08 = £6.26, or about £6.3.

41. Bezanson, Gray, and Hussey, *Prices,* p. 408.

42. The figure of £3 for the per-ton transport cost from Hopewell Forge to Philadelphia is from Walzer, "Transportation in the Philadelphia Trading Area," p. 315, n. 8. It has also been derived from the following letters: Peter Grubb to Attmore and Peters, Hopewell Forge, 17 February 1768; Attmore and Peters to Peter Grubb, Philadelphia, 8 April 1768; and Wishart and Edwards to Peter Grubb, Philadelphia, 8 April 1768, all in Grubb Collection, Box 1.

43. Bezanson, Gray, and Hussey, *Prices,* pp. 412-15.

44. Instructions Given and Left with Sam'l Hay at the Carlisle Iron Works, 4, 5 May 1769, by the Owners, Carlisle Iron Works.

45. For a thorough discussion of eighteenth-century Philadelphia's role as a central place see Lemon, *Best Poor Man's Country,* pp. 118-49, esp. pp. 118-31. Lemon correctly describes Philadelphia as "the nodal point of the province" (p. 125).

46. Instructions Given and Left with Sam'l Hay at the Carlisle Iron Works, 4, 5 May 1769, Carlisle Iron Works.

47. Hopewell Forge, in Lancaster County, frequently sold bar iron to merchants in York who often sent their wagons to the forge (see, for example, George Stake to Peter Grubb, York, 22 February 1770, 6 and 15 April and 20 August 1772; and Dan Spangler to Peter Grubb, York, 26 March 1772, all in Grubb Collection, Box 1. Moreover, Lancaster merchants who purchased bar iron from Hopewell Forge also sold the iron to buyers in York (see William Bell to Peter Grubb, Lancaster, 5 May 1772, ibid.).

48. See correspondence in Grubb Collection, Box 1, passim; and Hopewell Forge Ledgers A–G, 1765–75, passim.

49. Figure 8 is a plot of every recorded bar-iron transaction at Hopewell Forge during 1768. Each point represents a transaction, giving the number of tons involved and the price charged per ton. The deviation of many of the points from a smoothly deteriorating curve (negatively logarithmic) has several probable causes. First, normal fluctuations in supply and demand in the various markets would have affected the per-ton price of bar iron in any quantity. Second, weather conditions may well have been an influence in the manner described above and therefore may explain the eccentric point representing a transaction for 3.15 tons at £30.63 per ton. This particular transaction occurred in August, the month having the highest mean precipitation. This is significant because the mean monthly price per ton of bar iron rose fairly consistently as the amount of precipitation increased (for the twelve months of 1768 the correlation coefficient equaled 0.8096, significant at better than the 0.01 confidence level). Finally, there were apparently inelasticities of both price and quantity. The price inelasticity makes sense because the production cost for a ton of bar iron at Hopewell Forge in 1768 was between £19 and £20. The inelasticity with respect to quantity is also readily explained by the fact that a wagon could carry between 1.25 and 1.5 tons of bar iron. Therefore, orders smaller than one wagonload were not common.

50. Robert Ellis to Mr. Hollock, Philadelphia, 7 March 1739 / 40, Letter Book of Robert Ellis, 1736–48, Collection of Business, Professional, and Personal Account Books, Historical Society of Pennsylvania.

51. Charles Carroll, barrister, to Thomas Ringgold, Chester Town, Annapolis, 25 February 1761, in Holt, "Letters of Charles Carroll, Barrister," *Maryland Historical Magazine* 33 (1938): 195.

52. See Lemon, *Best Poor Man's Country,* pp. 131–40.

53. Ibid., fig. 11 (p. 48).

54. Ibid., table 31 (p. 187).

55. Omwake et al., *Conestoga Six-Horse Bell Teams,* p. 35; see also Shumway, Durell, and Frey, *Conestoga Wagon, 1750–1850,* pt. 3, passim.

56. Using data from an admittedly small sample of nine Conestoga-type wagons of the late eighteenth and early nineteenth centuries, the mean diameter of the rear wheels was found to be slightly more than 5 feet, while the mean diameter of the front wheels was about 3.8 feet (Shumway, Durell, and Frey, *Conestoga Wagon, 1750–1850,* p. 177). The procedure used for computing the number of cubic feet of iron per tire was as follows:

(1) 4 ft. x 3.14 (*pi*) = 12.5 ft. (approximately)
(2) 12.5 ft. x 0.3 ft. x 0.02 ft. = 0.075 ft.³

No figure could be found for the thickness of the tires, but from illustrations and scale drawings of wagons, 0.02 feet, or 0.25 inch, would seem to be a reasonable and conservative estimate (ibid.; Omwake et al., *Conestoga Six-Horse Bell Teams*). The density of wrought iron is given as 0.28 lbs. per cubic inch in American Society for Metals, *Metals Handbook,* vol. 1, *Properties and Selection of Metals,* 8th ed. (Novelty, Ohio: American Society for Metals, 1961), p. 52.

57. The number of wagons in Northampton County is rounded from the 1758 figure of 201 given in Walzer, "Transportation in the Philadelphia Trading Area," p. 275.

58. Lancaster County alone was said to have two thousand wagons in 1759 (see Lemon, *Best Poor Man's Country,* p. 278, n. 45).

59. Hopewell Forge Ledgers A–G, 1765–75. The actual annual number of tons sold by Hopewell Forge in these years was as follows: in 1767, 114.59; in 1768, 173.62; in 1769, 195.93; in 1770, 225.46; in 1771, 217.20; in 1772, 155.61; in 1773, 124.47; in 1774, 159.67; and in 1775, 117.04. The total number of tons sold for the years 1767–75 was 1,483.59, and the mean annual tons amounted to 164.84.

60. Cornwall Furnace made forge castings for Hopewell Forge (see Hopewell Forge Coal, Iron & Time Book, Etc., 1768–75, p. 91. For manufactured articles see, for example, Matthias Hough to Curttis or Peter Grubb [probably the latter], Lancaster, 29 November 1774, Grubb Collection, Box 1. See also Hough to Grubb, Lancaster, 11 April 1775, ibid.; and "List of Castings for which Patterns are now ready at the Carlisle Iron Works the 29th June 1765," Carlisle Iron Works). The Durham Company also made stove plates and other castings (see Laubach, "The Durham Iron Works," p. 244. For the products of New Jersey furnaces and forges see Peter O. Wacker, *The Musconetcong Valley of New Jersey: A Historical Geography* [New Brunswick: Rutgers University Press, 1968], p. 110; see also Bining, *British Regulation,* pp. 89, 91).

61. See Bining, *Pennsylvania Iron Manufacture,* pp. 45–46 and 171–73.

62. There are two possible reasons for the high percentage figure in York County. The first of these is simply that the one specialized facility in that county was a localized aberration — a possible but not very palatable explanation. The second possibility conforms more closely to what has been said of the town of York as a hinterland market center, that is, that since it was one of the largest of the country markets, sound business sense lay behind the decision to erect a specialized production facility.

63. For example, in 1751 and probably in 1752 a ton of pig iron sold for between £7 and £7.5 in Philadelphia. At the same time, pig iron purchased at Colebrookdale Furnace sold for £5 per ton. Transportation of a ton of Colebrookdale pig iron to Philadelphia cost £1.75, or 20 percent of the Philadelphia price (see Colebrookdale Furnace Ledger, 1750–52, Forges and Furnaces Account Books. Historical Society of Pennsylvania, pp. 22, 42, 61, 62, 66, and 82). Bining notes that in 1760 pig iron sold for £7 per ton at the furnaces and £9 per ton in Philadelphia. Thus, by the time a ton of pig iron reached Philadelphia, transportation costs accounted for 22 percent of its market price. By contrast, in 1758 the transportation costs incurred in transporting a ton of bar iron from Hopewell Forge in Berks County were also £2, but bar iron sold for about £27 in Philadelphia, and transportation costs represented only 7.4 percent of its market price (see Bining, *Pennsylvania Iron Manufacture,* p. 159; and Walzer, "Transportation in the Philadelphia Trading Area," pp. 315–17, n. 8).

64. Lemon, *Best Poor Man's Country,* p. 133.

65. Cf. Bining's contention that the "iron plantations" were "usually a great distance from the main highways" (Bining, *Pennsylvania Iron Manufacture,* p. 32).

66. See, for example, "Early Petitions," in *Pennsylvania Archives,* 6th ser., vol. 14, ed. Thomas Lynch Montgomery (Harrisburg, Pa.: Harrisburg Publishing Co., State Printer, 1907), pp. 259–63, 267–80, 287–96; *Pennsylvania Archives,* 1st ser., vol. 1, ed. Samuel Hazard (Philadelphia: State of Pennsylvania, 1852), p. 436; "Minutes of the Provincial Council of Pennsylvania," *Colonial Records,* vol. 9, pp. 440, 556–61, and vol. 10, pp. 46–47, 50–51, 55, 69–70, 112; *Pennsylvania Archives,* 1st ser., vol. 4, ed. Samuel Hazard (Philadelphia: State of Pennsylvania, 1853), pp. 362–63.

67. "Early Petitions," p. 274.

68. Ibid., pp. 274–75.

69. Robert Ellis to Lawrence Gordon, 15 March 1744 / 45, in Fackenthal, *Briefs of Title,* p. 147; see also map 2 in this volume.

70. "Early Petitions," p. 290.

71. Ibid., pp. 291–92.

## CHAPTER 4

1. Dr. Carroll to Messrs Sedgley and Cheston, 20 April 1753, in "Extracts," *Maryland Historical Magazine* 26 (1931): 49.

2. Sam Caldwell to Peter Grubb, Philadelphia, 15 April 1768, Grubb Collection, Box 1. The average price of twenty-four pounds per ton is from Bezanson, Gray, and Hussey, *Prices,* p. 408.

3. John Wall to Peter Grubb, [Philadelphia], 30 July 1772, Grubb Collection, Box 1.

4. Wall to Peter Grubb, 20 August 1772, in ibid.

5. See table 12.

6. Charles Carroll, barrister, to Messrs. John Stewart and Company, Annapolis, 30 November 1756, in Holt, "Letters of Charles Carroll, Barrister," *Maryland Historical Magazine* 31 (1936): 323.

7. Carroll to John Stewart and Company, 15 September 1757, ibid., p. 41.

8. Particularly useful discussions of some aspects of the English markets are contained in Johnson, "The Baltimore Company Seeks English Markets," pp. 41–59; R. H. Campbell, *Carron Company* (Edinburgh: Oliver and Boyd, 1961), pp. 2–153; Flinn, *Men of Iron,* pp. 136–46; and R. A. Pelham, "The West Midland Iron Industry and the American Market in the 18th Century," *University of Birmingham Historical Journal* 2, no. 2 (1950): 141–62.

9. Dr. Carroll to William Black, Maryland, 8 May 1754, in "Extracts," *Maryland Historical Magazine* 27 (1932): 219.

10. See, for example, various letters in Grubb Collection, Box 1; "Extracts," *Maryland Historical Magazine* 20-27, passim; and Holt, "Letters of Charles Carroll, Barrister," *Maryland Historical Magazine* 31-38, passim.

11. For a short but detailed discussion of the behavior of the Baltimore Company in the English markets vis-à-vis the variable transaction times see Johnson, "The Baltimore Company Seeks English Markets," pp. 39 40, 59 60.

12. See, for example, Holt, "Letters of Charles Carroll, Barrister," *Maryland Historical Magazine* 31-38, passim. Even in the 1740s, when the character of the London market was well known to the Baltimore Company's members, the slow transaction rate prompted Dr. Charles Carroll to write a sarcastic letter to a merchant to whom he had consigned his pig iron (see Dr. Carroll to Lawrence Williams, Maryland, 24 September 1742, in "Extracts," *Maryland Historical Magazine* 20 [1925]: 167). The ratio of the transaction times for London and Bristol are derived from figures given in Johnson, "The Baltimore Company Seeks English Markets," p. 59.

13. Johnson, "The Baltimore Company Seeks English Markets," pp. 39-40. See also Flinn, *Men of Iron,* passim.

14. See correspondence between various Philadelphia merchants and Peter Grubb, owner of Hopewell Forge, in Grubb Collection, Box 1.

15. Relations were not always cordial between a producer and the merchant who advanced him credit (see William Bell to Peter Grubb, Lancaster, 19 January 1772, Grubb Collection, Box 1). See also Carlton O. Wittlinger, "Early Manufacturing in Lancaster County, Pennsylvania, 1710-1840" (Ph.D. diss., University of Pennsylvania, 1953), pp. 103-4.

16. See, for example, an advertisement dated 17 December calling on those indebted to two operators of the Durham "iron works Bucks County" to "discharge their respective

debts" (*Pennsylvania Journal and Weekly Advertiser,* 3 January 1765; see also copy of a memorandum to John Morris, Jr., from Amos Strettell, Philadelphia, 20 July 1765, Carlisle Iron Works. Both Morris and Strettell were partners in the company).

17. Letter to Nathaniel Chapman, December 1736, Carewe Papers.

18. John Price to Charles Carroll, London, 2 March 1750, Carroll-Maccubbin Papers, Box 1750-56. A discussion of Price's proposal is also given in Johnson, "Establishment of the Baltimore Company," pp. 285-86.

19. Price to Carroll, 2 March 1750, Carroll-Maccubbin Papers, Box 1750-56.

20. Ibid.

21. Ibid. See also Johnson, "Establishment of the Baltimore Company," p. 286.

22. Price to Carroll, 2 March 1750, Carroll-Maccubbin Papers, Box 1750-56.

23. Dr. Carroll to William Black, Maryland, 4 July 1743, in "Extracts," *Maryland Historical Magazine* 20 (1925): 272.

24. Charles Carroll, barrister, to Messrs Gale and Pensonby, Annapolis, 20 August 1758, in Holt, "Letters of Charles Carroll, Barrister," *Maryland Historical Magazine* 32 (1937): 184.

25. Charles Carroll, barrister, to Williams Anderson, Annapolis, 25 September 1759, ibid., p. 358.

26. "The IRON-TRADE of Great-Britain Impartially Considered," in Papers Relating to Iron, Peltries, Trade, Etc., Penn Manuscripts, p. 4 (italics in the original).

27. Even in 1771, when colonial exports of iron to England were at their peak, colonial iron accounted for only 10-12.5 percent of all English iron imports (Wacker, *The Musconetcong Valley of New Jersey,* p. 103. For additional material on the significance of colonial iron to overall consumption in England see Pelham, "The West Midland Iron Industry," pp. 159-60 and passim).

28. Bezanson, Gray, and Hussey, *Prices,* pp. 413-14.

29. Paul Zantzinger to Peter Grubb, 20 January 1774, Grubb Collection, Box 1.

30. Curttis Grubb to Peter Grubb, 27 January 1774, ibid.

31. James Old to Curttis or Peter Grubb, Reading Furnace, 27 March 1774, ibid.

32. Bezanson, Gray, and Hussey, *Prices,* pp. 414-15.

33. See, for example, Bining, *Pennsylvania Iron Manufacture,* pp. 75, 193-94.

34. Anne Bezanson, *Prices and Inflation during the American Revolution: Pennsylvania, 1770-1790* (Philadelphia: University of Pennsylvania Press, 1951), p. 164.

35. Ibid., p. 332; and Bezanson, Gray, and Hussey, *Prices,* pp. 378-415.

36. Bezanson, *Prices and Inflation,* app. table 1 (p. 335).

37. New Pine Forge Ledgers, 1775-78, Forges and Furnaces Account Books, Historical Society of Pennsylvania.

38. See William Atlee to Peter Grubb, Lancaster, 1 August 1776; Paul Zantzinger to Peter Grubb, Lancaster, 25 November 1777; and Curttis Grubb to Peter Grubb, 24 January 1779, Grubb Collection, Box 1. Roughly twenty-two pounds of skelp bar iron were needed to make a barrel for a six- to eight-pound rifle. The loss of weight occurred in the reheating, hammering, and filing of the metal in the course of fabrication (see Elliot Wigginton, ed., *Foxfire 5: Ironmaking, Blacksmithing, Flintlock Rifles, Bear Hunting, and Other Affairs of Plain Living* [Garden City, N.Y.: Anchor Press, 1979], p. 226). Musket barrels required less iron than did rifle barrels because their walls did not have to be thick enough to accommodate the interior rifling.

39. Bezanson, *Prices and Inflation,* app. tables 1 (p. 337) and 8 (p. 332).

40. Ibid., chap. 3.

41. New Pine Forge Ledgers, 1775-78.

42. Ibid.

43. Ibid.

44. Bezanson, *Prices and Inflation*, table 8 (p. 322).

45. Ibid., app. table 1 (pp. 334-38).

46. New Pine Forge Ledgers, 1775-78.

47. Caleb and Amos Houlke to Peter Grubb, Philadelphia, 28 September 1778, Grubb Collection, Box 1. See also Bezanson, *Prices and Inflation*, pp. 167-70.

48. New Pine Forge Ledgers, 1775-78; Hopewell Forge Ledger I, 1780-83; and various letters to and from Peter Grubb, 1777-79, Grubb Collection, Box 1. "Light iron" — that is, "Light Flatts and Squares" — was much in demand from Hopewell Forge (see Matthias Hough to Peter Grubb, Lancaster, 28 November 1778, Grubb Collection, Box 1).

49. See Bezanson, *Prices and Inflation*, pp. 165-68; and Bining, *Pennsylvania Iron Manufacture*, pp. 124-25, 163-64. For a classic statement of the contrary view see Thomas C. Cochran, "Did the Civil War Retard Industrialization?" *Mississippi Valley Historical Review* 48 (1961): 200.

50. Pine Forge Bar Iron Book, 1787-90, and Pine Forge Receipts Book, 1787-90, in Forges and Furnaces Account Books, Historical Society of Pennsylvania.

51. For a breakdown of the population of Pittsburgh in 1792 see Hazard, *Register of Pennsylvania* 8, p. 223. The characterization of Pittsburgh in 1815 is from James M. Riddle, comp., *The Pittsburgh Directory for 1815* (Pittsburgh: James M. Riddle, 1815), p. 4. The composition of the city's iron industry is from John Taylor and R. Patterson, *The Honest Man's Extra Almanac for the City of Pittsburgh and the Surrounding Country for the Year 1813* (Pittsburgh: Patterson & Hopkins, 1813).

52. Coxe, *Statement of the Arts and Manufactures*, pp. 49-52.

53. Riddle, *Pittsburgh Directory for 1815*, pp. 2-3.

54. Diane Lindstrom, *Economic Development in the Philadelphia Region, 1810-1850* (New York: Columbia University Press, 1978), p. 25.

55. C. G. Childs, "Philadelphia and Reading Railroad — Its History, etc.," *Hunt's Merchants' Magazine* 16 (February 1847): 210.

56. See, for example, *McLane Report*, vol. 3, docs. 13 and 14, passim. The detailed records of specific furnaces and forges reveal the increased specialization in the industry (see Speedwell Forge Anchonies and Blooms Book, 1832-48, and Pequea Works Coal and Iron Book, 1828-32, Forges and Furnaces Account Books, Historical Society of Pennsylvania).

57. U.S., Congress, House, *Pennsylvania. Memorial of Manufacturers of Hardware, Smiths and Iron-Founders, of the City of Philadelphia to the Honorable the Senate and the House of Representatives of the United States of America in Congress Assembled*, 20th Cong., 1st sess., 17 March 1828, H. Exec. Doc. 202, pp. 3-8.

58. Flinn, *Men of Iron*, pp. 6-8, 98-99.

59. House, *Pennsylvania. Memorial of Manufacturers of Hardware, Smiths and Iron-Founders*, p. 3. An early statement of the pig- and bar-iron producers' view of the situation is Draft of a Memorial to the United States House of Representatives and Senate by Jonah Thompson, Mark Richards, and David C. Wood, "Committee of Iron Masters and Manufacturers of Iron," Philadelphia, 16 December 1823, enclosed in Jonah Thompson to Robert Coleman, Philadelphia, 19 December 1823, Eleutherian Mills Historical Library (hereafter EMHL).

60. See, for example, the memorial of the "Committee of Iron-Masters and Manufacturers of Iron," Philadelphia, 16 December 1823, EMHL; and House, *Pennsylvania. Memorial of Manufacturers of Hardware, Smiths and Iron-Founders*, pp. 3-4.

61. U.S., Congress, House, *Memorial of the Citizens of Philadelphia Engaged in the Manufacture of Iron to the Senate and House of Representatives of the United States in Congress Assembled*, 21st Cong., 2d sess., 21 February 1831, H. Exec. Doc. 109, p. 3.

62. For a thorough account of urban growth in the United States during the nineteenth century see Manuel Gottlieb, *Long Swings in Urban Development* (New York: National Bureau of Economic Research, 1976); and George Rogers Taylor, *The Transportation Revolution, 1815-1860* (New York: Harper Torchbooks, 1951). A more recent analysis of the connection between urban growth and aggregate demand is presented in Lindstrom, *Economic Development in the Philadelphia Region.*

In 1810 Tench Coxe reported a total of 170 naileries, which turned out about 3,200 tons (one ton = 2,240 lbs.) of nails. In 1832 the incomplete returns for the *McLane Report* listed 3 nailworks, which produced in excess of 400 tons of nails per year in eastern Pennsylvania. The *McLane Report*'s more complete returns for the west included 8 nailworks, which produced 2,759 tons of nails (see Coxe, *Statement of the Arts and Manufactures,* pp. 49-52; *McLane Report,* vol. 2, doc. 13, passim, and doc. 14, no. 323, pp. 638-41). A not unreasonable estimate of 7,000 and 40,000 tons as the nail production of Pennsylvania and of the United States, respectively, was given by one nail manufacturer in Chester County (see responses of Morton and Henry Coate's Nail Manufactory, *McLane Report,* vol. 2, doc. 13, no. 17, p. 216).

63. Peter Temin, *Iron and Steel in Nineteenth-Century America: An Economic Inquiry* (Cambridge, Mass.: M.I.T. Press, 1964), p. 15.

64. Responses to the questionnaire distributed under Treasury Secretary Louis McLane's authority were often hostile in tone, expressing "an universal objection to several of the queries proposed by the department" (see "Report of Andrew M. Prevost to the Commissioners [Mathew Carey and Clement C. Biddle]," Philadelphia, 20 April 1832, *McLane Report,* vol. 2, doc. 13, no. 2, p. 197). The inadequacies of the 1849 report are discussed in Robert William Fogel, *Railroads and American Economic Growth: Essays in Econometric History* (Baltimore: The Johns Hopkins Press, 1964); pp. 153, 160-61.

65. See Speedwell Forge Record Book, 1840-60; Colebrook Furnace Castings Book, 1837-43; and Pequea Works Coal and Iron Book, 1828-32, Forges and Furnaces Account Books, Historical Society of Pennsylvania. See also *McLane Report,* vol. 2, doc. 13, no. 1, and docs. 13 and 14, passim.

66. Frank W. Taussig, *The Tariff History of the United States,* 8th ed. (New York: G. P. Putnam's Sons, 1931), p. 134.

67. See Temin, *Iron and Steel,* pp. 21-22.

68. The literature on this point is extensive and includes Temin, *Iron and Steel,* pp. 17-18; and Taussig, *Tariff History of the United States,* pp. 126-28. For a contemporary account see "Memorial of the Iron Manufacturers of New England Asking for a Modification of the Tariff of 1846," Philadelphia, 1850, EMHL, pp. 35-56.

69. "Memorial of the Iron Manufacturers of New England," p. 37.

70. For example, see *McLane Report,* vol. 2, doc. 13, nos. 10, p. 208, and 24, p. 225; and doc. 14, no. 2, p. 236.

71. Temin, *Iron and Steel,* p. 22; Nathan Rosenberg, *Technology and American Economic Growth* (New York: Harper Torchbooks, 1972), p. 74.

72. Fogel, *Railroads and American Economic Growth,* table 5.15 (p. 194).

73. See U.S., Congress, Senate, *Memorial on Duty on Railroad Iron Praying an Extension of the Law Exempting Railroad Iron from Duty of the Georgia Railroad Company,* 28th Cong., 1st sess., 16 January 1844, S. Doc. 58; *Memorial against Duties on Railroad Iron Praying a Remission of the Duties on Certain Railroad Iron of the Long Island Railroad Company,* 28th Cong., 1st sess., 19 January 1844, S. Doc. 55; and *Memorial of the Presidents and Directors of Sundry Railroad Companies in Virginia, Praying the Repeal of the Duty on Railroad Iron,* 28th Cong., 1st sess., 11 March 1844, S. Doc. 176.

74. Taussig, *Tariff History of the United States,* pp. 111 and n, 120-21, 114.

75. See, for example, U.S., Congress, Senate, *Memorial of a Number of Citizens of Pennsylvania Praying a Repeal [sic] of the Duty upon Railroad Iron*, 28th Cong., 1st sess., 27 February 1844, S. Doc. 148; and *Proceedings of a Meeting of Democratic Citizens of Sunbury, Pa., . . . ,* 29th Cong., 1st sess., 23 July 1846, S. Doc. 446. The happy position in which the textile industry found itself is described in Taussig, *Tariff History of the United States,* pp. 137-40.

76. Taussig, *Tariff History of the United States,* p. 115.

77. "Memorial of the Iron Manufacturers of New England," pp. 32-33.

78. Ibid., p. 19; Charles E. Smith, "The Manufacture of Iron in Pennsylvania," *Hunt's Merchants' Magazine* 25 (November 1851): 578.

79. "Memorial of the Iron Manufacturers of New England," p. 16; Taussig, *Tariff History of the United States,* pp. 127-28, 134.

80. "Memorial of the Iron Manufacturers of New England," p. 17.

81. Ibid., pp. 17, 18, 16, and 33-34, respectively.

82. Ibid., pp. 23-24; and House, *Memorial of the Citizens of Philadelphia Engaged in the Manufacture of Iron,* p. 3.

83. House, *Memorial of the Citizens of Philadelphia Engaged in the Manufacture of Iron,* p. 3.

84. House, *Pennsylvania. Memorial of Manufacturers of Hardware, Smiths and Iron-Founders,* p. 7.

85. The *Journal of the Franklin Institute* published a number of accounts of experiments on iron conducted in the United States and Great Britain. See, for example, Walter R. Johnson, "Experiments on Two Varieties of Iron, Manufactured at the Adirondack Works Directly from the Magnetic Ore of McIntyre, Essex County, New York," *Journal of the Franklin Institute,* N.S., 23 (January 1839): 1-10; and Eaton Hodgkinson, "On the Relative Strength and Other Mechanical Properties of Cast Iron Obtained by Hot and Cold Blast," ibid., 24 (September 1839): 184-96 and (October 1839): 238-57. See also, Walter R. Johnson, "Letters from Professor W. R. Johnson, on the Subject of Further Experiments on Iron, Copper and Coal," in "Special Studies," *New American State Papers,* ed. Thomas C. Cochran, vol. 11 (Wilmington, Del.: Scholarly Resources, 1973), pp. 676-81.

86. "Memorial of the Iron Manufacturers of New England," pp. 20-21.

87. Letter to Captain Beverly Kennon, Washington, D.C., 4 September 1843, in Johnson, "Letters from Professor W. R. Johnson," p. 677.

88. "Memorial of the Iron Manufacturers of New England," pp. 20-22. The memorial cites the "reports of Major Wade, a scientific metallurgist, made to the Ordinance Bureau" in the late 1840s (pp. 21-22). A Major Wade, formerly of the United States Army, is credited with the invention of a "beautiful and ingenious machine . . . which is so contrived as to give in pounds per square inch of the material, the resistance to crushing, to twisting, and to longitudinal and traverse fracture" (Board of Regents of the Smithsonian Institution, *Ninth Annual Report,* 33d Cong., 2d sess., 1855, H. Misc. Doc. 37, p. 18). See also the response to query 7 — "Cause of increase [or decrease as the case may be] of profit?" — of "Roland Curtin & Sons, Eagle Iron Works, Centre County, West Pennsylvania," *McLane Report,* vol. 3, doc. 14, no. 33, p. 289.

89. "Memorial of the Iron Manufacturers of New England," p. 31; and Smith, "The Manufacture of Iron in Pennsylvania," p. 581. Data are drawn from "Documents Relating to the Manufacture of Iron in Pennsylvania," tables following p. 72. These tables were widely published in the journals of the day, including *Hunt's Merchants' Magazine* 25 (November 1851) and Henry Varnum Poor's *American Railroad Journal* 23 (27 July; 3, 17, 24, 31 August 1850).

90. *McLane Report,* vol. 2, doc. 13, no. 10, pp. 207-8.

91. "Memorial of the Iron Manufacturers of New England," p. 7; Smith, "The Manufacture of Iron in Pennsylvania," 581.

92. *McLane Report,* vol. 2, doc. 13, no. 1, query 32, p. 197; doc. 13, no. 9, pp. 204-5; and doc. 14, no. 87, pp. 381-82.

93. The Coate brothers and McCalmont are not listed in "Documents Relating to the Manufacture of Iron in Pennsylvania," tables following p. 72. Also, neither name appears in a less extensive compilation published in 1846 which listed a total of 334 facilities (see "Iron and Coal Statistics: Being Extracts from the Report of a Committee to the Iron and Coal Association of the State of Pennsylvania," *Journal of the Franklin Institute,* 3d ser., 12 [August 1846]: 124-35).

94. *McLane Report,* vol. 2, doc. 13, no. 2, p. 197.

95. Speedwell was owned by either Nicholas or Daniel Yocum or both — the record is unclear (see "Documents Relating to the Manufacture of Iron in Pennsylvania," table entitled "A Detailed Statement of the Charcoal Forges in Eastern Pennsylvania in the Year 1850," following p. 72). In 1850, 50 percent of the forges in eastern Pennsylvania and 96 percent of the 23 in Berks County used waterpower. Similarly, 92 percent of those in the eastern part of the state and 96 percent of those in Berks County used charcoal as their fuel. Fifty-six percent of the forges in the region and 74 percent of the forges in Berks County were owned by individuals, as opposed to partnerships or companies. Speedwell Forge produced an average of 260 tons of blooms and bar iron during the period 1840-47 (Speedwell Forge Anchonies and Blooms Book, 1832-48). By comparison, incomplete data for 119 forges in eastern Pennsylvania indicate that in 1849 output per forge was 238 tons, but only 206 tons for 21 forges in Berks County. The latter figure is probably considerably lower than it should be because of missing data. In 1849, 119 forges in eastern Pennsylvania and the 21 in Berks County employed 26 and 20 "men and boys," respectively. The source for the 1849 data is "Documents Relating to the Manufacture of Iron in Pennsylvania," table entitled "A Detailed Statement of the Charcoal Forges in Eastern Pennsylvania in the Year 1850," following p. 72.

96. Speedwell Forge Time Book, 1832-42, Forges and Furnaces Account Books, Historical Society of Pennsylvania.

97. Price data for blooms are spotty for the nineteenth century. A sample of twenty-seven forges from the *McLane Report,* doc. 14, for western Pennsylvania provides fifteen price quotations for blooms and twelve for bar iron in 1832. The mean price for blooms was sixty-seven dollars per ton; and the mean price for bar iron was eighty-five dollars per ton.

98. Speedwell Forge Anchonies and Blooms Book, 1832-48.

99. The reduction was to $3.50 per ton from some unknown wage. That it may have been a substantial reduction is suggested by the fact that in 1832 the owner of Juniata Forge reported that his forgemen made $6.00 per ton (see *McLane Report,* vol. 2, doc. 14, no. 23, p. 319, replies of J. Steinman for Peter Shoenberger, owner of Juniata Forge, in Huntingdon County, West Pennsylvania). Juniata's forgemen worked "by turns during night and day" (ibid.).

## CHAPTER 5

1. "Documents Relating to the Manufacture of Iron in Pennsylvania," tables following p. 72.

2. The association of the adoption of new techniques with the formation of more advanced types of business organization is usually made with respect to the integrated man-

ufacturing establishments of the nineteenth century before 1860. Thus, Peter Temin, in discussing the integrated rolling mills of the 1840s and 1850s in Pennsylvania — about half of which were owned by companies — points out that the capital costs of rail mills were higher than those of other rolling mills because of the need in the rail mills for heavy, costly machinery (see Temin, *Iron and Steel,* pp. 106-14, esp. p. 113). A similar point is made by Alfred D. Chandler, Jr., with respect to the rise of integrated textile mills in Massachusetts after the War of 1812. He notes that one of the chief virtues of the integrated mill was its large output capacity, made possible by its use of power-driven machinery. The use of this machinery entailed large capital costs which could be met only by incorporation of the ventures (see Chandler, *The Visible Hand: The Managerial Revolution in American Business* [Cambridge, Mass.: Belknap Press, 1977], pp. 58-59).

3. Temin observes: "The expensiveness of the initial investment [in a large rail mill] required a large volume of production to spread the fixed cost over many items and keep down the cost of any one. The size of the plant required thus implied large scale and limited entry [into the industry], while large scale provided the impetus toward integration" (Temin, *Iron and Steel,* p. 113). Referring specifically to Francis Cabot Lowell's textile factory, the Boston Manufacturing Company of Waltham, Massachusetts (soon incorporated to provide needed additional capital), Alfred Chandler notes that "by integrating all the activities involved in these two basic processes [spinning and weaving], Lowell's Boston Manufacturing Company was able to turn out a far greater volume of cloth at a much lower unit cost than any other textile producer" (Chandler, *The Visible Hand,* p. 58).

4. Eighteenth-century data are drawn largely from Bining, *Pennsylvania Iron Manufacture,* pp. 171-76. The 1832 data are contained in *McLane Report,* vol. 2, docs. 13 and 14. Data for 1842 are printed in "Iron and Coal Statistics," pp. 124-36. The 1849 data are contained in "Documents Relating to the Manufacture of Iron in Pennsylvania," tables following p. 72.

5. See "Report of Andrew M. Prevost to the Commissioners [Matthew Carey and Clement C. Biddle]," Philadelphia, 20 April 1832, *McLane Report,* vol. 2, doc. 3, no. 2, p. 197.

6. Temin, *Iron and Steel,* p. 59; "Documents Relating to the Manufacture of Iron in Pennsylvania," tables following p. 72.

7. "Documents Relating to the Manufacture of Iron in Pennsylvania," tables following p. 72; *McLane Report,* vol. 2, docs. 13 and 14.

8. For capitalization levels of different types of production facilities see "Statement, Showing the Number and Condition of Each Sort of Iron Works, and the Capital Invested in the Land and Buildings in Each County in Eastern Pennsylvania, in the Year 1850" and a similar statement for western Pennsylvania in "Documents Relating to the Manufacture of Iron in Pennsylvania," tables following p. 72. A useful caveat concerning capitalization figures such as those given in the *McLane Report* is offered in Glenn Porter and Harold C. Livesay, *Merchants and Manufacturers: Studies in the Changing Structure of Nineteenth-Century Marketing* (Baltimore: The Johns Hopkins Press, 1971), p. 49.

9. I have assumed that the mean numbers of puddling furnaces, heating furnaces, and rollers were a rough but reliable reflection of capitalization, the obvious but sound principle being that two furnaces or rollers cost more than one furnace or roller.

10. Porter and Livesay, *Merchants and Manufacturers,* p. 48.

11. Ibid., pp. 47-48; see also "Iron and Coal Statistics," p. 126.

12. Porter and Livesay, *Merchants and Manufacturers,* p. 48; "Documents Relating to the Manufacture of Iron in Pennsylvania," tables following p. 72.

13. "Documents Relating to the Manufacture of Iron in Pennsylvania," tables following p. 72.

14. Ibid., p. 72. One furnace was owned by a bank.

15. Less than 8 percent of the furnaces and forges used steam or steam and water, whereas almost 39 percent of the rolling, slitting, and wire mills, nailworks and other specialized facilities made use of steam, either exclusively or in combination with water-power. Predictably enough, foundries and steam-engine works relied heavily on steam-power: about 78 percent used only steam; 11 percent used waterpower; and 11 percent used horses (derived from *McLane Report,* vol. 2, doc. 14, no. 323, abstract).

16. "Documents Relating to the Manufacture of Iron in Pennsylvania," tables following p. 72. Of the hot-blast charcoal furnaces constructed as hot-blast furnaces — that is, not converted from cold-blast operation — after 1829, seventeen were entirely or in part powered by steam. An 1832-vintage steam-powered furnace was erected by a partnership. A furnace built in the same year and owned by a company was powered by water and steam. Four years later a company built a furnace powered entirely by steam.

17. "Iron and Coal Statistics," p. 131.

18. Ibid., pp. 129–30.

19. "Documents Relating to the Manufacture of Iron in Pennsylvania," tables following p. 72.

20. "Iron and Coal Statistics," p. 125.

21. Ibid., p. 127.

22. Ibid.

23. See *Laws of the General Assembly of the State of Pennsylvania* (Harrisburg: Published by authority, 1830–50). These contain the special charters of incorporation issued by the state to petitioners.

24. Ibid.; Porter and Livesay, *Merchants and Manufacturers,* p. 40.

25. An additional thirty-five firms, or 10 percent of the total number, owned both furnaces and forges. Of these thirty-five, twenty-one were owned by individuals, nine by partnerships, and five by companies. The combined total of "integrated" firms (the use of the term is Temin's), therefore, is fifty-five, or about 16 percent of the 350 firms. This is roughly comparable to the 20 percent figure for 1820 and 1857 given by Temin in *Iron and Steel,* p. 94.


CHAPTER 6

1. Survival rates are derived from "Iron and Coal Statistics," p. 126; and "Documents Relating to the Manufacture of Iron in Pennsylvania."

2. Joseph A. Schumpeter, *Capitalism, Socialism and Democracy,* 3d ed. (New York: Harper Torchbooks, 1962), p. 83. Here Schumpeter describes "Creative Destruction" as a "process of industrial mutation . . . that incessantly revolutionizes the economic structure *from within,* incessantly destroying the old one, incessantly creating a new one. This process of Creative Destruction is the essential fact about capitalism" (italics in the original).

3. Ibid.

4. Three new charcoal furnaces were erected in eastern Pennsylvania between 1850 and 1857. All of them had failed or stopped within that period (see J. P. Lesley, *The Iron Manufacturer's Guide to the Furnaces, Forges and Rolling Mills of the United States* [New York: John Wiley, 1859], pp. 37–61, 87–108).

5. See William D. Walsh, *The Diffusion of Technological Change in the Pennsylvania Pig Iron Industry, 1850–1870,* Dissertations in American Economic History, ed. Stuart Bruchey (New York: Arno Press, 1975), app. table A.1 (p. 207).

6. These figures are calculated from the total-furnace-output and total-furnace-capacity values for all furnaces except coke- and bituminous coal–fueled facilities, contained in tables 37 and 38, respectively.

7. The anthracite furnaces were more cost-efficient than other furnaces because of their large output capacities and their use of a more efficient fuel (see Walsh, *The Diffusion of Technological Change,* app. tables B.1 and B.2 [pp. 211–12]; and Temin, *Iron and Steel,* table 3.1 [p. 64]).

8. These figures for the 1840s and 1850s are computed from data contained, respectively, in "Documents Relating to the Manufacture of Iron in Pennsylvania," tables following p. 72; and Lesley, *The Iron Manufacturer's Guide,* pp. 229–40, 247–53.

9. This conclusion is based on the lack of concentration evident in the data for these periods. For the eighteenth century see Bining, *Pennsylvania Iron Manufacture,* pp. 171–76. Data for the period in the nineteenth century prior to 1832 are found in the *McLane Report,* passim.

10. These figures are derived from the tabular data presented in "Iron and Coal Statistics," table entitled "List of New Anthracite Furnaces in Pennsylvania," p. 131.

11. Temin, *Iron and Steel,* p. 106; and Harold C. Livesay, "Marketing Patterns in the Antebellum American Iron Industry," *Business History Review* 45 (Autumn 1971): 290.

12. Temin, *Iron and Steel,* p. 111.

13. Ibid., p. 112.

14. Survival rates are derived from "Documents Relating to the Manufacture of Iron in Pennsylvania"; and Lesley, *The Iron Manufacturer's Guide,* pp. 229–40, 247–53.

15. Livesay, "Marketing Patterns," p. 289; Temin, *Iron and Steel,* p. 111.

16. Temin, *Iron and Steel,* p. 111.

17. "Documents Relating to the Manufacture of Iron in Pennsylvania"; and Lesley, *The Iron Manufacturer's Guide,* passim.

18. Lesley, *The Iron Manufacturer's Guide,* pp. 750, 759.

19. In 1849 five integrated mill firms owned thirteen anthracite blast furnaces with a mean capacity of 4,312 tons and a mean volume of 4,559 cubic feet. The mean capacity and mean volume for the industry as a whole in 1849 were 4,025 tons and 4,168 cubic feet, respectively. In 1859 nine integrated mill firms owned eighteen anthracite furnaces with a mean volume of 7,163 cubic feet. The mean volume for the entire industry in 1859 was 5,840 cubic feet (figures for 1849 are derived from "Documents Relating to the Manufacture of Iron in Pennsylvania"; those for 1859 are derived from Lesley, *The Iron Manufacturer's Guide,* pp. 6–23).

20. Walt W. Rostow, *The Stages of Economic Growth: A Non-Communist Manifesto* (Cambridge: At the University Press, 1960), p. 55; and idem, ed., *The Economics of Take-off into Sustained Growth* (New York: St. Martin's Press, 1963), p. 5.

21. Fogel, *Railroads and American Economic Growth,* pp. 232–33; and Albert Fishlow, *American Railroads and the Transformation of the Antebellum Economy,* Harvard Economic Studies, vol. 127 (Cambridge, Mass.: Harvard University Press, 1965), p. 143.

22. See Fishlow, *American Railroads and the Transformation of the Antebellum Economy,* pp. 104 and 115.

23. This estimate is derived in a restrictive manner. Only the rolling mills specifically identified as having produced rails or railroad iron were included in the calculations. Thus, several mills that produced spikes or other iron products consumed by the railroad are not considered.

24. Temin, *Iron and Steel,* p. 21; Fishlow, *American Railroads and the Transformation of the Antebellum Economy,* pp. 136–37.

25. Fishlow, *American Railroads and the Transformation of the Antebellum Economy,* p. 149.

26. Livesay, "Marketing Patterns," pp. 288, 292. See also Fishlow, *American Railroads and the Transformation of the Antebellum Economy,* pp. 144–45.

27. The rolling mill of Reeves, Buck & Company produced bar and sheet at a rate of 40.4

tons per worker and consumed 1.33 tons of anthracite coal per ton of output. Its nearest competitor in terms of efficiency was M. A. & S. Bertholet & Company, a nonintegrated mill firm that made sheet iron, bars, and rods at a rate of 25 tons per worker but in the process consumed 2.67 tons of anthracite coal per ton of output. These figures are derived from "Documents Relating to the Manufacture of Iron in Pennsylvania."

28. Ibid.; and Lesley, *The Iron Manufacturer's Guide,* pp. 229-40, 247-53.

29. Livesay, "Marketing Patterns," p. 288.

30. Temin, *Iron and Steel,* p. 68. The capitalization levels for the ante-bellum iron industry are suspect, primarily because "it is not possible to ascertain what, if any, uniform system of valuation is used to obtain the capital investment figures" (Walsh, *The Diffusion of Technological Change,* p. 17).

31. Smith and Cole, *Fluctuations in American Business,* app. table 74 (pp. 192-94).

32. Ibid., p. 127.

33. Ibid., p. 125.

34. Ibid., chart 44, (p. 126); see also p. 127.

35. Ibid., pp. 83-84, 136-37.

36. "Iron and Coal Statistics," p. 131; "Documents Relating to the Manufacture of Iron in Pennsylvania."

37. Figures are derived from Fogel, *Railroads and American Economic Growth,* table 5.14 (p. 192).

38. See, for example, Smith, "The Manufacture of Iron in Pennsylvania," p. 581.

39. Apart from the empirical evidence presented in table 48, indirect support for this conclusion is found in an article nearly contemporaneous with the period under discussion. In an article by James George Beckton originally published in the periodical *Newton's London Journal of Arts,* August 1865, the author notes that "the area of the boshes in the large furnace [is] double that in the small furnace, while the quantity of iron produced by the large furnace and, consequently, the quantity of blast supplied is only one and a half times as much as in the small furnace." He goes on to surmise that because the "ascending gases pass through the materials at a slower velocity and at a lower temperature in the larger furnace," the larger furnaces are more fuel-efficient (see James George Beckton, "On the Construction of Blast Furnaces and the Manufacture of Pig Iron in the Cleveland District," *Journal of the Franklin Institute,* 3d ser., 51 [January 1866]: 39).

40. Louis C. Hunter, "The Influence of the Market upon Technique in the Iron Industry in Western Pennsylvania up to 1860," *Journal of Economic and Business History* 1 (February 1929): 241-81; and Temin, *Iron and Steel,* pp. 51-76.

41. Hunter, "The Influence of the Market."

42. Temin, *Iron and Steel,* p. 76.

43. In *Railroads and American Economic Growth,* Robert Fogel uses the figures for largest previous product "as a measure of capacity (rather than the higher but more questionable capacity ratings)" (p. 153). The reasons behind his objection to the use of rated capacity figures are not clear. Furnace volume is far more closely related to the rated capacity of a furnace than to the furnace's largest previous product. The latter was only indirectly tied to furnace volume. It reflected market conditions since the time of the construction of the furnace.

44. Because of the much smaller size and lower level of capitalization of charcoal furnaces, no lag is introduced between capacity and the discount rate. The assumption is that the financing and construction of a charcoal furnace occurred during the same year in which the furnace went into blast.

45. "Documents Relating to the Manufacture of Iron in Pennsylvania," tables following p. 72. Three other charcoal furnaces were listed: two owned by the heirs of deceased operators, one by a bank.

## CHAPTER 7

1. Commonwealth of Pennsylvania, "Statistical Table of the Blast Furnaces of Pennsylvania, Giving Location, Name of Furnace, Owner or Lessee, Post Office Address, Fuel, Ores and Production in 1872, Taken Mainly from the 'American Manufacturer,' as Compiled by the Editor, Joseph D. Weeks," *First Annual Report of the Bureau of Statistics of Labor and Agriculture, for the Years 1872–3* (Harrisburg: Benjamin Singerly, State Printer, 1874), pp. 238–45.

# Selected Bibliography

Although a large body of sources, both manuscript collections and published materials, has informed this history, only those sources that are cited in the notes or bear directly on a point made in the text are listed here.

## PRIMARY SOURCES

### Manuscript Sources

Baltimore, Md.   Maryland Historical Society.
  Baltimore Company Records, 1703–37.
  Carroll-Maccubbin Papers, 1730–37. Records of the Baltimore Iron Works.
  Hanson Family Papers, 1731–87. Elk Ridge Company (Caleb Dorsey and Co. Iron Works), 1757–87. Accounts and Other Business Papers.
Newark, N.J.   New Jersey Historical Society.
  Manuscripts Collection. K26.31. Letter Book of Robert Erskine No. 1, May 1772; September–December 1773.
  Manuscripts Collection. N.J. III 21. Peter Hasenclever to James Parker, London, 20 February 1767.
New York, N.Y.   New York Public Library.
  Special Collections. Peter Hasenclever. *The Remarkable Case of Peter Hasenclever, Merchant.* London, 1773. Photocopy of the original.
Philadelphia, Pa.   Historical Society of Pennsylvania.
  Additional Manuscripts. Durham Iron Company Briefs of Title, 1773.
  Collection of Business, Professional, and Personal Account Books. Letter Book of Robert Ellis, 1736–48.
  Forges and Furnaces Account Books.
    Colebrook Furnace Castings Book, 1837–43.
    Colebrookdale Furnace Ledger, 1750–52.
    Mary Ann Furnace Time Book & Miscellaneous, 1765–71.
    New Pine Forge Cole Book, 1744–60.
    New Pine Forge Ledger A, 1760–62.
    New Pine Forge Ledger B, 1762–63.
    New Pine Forge Ledgers, 1775–78.
    New Pine Forge Time Book, 1760–63.

163

Pequea Works Coal and Iron Book, 1828–32.
Pine Forge Bar Iron Book, 1787–90.
Pine Forge Receipts Book, 1787–90.
Speedwell Forge Anchonies and Blooms Book, 1832–48.
Speedwell Forge Cordwood and Coal Book, 1832–45.
Speedwell Forge Cordwood and Coal Book, 1846–61.
Speedwell Forge Record Book, 1840–60.
Speedwell Forge Time Book, 1832–42.
Grubb Collection. Box 1. Correspondence.
Grubb Collection. Grubb Furnace and Forge Account Books.
Cornwall Furnace Blast and Pig Iron Book, 1776–92.
Cornwall Furnace Coal and Cordwood Book, 1776–92.
Cornwall Furnace Time Book, 1776–85.
Hopewell Forge Coal, Iron & Time Book, Etc., 1768–75.
Hopewell Forge Ledger A, 1765–67.
Hopewell Forge Ledger B, 1767–68.
Hopewell Forge Ledger C, 1768–69.
Hopewell Forge Ledger D, 1769–70.
Hopewell Forge Ledger E, 1770–71.
Hopewell Forge Ledger F, 1771–74.
Hopewell Forge Ledger G, 1774–75.
Hopewell Forge Ledger I, 1780–83.
Hopewell Forge Ledger K, 1783–86.
Iron Industry and Trade Autograph Collection. Carlisle Iron Works. Papers.
Logan Papers. Letter Books of James Logan, 1716–29.
Penn Manuscripts. Papers Relating to Iron, Peltries, Trade, Etc., 1712–1817.
Potts Manuscripts. Potts Grove Ledger B, XVII, 1762.
Washington D.C. Library of Congress.
British Museum Additional Manuscripts. 29600. Carewe Papers. Papers Relating to America, 1725–76. Photocopy of the original.
Wilmington, Del. Eleutherian Mills Historical Library.
Draft of a Memorial to the United States House of Representatives and Senate by Jonah Thompson, Mark Richards, and David C. Wood, "Committee of Iron Masters and Manufacturers of Iron," Philadelphia, 16 December 1823. Enclosed in Jonah Thompson to Robert Coleman, Philadelphia, 19 December 1823.
"Memorial of the Iron Manufacturers of New England Asking for a Modification of the Tariff of 1846," Philadelphia, 1850.

### PRINTED PRIMARY SOURCES

*American Railroad Journal,* 1830–60.
Balch, Thomas. *Letters and Papers Relating Chiefly to the Provincial History of Pennsylvania, With Some Notices of the Writers.* Philadelphia: Privately printed, 1855.

Beckton, James George. "On the Construction of Blast Furnaces and the Manufacture of Pig Iron in the Cleveland District." *Journal of the Franklin Institute,* 3d ser., 51 (January 1866): 37-44.

Board of Regents of the Smithsonian Institution. *Ninth Annual Report.* 33d Cong., 2d sess., 1855, H. Misc. Doc. 37.

Burnaby, Andrew. *Travels through the Middle Settlements of North America, 1759-1760.* 3d ed. 1798. Reprinted in *Burnaby's Travels through North America,* edited by Rufus Rockwell Wilson. New York: A. Wessels Co., 1904.

Childs, C. G. "The Iron Trade of Europe and the United States: With Special Reference to the Iron Trade of Pennsylvania," *Hunt's Merchants' Magazine* 16 (June 1847): 584-85.

_____. "Philadelphia and Reading Railroad — Its History, etc." *Hunt's Merchants' Magazine* 16 (February 1847): 210-12.

Commonwealth of Pennsylvania. "Statistical Table of the Blast Furnaces of Pennsylvania, Giving Location, Name of Furnace, Owner or Lessee, Post Office Address, Fuel, Ores and Production in 1872, Taken Mainly from the 'American Manufacturer,' as Compiled by the Editor, Joseph D. Weeks." *First Annual Report of the Bureau of Statistics of Labor and Agriculture, for the Years 1872-3,* pp. 238-45. Harrisburg: Benjamin Singerly, State Printer, 1874.

Coxe, Tench. *A Statement of the Arts and Manufactures of the United States of America for the Year 1810.* Philadelphia, 1814. Copy in the Eleutherian Mills Historical Library, Wilmington, Del.

"Diary of a Journey of Moravians from Bethlehem, Pennsylvania, to Bethabara in Wachovia, North Carolina, 1753." In *Travels in the American Colonies,* ed. Newton D. Mereness, pp. 327-56. New York: The Macmillan Co., 1916.

"Documents Relating to the Colonial History of the State of New Jersey." *New Jersey Archives,* 1st ser., vol. 9. Newark, N.J.: State of New Jersey, 1885.

"Documents Relating to the Manufacture of Iron in Pennsylvania." *Journal of the Franklin Institute,* 3d ser., 21 (January 1851), tables following pp. 69-72.

"Extracts from Account and Letter Books of Dr. Charles Carroll of Annapolis." *Maryland Historical Magazine* 18-27 (1923-32).

Fackenthal, B. F., Jr., comp. *Briefs of Title to Real Estate in Durham and Adjoining Townships in Pennsylvania and the Partition and Allottment of the Durham Iron Company among the Partners as of December 24, 1773 and its SUBSEQUENT OWNERS. Also Briefs of OTHER LAND Titles in Springfield Township and Nockamixon Townships in Bucks County and in Williams and Lower Saucon Townships Northampton County Pennsylvania together with Other Historical Data.* Riegelsville, Pa.: Historical Society of Pennsylvania, 1936.

Hazard, Samuel, ed. *The Register of Pennsylvania. Devoted to the Preservation of Facts and Documents, and every Kind of useful Information Respecting the State of Pennsylvania* 8 (July–December 1831).

Hodgkinson, Eaton. "On the Relative Strength and Other Mechanical Properties of Cast Iron Obtained by Hot and Cold Blast." *Journal of the
Franklin Institute,* 3d ser., 14 (September 1839): 184–96 and (October 1839):
223–57.

Holt, W. Stull, ed. "Letters of Charles Carroll, Barrister." *Maryland
Historical Magazine* 31–38 (1936–43).

"Iron and Coal Statistics: Being Extracts from the Report of a Committee
to the Iron and Coal Association of the State of Pennsylvania." *Journal of
the Franklin Institute,* 3d ser., 12 (August 1846): 124–36.

Johnson, Walter R. "Experiments on Two Varieties of Iron, Manufactured at
the Adirondack Works Directly from Magnetic Ore of McIntyre, Essex
County, New York." *Journal of the Franklin Institute,* N.S., 23 (January
1839): 1–10.

———. "Letters from Professor W. R. Johnson, on the Subject of Further
Experiments on Iron, Copper and Coal," Philadelphia, 23 June 1841;
Washington, D.C., 4 September 1843; Philadelphia, 11, 13, and 16
November 1844. In "Special Studies," *New American State Papers,* edited by
Thomas C. Cochran, vol. 11, pp. 676–81. Wilmington, Del.: Scholarly
Resources, 1973.

Jones, Anna I., and Stone, George W. "Topographic Map of Lancaster
Quadrangle." In *Topographic and Geographic Atlas of Pennsylvania, Lancaster Quadrangle,* sheet 168, pl. 1. Harrisburg: Pennsylvania Department
of Internal Affairs, Topographic and Geologic Survey, 1930.

Kalm, Peter. *The America of 1750: Peter Kalm's Travels in North America,
The English Version of 1770.* Edited and translated by Adolph B. Benson. 2
vols. 1937. Reprint. New York: Dover Publications, 1966.

Lathem, Edward Connery, comp. *Chronological Tables of American
Newspapers, 1690–1820.* Barre, Mass.: American Antiquarian Society and
Barre Publishers, 1972.

*Laws of the General Assembly of the State of Pennsylvania.* Harrisburg:
Published by authority, 1830–50.

Lesley, J. P. *The Iron Manufacturer's Guide to the Furnaces, Forges and
Rolling Mills of the United States.* New York: John Wiley, 1859.

McLane, Louis. *Documents Relative to the Manufactures of the United
States.* 4 vols. 1833. Reprint (4 vols. in 3). New York: Burt Franklin, 1969.

"A Map of Pennsylvania exhibiting not only the improved parts of that
Province, but also its extensive frontiers: Laid down from actual surveys,
and chiefly from the late Map of W. Scull Published in 1770. Published by
Robert Sayer & J. Bennett, 10 June 1775." Milton S. Eisenhower Library,
The Johns Hopkins University, Baltimore, Md.

*Maryland Gazette,* 1767.

Miller, Herman P. *Outline Maps of the Counties of Allegheny, Berks, Bucks,
Cambria, Dauphin, Fayette, Lackawanna, Lancaster, Luzerne, Mont-
gomery, Philadelphia, Schuylkill, Westmoreland and York. . . .* Harrisburg:
Pennsylvania General Assembly, 1901.

"Minutes of the Provincial Council of Pennsylvania from the Organization to
the Termination of the Proprietary Government." In *Colonial Records,* vols.
9 and 10. Harrisburg: Published by the State, 1852.

*Pennsylvania Archives.* 1st ser., vol. 1. Edited by Samuel Hazard. Philadelphia: State of Pennsylvania, 1852.

_____. 1st ser., vol. 4. Edited by Samuel Hazard. Philadelphia: State of Pennsylvania, 1853.

_____. 3d ser., vol. 17. Edited by William Henry Egle. Philadelphia: State of Pennsylvania, 1898.

_____. 6th ser., vol 14. Edited by Thomas Lynch Montgomery. Harrisburg, Pa.: Harrisburg Publishing Co., State Printer, 1907.

*Pennsylvania Chronicle,* 1767–74.

*Pennsylvania Chronicle and Universal Advertiser,* 1767.

*Pennsylvania Journal and Weekly Advertiser,* 1765.

Riddle, James M., comp. *The Pittsburgh Directory for 1815.* Pittsburgh: James M. Riddle, 1815.

Schoepf, Johann David. *Travels in the Confederation [1783–84].* Edited and translated from the German edition of 1788 by Alfred J. Morrison. Philadelphia: William J. Campbell, 1911.

Smith, Charles E. "The Manufacture of Iron in Pennsylvania." *Hunt's Merchants' Magazine* 25 (November 1851): 574–81 and tables following p. 656.

*The State of Maryland Historical Atlas: A Review of Events and Forces that have Influenced the State.* Washington, D.C.: The State of Maryland, Department of Economic and Community Development, Department of State Planning, 1973.

Taylor, John, and Patterson, R. *The Honest Man's Extra Almanac for the City of Pittsburgh and the Surrounding Country for the Year 1813.* Pittsburgh: Patterson & Hopkins, 1813.

"Travel Diary of Bishop and Mrs. Reichel and their Company from Lititz to Salem in Wachau (Wachovia) from May 22, to June 15, 1780." In *Travels in the American Colonies,* edited by Newton D. Mereness, pp. 586–99. New York: The Macmillan Co., 1916.

U.S. Congress, House, *Memorial of the Citizens of Philadelphia Engaged in the Manufacture of Iron to the Senate and House of Representatives of the United States in Congress Assembled.* 21st Cong., 2d sess., 21 February 1831, H. Exec. Doc. 109.

U.S. Congress, House, *Pennsylvania. Memorial of Manufacturers of Hardware, Smiths and Iron-Founders of the City of Philadelphia to the Honorable the Senate and the House of Representatives of the United States in Congress Assembled.* 20th Cong., 1st sess., 17 March 1828, H. Exec. Doc. 202.

U.S. Congress, Senate, *Memorial against Duties on Railroad Iron Praying a Remission of the Duties on Certain Railroad Iron of the Long Island Railroad Company,* 28th Cong., 1st sess., 19 January 1844, S. Doc. 55.

U.S. Congress, Senate, *Memorial of a Number of Citizens of Pennsylvania Praying a Repeal [sic] of the Duty upon Railroad Iron.* 28th Cong., 1st sess., 27 February 1844, S. Doc. 148.

U.S. Congress, Senate, *Memorial of the Presidents and Directors of Sundry Railroad Companies in Virginia, Praying the Repeal of the Duty on Railroad Iron.* 28th Cong., 1st sess., 11 March 1844, S. Doc. 176.

U.S. Congress, Senate, *Memorial on Duty on Railroad Iron Praying an Extension of the Law Exempting Railroad Iron from Duty of the Georgia Railroad Company.* 28th Cong., 1st sess., 16 January 1844, S. Doc. 58.

U.S. Congress, Senate, *Proceedings of a Meeting of Democratic Citizens of Sunbury, Pa., Expressing Their Opposition to the Bill for Reducing the Duties on Imports, and Requesting the Senators from the State of Pennsylvania to Use All Honorable Means to Defeat Its Passage.* 29th Cong., 1st sess., 23 July 1846, S. Doc. 446.

U.S. Department of the Interior, Geological Survey. *State of Pennsylvania Base Map with Highways and Contours.* Washington, D.C.: U.S. Department of the Interior, 1955.

## SECONDARY SOURCES

Abler, Ronald; Adams, John S.; and Gould, Peter. *Spatial Organization: The Geographer's View of the World.* Englewood Cliffs, N.J.: Prentice-Hall, 1971.

Alotta, Robert I. *Street Names of Philadelphia.* Philadelphia: Temple University Press, 1975.

American Society for Metals. *Properties and Selection of Metals.* Vol. 1 of *Metals Handbook.* 8th ed. Novelty, Ohio: American Society for Metals, 1961.

Ashton, Thomas S. *Iron and Steel in the Industrial Revolution.* University of Manchester Economic History Series, no. 11. Manchester, 1924.

Bezanson, Anne. *Prices and Inflation during the American Revolution: Pennsylvania, 1770–1790.* Philadelphia: University of Pennsylvania Press, 1951.

———; Gray, Robert D.; and Hussey, Miriam. *Prices in Colonial Pennsylvania.* Philadelphia: University of Pennsylvania Press, 1935.

———. *Wholesale Prices in Philadelphia, 1787–1861.* 2 vols. Philadelphia: University of Pennsylvania Press, 1937.

Bining, Arthur Cecil. "The Iron Plantations of Early Pennsylvania." *Pennsylvania Magazine of History and Biography* 57 (1933): 117–37.

———. *British Regulation of the Colonial Iron Industry.* Philadelphia: University of Pennsylvania Press, 1933.

———. *Pennsylvania Iron Manufacture in the Eighteenth Century.* Publications of the Pennsylvania Historical Commission, vol. 4. 1938. Reprint. Harrisburg: Pennsylvania Historical and Museum Commission, 1973.

———. "Early Ironmasters of Pennsylvania." *Pennsylvania History* 18 (1951): 93–103.

Bridenbaugh, Carl. *Cities in Revolt: Urban Life in America, 1743–1776.* New York: Alfred A. Knopf, 1968.

Campbell, R. H. *Carron Company.* Edinburgh: Oliver and Boyd, 1961.

Chandler, Alfred D., Jr. *The Visible Hand: The Managerial Revolution in American Business.* Cambridge, Mass.: Belknap Press, 1977.

Cochran, Thomas C. "Did the Civil War Retard Industrialization?" *Mississippi Valley Historical Review* 48 (1961): 197–210.

Cole, Arthur Harrison. *Wholesale Commodity Prices in the United States, 1700–1861: Statistical Supplement; Actual Wholesale Prices of Various Commodities.* Cambridge, Mass.: Harvard University Press, 1938.

Dunbar, Seymour. *A History of Travels in America.* 4 vols. Indianapolis: Bobbs-Merrill Co., 1915.

Durnbaugh, Donald F. "Two Early Letters from Germantown." *Pennsylvania Magazine of History and Biography* 84 (1960): 219–33.

Ellis, F. *History of Northampton County, Pennsylvania.* Philadelphia: P. Fritts, 1877.

Ernst, Joseph Albert. *Money and Politics in America, 1755–1775: A Study in the Currency Act of 1764 and the Political Economy of Revolution.* Chapel Hill: University of North Carolina Press, 1973.

Fackental, B. F., Jr. "The Durham Iron Works in Durham Township." In *Papers Read before the Society and Other Historical Papers. The Bucks County [Pa.] Historical Society* 7 (1937): 59–93.

Fishlow, Albert. *American Railroads and the Transformation of the Ante bellum Economy.* Harvard Economic Studies, vol. 127. Cambridge, Mass.: Harvard University Press, 1965.

Flinn, Michael W. *Men of Iron: The Crowleys in the Early Iron Industry.* Edinburgh: At the University Press, 1962.

Flueckiger, Gerald Eugene. "The Structure and Behavior of Technological Change in the Iron and Steel Industry, 1700–1899." Ph.D. diss., Purdue University, 1970.

Fogel, Robert William. *Railroads and American Economic Growth: Essays in Econometric History.* Baltimore: The Johns Hopkins Press, 1964.

Gemmell, Alfred. "The Charcoal Iron Industry in the Perkiomen Valley." Master's thesis, University of Pennsylvania, 1947.

Gottlieb, Manuel. *Long Swings in Urban Development.* New York: National Bureau of Economic Research, 1976.

Habakkuk, H. J. *American and British Technology in the Nineteenth Century: The Search for Labour-Saving Inventions.* Cambridge: At the University Press, 1962.

Holt, W. Stull. "Charles Carroll, Barrister: The Man." *Maryland Historical Magazine* 31 (1936): 112–36.

Hunter, Louis C. "The Influence of the Market upon Technique in the Iron Industry in Western Pennsylvania up to 1860." *Journal of Economic and Business History* 1 (February 1929): 241–81.

Johnson, Keach. "The Establishment of the Baltimore Company." Ph.D. diss., University of Iowa, 1949.

_____. "The Genesis of the Baltimore Ironworks." *Journal of Southern History* 19 (1953): 157–79.

_____. "The Baltimore Company Seeks English Markets: A Study of the Anglo-American Iron Trade, 1731–1755." *William and Mary Quarterly,* 3d ser., 16 (1959): 37–60.

Land, Aubrey C. *The Dulaneys of Maryland: A Biographical Study of Daniel*

*Dulaney, The Elder (1685–1753) and Daniel Dulaney, The Younger (1722–1797)*. Baltimore: The Johns Hopkins Press, 1955.

Lane, Wheaton J. *From Indian Trail to Iron Horse: Travel and Transportation in New Jersey, 1620–1860*. Princeton: Princeton University Press, 1939.

Laubach, Charles. "The Durham Iron Works." In *A Collection of Papers Read before the Bucks County Historical Society* 1 (1908): 232–49.

Lemon, James T. "Urbanization and the Development of Eighteenth-Century Southeastern Pennsylvania and Adjacent Delaware." *William and Mary Quarterly,* 3d ser., 24 (1967): 501–42.

———. *The Best Poor Man's Country: A Geographical Study of Early Southeastern Pennsylvania*. Baltimore: The Johns Hopkins Press, 1972.

Lindstrom, Diane. *Economic Development in the Philadelphia Region, 1810–1850*. New York: Columbia University Press, 1978.

Livesay, Harold C. "Marketing Patterns in the Antebellum American Iron Industry." *Business History Review* 45 (Autumn 1971): 269–95.

McCormick, Richard P. *New Jersey from Colony to State, 1609–1789*. The New Jersey Historical Series, vol. 1. Princeton: D. Van Nostrand Co., 1964.

Montgomery, Morton L. "Early Furnaces and Forges of Berks County, Pennsylvania." *Pennsylvania Magazine of History and Biography* 8 (1884): 56–81.

Morison, Samuel Eliot. *The Oxford History of the American People*. New York: Oxford University Press, 1965.

Neu, Irene D. "The Iron Plantations of Colonial New York." *New York History* 33 (1952): 3–24.

North, Douglass, C. *The Economic Growth of the United States, 1790–1860*. Englewood Cliffs, N.J.: Prentice-Hall, 1961.

Omwake, John; with Frey, H. C.; Landis, H. K.; and Hargrave, Catherine P. *The Conestoga Six-Horse Bell Teams of Eastern Pennsylvania*. Cincinnati: John Omwake, 1930.

Pelham, R. A. "The West Midland Iron Industry and the American Market in the 18th Century." *University of Birmingham Historical Journal* 2, no. 2 (1950): 141–62.

Peterson, Merrill: *Olive Branch and Sword: The Compromise of 1833*. Baton Rouge: Louisiana State University Press, 1982.

Porter, Glenn, and Livesay, Harold C. *Merchants and Manufacturers: Studies in the Changing Structure of Nineteenth-Century Marketing*. Baltimore: The Johns Hopkins Press, 1971.

Pred, Allan R. *Urban Growth and the Circulation of Information: The United States System of Cities, 1790–1840*. Cambridge, Mass.: Harvard University Press, 1973.

Redlich, Fritz. "Soderfors in Context: The Production of Iron in the Charcoal Era." Introduction to *Soderfors Anchor-Works History,* by Johan Lundstrom, trans. Lars-Erik Hedin. Boston: Baker Library, Harvard Graduate School of Business Administration, 1970.

Ringwalt, J. L. *Development of Transportation Systems in the United States*. Philadelphia: J. L. Ringwalt, 1888.

Robbins, Michael Warren. "The Principio Company: Iron-Making in Colonial

Maryland, 1720–1781." Ph.D. diss., The George Washington University, 1972.
Rogers, James E. Thorold. *A History of Agriculture and Prices in England.* Vol. 7, pt. 1. Oxford: Clarendon Press, 1902.
Rosenberg, Nathan. *Technology and American Economic Growth.* New York: Harper Torchbooks, 1972.
Rostow, Walt W. *The Stages of Economic Growth: A Non-Communist Manifesto.* Cambridge: At the University Press, 1960.
_____. *The Process of Economic Growth.* 2d ed. New York: W. W. Norton, 1962.
_____. *The World Economy: History & Prospect.* Austin: University of Texas Press, 1978.
_____, ed. *The Economics of Take-off into Sustained Growth.* New York: St. Martin's Press, 1963.
Sachs, William S., and Hoogenboom, Ari. *The Enterprising Colonials: Society on the Eve of the Revolution.* Chicago: Argonaut, 1965.
Salinger, Susan Vineberg. "Labor and Indentured Servants in Colonial Pennsylvania." Ph.D. diss., University of California at Los Angeles, 1980.
Schumpeter, Joseph A. *Capitalism, Socialism and Democracy.* 3d ed. New York: Harper Torchbooks, 1962.
Shumway, George; Durell, Edward; and Frey, Howard C. *Conestoga Wagon, 1750–1850: Freight Carrier for 100 Years of America's Westward Expansion.* York, Pa.: Early American Industries Association and George Shumway, 1964.
Skaggs, David Curtis. *Roots of Maryland Democracy, 1753–1776.* Contributions in American History, no. 30. Westport, Ct.: Greenwood Press, 1973.
Smith, Walter Buckingham, and Cole, Arthur Harrison. *Fluctuations in American Business, 1790–1860.* Cambridge, Mass.: Harvard University Press, 1935.
Taussig, Frank W. *The Tariff History of the United States.* 8th ed. New York: G. P. Putnam's Sons, 1931.
Taylor, George Rogers. *The Transportation Revolution, 1815–1860.* New York: Harper Torchbooks, 1951.
Temin, Peter. *Iron and Steel in Nineteenth-Century America: An Economic Inquiry.* Cambridge, Mass.: M.I.T. Press, 1964.
Thayer, Theodore. *Israel Pemberton, King of the Quakers.* Philadelphia: Historical Society of Pennsylvania, 1943.
Tolles, Frederick B. *James Logan and the Culture of Provincial America.* The Library of American Biography, edited by Oscar Handlin. Boston: Little, Brown, and Company, 1957.
_____. *Meeting House and Counting House: The Quaker Merchants of Colonial Philadelphia, 1682–1763.* New York: W. W. Norton and Company, 1963.
Wacker, Peter O. *The Musconetcong Valley of New Jersey: A Historical Geography.* New Brunswick: Rutgers University Press, 1968.
Walsh, William D. *The Diffusion of Technological Change in the Pennsyl-

*vania Pig Iron Industry, 1850–1870.* Dissertations in American Economic History, edited by Stuart Bruchey. New York: Arno Press, 1975.

Walton, Gary M., and Shepherd, James F. *The Economic Rise of Early America.* Cambridge: At the University Press, 1979.

Walzer, John Flexer. "Transportation in the Philadelphia Trading Area, 1740–1775." Ph.D. diss., University of Wisconsin, 1968.

Wigginton, Elliot, ed. *Foxfire 5: Ironmaking, Blacksmithing, Flintlock Rifles, Bear Hunting, and Other Affairs of Plain Living.* Garden City, N.Y.: Anchor Press, 1979.

Wittlinger, Carlton O. "Early Manufacturing in Lancaster County, Pennsylvania, 1710–1840." Ph.D. diss., University of Pennsylvania, 1953.

Zabler, Jeffrey Francis. "A Microeconomic Study of Iron Manufacture, 1800–1830." Ph.D. diss., University of Pennsylvania, 1970.

# Index

173

## ABOUT THE AUTHOR

PAUL F. PASKOFF teaches history at Louisiana State University. He is coeditor (with Daniel J. Wilson) of *The Cause of the South: Selections from De Bow's Review, 1846–1867.*

The Johns Hopkins University Press

INDUSTRIAL EVOLUTION

This book was composed in Times Roman and Americana
Compugraphic by Capitol Communication Systems
from a design by Gerard A. Valerio.
It was printed on 50-lb. Glatfelter paper and bound
in Holliston Kingston cloth by Thomson-Shore, Inc.